WOMEN
IN
MID-LIFE
CRISIS

JIM and SALLY CONWAY

WOMEN IN MIDLIFE CRISIS

Tyndale House Publishers, Inc.
WHEATON, ILLINOIS

Unless otherwise indicated, the Scripture verses
quoted in this book are from *The Living Bible*,
© 1971 by Tyndale House Publishers, and are used
by permission.

Certain concepts which appear in this book are
also in *Men in Mid-Life Crisis*, © 1978, David C.
Cook Publishing Co., Elgin, IL 60120. Used by
permission.

First printing, October 1983
Library of Congress Catalog Card Number 83-50127
ISBN 0-8423-8382-4, cloth
Copyright © 1983 by Jim and Sally Conway
All rights reserved
Printed in the United States of America

To Our Daughters
  Barbara Conway Schneider
  Brenda Conway Russell
  Becki Conway Sanders

Who have helped us to more fully understand
  Life
  People
  God
  and Ourselves

Contents

Foreword

My daughter came home with a stress test from her high school psychology text and gave it to me. I tested out at about 450 points—a healthy recommended average was about 230 points!

It has been another hard year. (I've stopped saying, "Last year was the hardest year of our lives," because I've learned that the middle years of life are often just as difficult.) Oh, the normal demands I've learned to juggle: writing deadlines and raising children and needy people living in our home. But the outward circumstances over which I have no control often raise my stress quotient—such as the death of a parent. . . .

Mother died on my birthday, my thirty-ninth birthday, and all this year I have known I would turn forty on the first anniversary of my mother's death.

Unconsciously, I began preparing myself for mid-life passage when I was twenty-nine years old. I realized then that the woman I would become at forty was the one I decided to be at thirty. I think I would probably have flown through this year's birthday with raised colors and little hesitation . . . but my mother died on my birthday, two years after my father's death. And the sudden realization that life, *no one's life*, is permanent plunged me into a year of intense personal evaluation.

In some ways, it has been a ruthless evaluation—I am learning not to be sparing when it comes to personal growth. There was fatigue to identify, depression to refuse, healthy work of grief to endure. But deeper, much deeper than this was the question: What do I want to do with the rest of my life, with the rest of whatever life is remaining to me?

The Lord and I have been battling this year, not in the adversarial sort of way but in the co-unioned sort of way; and as all spiritual journeys are, this has been a sociological journey as well.

What gifts have I been given that enable me to do a job that few others in the Kingdom can do? What is the inward calling that is stronger than any other and how is it being diffused into less meaningful activities and commitments?

I discovered that, after ten years of writing, writing is still my deepest calling; but it is a new kind of writing, a writing I have never before done. It has a sharp and different edge.

I discovered a longing for the contemplative life. Though my life is filled with people, I am basically an introvert in that I draw my strength from silence, from quiet, from thought. I began to design a new life style in which prayer and silence are the center and have refused speaking invitations for the next several years.

As the older children are leaving home to go to college, I have discovered areas of neglect in the two younger boys. I only have a few years left for corrective parenting. These are dangerous years for my boys and I want to be near.

Well, the discoveries have gone on and on, and I would not have missed this inward sociological examination of my soul, this mid-life passage I might have overlooked or stored away for a more opportune moment, had Mother not died on my birthday.

In essence, I have reorganized all my intentions, begun scraping away at the gathered barnacles collected while passing through the seas of thirty. I feel good, I feel very good about this year forty.

Even more important, I think I am going to enjoy the woman I will be at fifty.

I highly recommend Jim and Sally Conway's book, *Women in Mid-Life Crisis*, for every woman (and every man who cares about a woman), whether she is in mid-life passage or only looking ahead to one, or wondering what it was that hit her a while back.

This is a book that will stimulate and expose and explain the inward journey. But it also gives wonderful, practical handles on healthy ways to make the inward journey and return whole. It forces on us the questions we should all be asking if we are best to fulfill the promise of this life as it is measured in the cadences of decades.

Karen Burton Mains

PART I

SURPRISED BY MID-LIFE CRISIS

Chapter One

COLLISION OF EXPECTATIONS AND REALITY

I wanted to crawl under the bed. Or better yet, I just wanted to disappear. I didn't want to run away and be somewhere else on the earth. I just wanted to be gone. I didn't want to commit suicide. I simply wanted to cease existing.

I felt so frustrated, and my husband just lay there, going off to sleep. I wanted him to talk to me, but I didn't know how to bring it about without making him angry. I finally gave a big sigh and crawled out of bed. In the dark I walked into the living room. Strange emotions were boiling inside me—emotions that had once been unfamiliar but were now all too common. Most of all, I was wishing that Jim would be concerned enough to come find me. I wanted to feel loved and comforted; instead I felt terribly alone. I didn't feel openly rejected by him, but he didn't seem to care about this raging turmoil I was in.

Of course, I chided myself, I should understand that he was very busy with a growing church to manage, and tomorrow was a full day for him, with lots of meetings and appointments. He needed to get his sleep, so I shouldn't expect him to put up with my troubles. Besides, when we did talk, I couldn't seem to help him understand

me. I just got more confused and frustrated, and we usually ended up with even more bad feelings toward each
other. There wasn't time or emotional energy (or, as I see
now, wisdom) to work it all out. It was just better to try to
go to sleep and forget. I also had a busy day tomorrow—I
always did—but my daily life as a pastor's wife seemed
part of another world, foreign and misty and not quite
real.

Sure, I would get up as usual and have my devotions
("Please, dear God, today help me to die to self, help me
not to feel hurt and mad"). Then I'd help Jim and the girls
get off to their day's activities and I'd really dig into my
work around the house. I also would make several phone
calls for a committee meeting later in the week, run some
errands, get a letter off for someone's birthday, keep some
appointments with people either in my home or theirs,
and have a nice meal ready for everyone in the evening.
Afterwards I'd see that our three girls got off to some
evening activity, or I'd help them with homework and
piano practice. I would answer the phone several times, do
an unplanned load of wash to have one of the girls' gym
suit clean for the next day, let the dog in and out several
times, and feel guilty that I hadn't had time to do more for
a friend who was sick. I would enjoy hearing the girls tell
bits and pieces about their day at school or listen to one of
them share some new insight that was unfolding in her as
I spent time "tucking" them all into bed. After telling them
goodnight, I would get a few more things done before Jim
would get home from a meeting, and we'd drop into bed.

And then that gnawing uneasiness I had felt off and on
all day would grow stronger and stronger. I wanted to
share it with Jim and have him help me get rid of it. He
counseled everyone else and received their praise for being
so wise and helpful, why wouldn't he help me? Sometimes
he did, but too often, I thought, his perception of my need
missed the boat. More often, he just didn't seem even to
try to understand. He was preoccupied with his work at

the church—new programs, plans for spiritual and nu-merical growth, stimulating meetings with students—great things happening as God worked in other people's lives. I had always shared in his "pastoring"; now I felt left out and unneeded, like a discarded old box. When I looked at the facts, my life wasn't any different than be-fore. I was still active, involved, and included, but I didn't *feel* the same as I had previously.

A wave of self-pity would wash over me. Right after that, a bigger wave of jealousy would slam into me. And before I could get myself righted from that blow, a third wave of just plain rejection and hurt would hit me. An old box—yes, I felt like a soggy cardboard box, bobbing just offshore. Soon I would be hopelessly saturated and sink.

But I didn't want to sink! Well, yes, often I did want to vanish from life, but what I really wanted was for all the inner confusion I felt to be straightened out so I could get on with the happy life I was supposed to be living. Part of me *was* happy, but a big chunk of me was miserable, and I didn't know why.

Experiences like this were common to me, off and on, during the last half of my thirties. My frustration and confusion were especially critical from about age thirty-six through thirty-nine. Jim and I thought the problem was simply unique to me—some personal quirks I needed to work out. I struggled desperately with feeling unspiritual and went through various spiritual exercises to try to "die to self" and "crucify the flesh."

LIFE *BEGINS* AT FORTY ??

Now we see that the problem was my transition into mid-life. Ever since *Men in Mid-Life Crisis* (Jim Conway, De-cember 1978) and *You and Your Husband's Mid-Life Crisis* (Sally Conway, November 1980) were published, we have been contacted by many women from around the United

States and Canada who feel they also are experiencing a
mid-life crisis. We have heard heart-wrenching stories
from single and married women from all circumstances of
life. The severity of problems varies, but all are seeing age
forty on the horizon, or have just passed it. They talk about
a change in their emotions and their perceptions of life.
Many have had a strong compulsion to run away; some
actually have. Some feel the turmoil less intensely but still
are unsettled by it.

We searched to see if there were studies about women in
mid-life, and, although some involved women in their late
thirties and early forties, none at that time had been done
to determine if women experience a "crisis" similar to a
man's crisis at mid-life and at an earlier time than the well-
recognized menopausal stress of the late forties or early
fifties. If there is such a time, what causes it? What can be
done to help ease the pressures? We both began to do
research about the matter and will be reporting what we
learned throughout this book.

COLLIDING EMOTIONS

The mid-life transition hits women in many different
ways.

At a Bible conference, Ellen* had asked to talk to me
(Jim) privately. Her lower lip quivered. Her eyes darted
back and forth as she scanned my face. She looked desperate. She needed to talk to someone, yet she was afraid,
because she was a Christian leader in her church.

We went to a quiet place where we could have privacy,
and the story began to pour out. The family had spent the
summer in a cabin by a mountain lake. Her husband,
Fred, stayed in the city to work during the week, but he
would come up each weekend. Her oldest son had
brought along his friend Jeff, age seventeen, to stay with

---

*In this illustration and throughout the book, we have changed names and
disguised circumstances to protect the privacy of the people involved.

them for the summer. Ellen said that on several occasions when Jeff had been at their house in the city, she had felt that he was watching her. Frequently their eyes had met and their prolonged gaze had silently communicated a mutual appreciation and stimulation.

"At the time," she said, "I didn't think too much about it, other than that it was flattering to have a good-looking young man look at me with such admiration, especially since my husband seemed too busy even to notice me."

The family had been at the cabin for about two weeks. Fred had joined them for the weekend and had returned to the city on Sunday night. All the kids got up early the next morning to go fishing, except Jeff, who decided to sleep in.

"I had fed them all breakfast and cleared up the kitchen after they left. Then decided to wake Jeff. As I pushed open his bedroom door, I saw him sleeping face down with the top half of his muscular body uncovered. I softly whispered his name. He didn't respond, so I sat on the edge of the bed and began to gently rub his back to try to awaken him. He slowly rolled over and said, 'That feels good.' Before I knew what was happening, we were kissing each other and one thing led to another."

Ellen fidgeted in the chair and kept her eyes down, staring at her hands as she clasped and unclasped her fingers. Slowly, but with great feeling, she said, "I was a very willing partner. Sex with him was not a duty as it was with my husband. It was exhilarating.

"It didn't end with that morning. I found excuses to be alone with him all summer long. Now that we are back in the city for the school year, I constantly long to be with him.

"What's happening to me? I'm a Christian. I am a leader in my church. I know this is wrong. I don't want to lose my family. I don't believe in divorce. I know he is only seventeen years old, but the fantasies are running wild in my brain. Someone really loves me and makes me feel like a woman. He has taken away that terrible sense of loneliness and exploitation that I feel with my children and my husband. I know I've got to stop seeing him, but I don't want to go back to living the life I had before—a sweet, smiling homemaker, meeting everybody's needs and not even noticed by my husband."

EVEN IN THE BEST OF WOMEN

We have found that the mid-life transition can be difficult for all types of women—married, never-married, formerly married; women with children and women without; women with previously satisfying careers; and women in a variety of socioeconomic circumstances.

Some single women, who have always hoped to marry, tell us that the prospect of turning forty seems like the absolute end to all their hopes. Other single women, who made a choice not to marry so they could throw their energies into education and career, begin to have second thoughts when they near forty.

Some have said, "I see now that I don't want to grow old alone." One confessed, "Until now I felt that a husband and kids would just be a big barrier to what I wanted to do in life; now I wish I at least had a husband for companionship."

Some women, whether married or unmarried, have a rough, explosive, crisis-type transition to mid-life. Others experience only a quiet restlessness and inner confusion without much disruption in their lives and relationships.

Between sessions at a women's retreat where I (Sally) was speaking, I was standing in line at the bookstore, waiting to pay for some greeting cards. Although I was not at the retreat to speak on mid-life problems, I had been introduced as an author and wife of an author of mid-life books. As the check-out line moved slowly toward the counter, the pretty, trim woman ahead of me turned and asked, "When are you going to write a book about women's mid-life crisis?" She then began to pour out her confusion. It was a story very similar to many others we had been hearing in recent months.

"I am thirty-six, but feel like I'm going on fourteen. I'm struggling with some of the same feelings I had when I was a young teenager," this composed-looking woman told me. I'm sure others around couldn't detect the disorder she was feeling inside.

"I have a wonderful husband and love him very much. We have two children and I enjoy being a mother. I have everything that should make a woman happy, but I feel so torn up and restless inside. I feel empty, and I don't know what's missing. I just want to run away."

She was an active, growing Christian, and what she was experiencing internally was very bewildering to her. On the one hand, she knew with her mind who she was and what she valued in life; but emotionally everything was scrambled. Sometimes life seemed hollow and she herself felt vacant; at other times there were so many issues pressing in on her and strange thoughts bombarding her mind that she felt too full, almost stuffed.

NO PAT ANSWERS

For about three-and-a-half years we have been doing serious research on women at mid-life, not centering so much on the age of menopause and the empty nest but looking at the era from mid-thirties up to menopause. We've discovered that a number of women go through an emotional trauma of crisis proportion during this time. In this book we'll be referring to this experience as "mid-life crisis."

There are no neat conclusions about exact causes and specific cures for a woman's mid-life crisis. In fact, the actual feelings and events are not alike for any two women. Human behavior and emotions are too complex for cut-and-dried answers that will apply in all instances for every person. Some *generalizations*, however, can be made from our research data and from the women we have counseled and interviewed. Some or all of the following factors may produce stress or cause a crisis for a woman in the last half of her thirties and very early forties:

1. Our present-day cultural view of women
2. An unhappy marital situation or lack of a marriage
3. Her husband's own mid-life crisis
4. Demands from children and their growing independence
5. Career priorities related to other life priorities
6. An accumulation of traumatic losses such as death, illnesses, or aging
7. Urgency from her inner clocks to accomplish her life dreams
8. Imperative reevaluation time to review the past and plan the future

Some of these factors are sharpened by the mere passing of time and the fact that a woman is now forced to realize that some of her expectations are never going to be met. For example, she can put up with a poor marriage for years, thinking that "someday soon" it will change; or she may keep hoping to see some of her other personal dreams come true. By mid-life she is faced with the hard reality that not all of her dreams will be realized. There is truly a "collision of expectations and reality."

Every woman will go through the transition from being a young adult to being a mid-life adult. Not all women will have a crisis. Our studies, however, show that more than two-thirds of the women do. It is our hope that understanding more about the transition—and potentially crisis—time will provide help for mid-life women, their families, friends, and everyone concerned.

INNER FEELINGS AT MID-LIFE

How do you describe what it feels like when you are in mid-life crisis? A Christian midwestern woman who is forty-four and is a frequent speaker at women's clubs described her own mid-life crisis in one word: *lonely.* "You feel as if no one understands, and if they do understand, they don't care. You are in it by yourself."

Another woman, age thirty-four, commented, "For the first time in my life I am admitting to myself and to everyone around me who I really am and what I really want to be. First, I always did what my parents wanted me to do, and then I did what my husband wanted. My parents think I'm acting strangely now, but for the first time in my life I am really acting like myself." This woman had just left her husband and three young children and started working fulltime in her profession to fulfill an earlier dream she had had when she was a young adult.

A thirty-eight-year-old East Coast woman declared, "I feel as if I am drowning. Pressures are coming at me from all sides—caring for my children, making my husband successful, meeting responsibilities at church, PTA, and my part-time job. And now my dad has just had a heart attack. I'm caring for everybody. But who am I? And who cares for me?"

IN THE PITS

Many women report that they don't know who they are by mid-life. Many experience varying degrees of depression. They sense some loss—or many losses. They may feel hopeless and worthless. They often interpret the actions of their husband, children, employers, or fellow workers to mean that they are unneeded, unwanted, and unattractive. They feel burned out and exploited. Their lives seem out of control. They are angry at the tell-tale signs of aging.

In adolescence a girl struggles to establish an identity and considers who she will become. At mid-life she is asking, "Who have I become? And do I like who I am?" She probably has been so busy caring for others that she is not very well acquainted with herself.

Depression is a common feeling of a woman in mid-life crisis. True depression incapacitates its victims. Depressed people have trouble making decisions and carrying out normal life. They may complain frequently of fatigue and experience real or imaginary physical disorders.

Depression almost always involves a deep sense of loss. Many women at mid-life feel that they have lost their youth, sex appeal, beauty, their chance to do what is most fulfilling—in short, the best years of life. Some may have lost their husbands through death or divorce. Married women with children often feel they've lost the opportunity to develop and use talents other than those needed for keeping house and mothering. The single and married women without children may feel they are getting past the age when they can give birth to their own healthy babies. Unmarried women, whether or not they are single by choice, may by this age want to marry but recognize that the probability of meeting a suitable mate is slim.

An unmarried career missionary woman in her late thirties, facing a hysterectomy, writes poignantly of her loss:

FOR WHAT MIGHT HAVE BEEN

It would have been an ecstatic conception.
Then, to know the being under my heart.
Oh, the thrill at the first sense of movement . . .
Possibly there would have been discomfort.
Then the increasing ungainliness of size.
Finally the pains would have come.
(They say it is the pain most easily forgotten.)
Joy and warmth with the nuzzling at breast,
The gift of the life-sustaining flow.
There would have been wonder at that little person.

No ecstasy—empty womb, bare breast.

Lord, channel that love and longing
  which YOU built into me.
Still my grief, renew my joy.
  Fulfill me as your person.[1]

—Written on the eve of my hysterectomy

Hopelessness is a common feeling at mid-life. How does a woman go back and relive life? How can she return to her youth with the mature insights she now has about herself and change the course of life? She can't go back, because life doesn't work that way. Even if she could start over, could she really change the circumstances of her life? If the future seems no better than the past or present— which right now look dreadful—her feeling of hopelessness is increased.

WHO AM I?

The mid-life woman often feels worthless and unnecessary as a person. Oh, she is needed to do the laundry, cook the meals, clean the house, run the errands for her children, be the gracious hostess for her husband's business entertaining, smiling pleasantly at the guests as she stands half a step behind him at his side. Yes, she is even important at work. She makes all those people successful by her careful attention to detail, writing letters for her boss that make him look like an insightful genius, and covering for him with gracious apologies for appointments that he misses. The woman who is a successful, effective executive is often treated as if she is working only so she can catch a man, get married, and raise children.

But the real question is whether she is seen as a person, or just as a geisha girl, chauffeur, secretary, and scrub woman.

The Hindus in India used to burn the widow on her husband's funeral pyre. It was a rather frank admission that this woman had lost her usefulness in life, and, supposedly, was being sent on to accompany her husband in the afterlife. In the United States we tell the average mid-life woman, who is frustrated and wondering who she is, to amuse herself with a hobby or with volunteer service.

WHERE DO I GO FROM HERE?

Taking up a hobby or doing volunteer work at mid-life, while ignoring the important value questions of "Who am I?" and "What is life all about?" is like allowing someone to put a chloroform-saturated cloth over your nose. "Stop protesting. Just lie back. Breathe deeply." Give up . . . forget about being a person . . . stay removed from reality.

The reality is that God has created you to be a useful person. He has given you specific gifts and talents, and those need to be used. God has also given you an identity that is rooted in who you are as a person. It is bigger than your activities of serving your family and people at work or at church.

Many mid-life women feel that their lives are out of control. They feel trapped by a lack of experience, lack of self-identity, and lack of encouragement from their husbands (or lack of a *husband*). They may also feel a lack of support from family or employers and a lack of the community with other women that would allow them to verbalize their real feelings. They are squeezed by too much to do in a day or week. No matter how organized and efficient they are or how fast they run, they are always behind. They often have unsatisfying relationships with their husband, children, or other people and feel they don't have enough power to improve those relationships. After all, they can't force people to cooperate, give them their attention, or love them.

IN SPITE OF HAVING IT ALL TOGETHER. . . .

Joan Israel, a psychotherapist from Detroit who has done extensive research on women's issues, thought she would never be troubled by mid-life because she was educated, aware of the problems, and a liberated woman. She had little concern about her appearance. She was sure she would age "with confidence, with security, with adventure." She says, "I became a feminist therapist, helping other women explore new facets of themselves so that they would not be dependent on youth and beauty for feeling good about themselves or secure with the men in their lives."[2]

In her chapter "Confessions of a 45-Year-Old Feminist" she continues, "One day, a few weeks after my 45th birthday, I looked into the mirror and said to myself, 'Joan, you look old!' The skin under my chin and neck suddenly sagged and wrinkled. . . . I tried pulling the skin to one side and agreed that this made me look better (younger).

"There I was, face to face with me. I did not like what I saw, but I was finding it hard to admit this. I had never felt like this before. I had always been happy with me; with my body, my face, my skin.

"After I got over the shock of my neck, I examined my hands. Gee, they looked wrinkled! All of a sudden, there was a lot of gray in my hair. My skin was dryer and flabbier. My breasts drooped.

"But why was I so upset? Was this simply egotism? Would getting older mean I was less attractive as a person? Less attractive to whom? To men in general? This had never been my bag, even when I was younger. Less attractive to my husband? He gave no indication of being turned off. Maybe it was the promise of things to come: aging, illness, death. I still do not know for sure. All I know is I was overwhelmed with concern about getting old."[3]

SAGGING AND DROOPING
Her personal concern with aging threw her even more intensely into research on what women her age were feeling. She discovered that women in their late thirties are commonly concerned about losing their attractiveness and

that most women wrestle with the aging factors in their late thirties or early forties. Perhaps for her the process had been postponed slightly or "I had deluded myself that it wouldn't happen to me."[4]

She goes on to speak of her research: "I was interested to see that most of the women I asked showed generalized concern about wrinkled skin and drooping breasts and buttocks. The dream merchants, advertisers, cosmetics and foundation manufacturers know what they are doing. On the other hand, all of the women felt their sexual organs had improved with age and expected this would continue. Their main fear, like mine, was not that their sexual urge or capacity for enjoying sex would decrease but that their outward appearance would get in the way of finding a partner. They seemed to be saying, 'It doesn't matter who I am, after all, just what I look like.' "[5]

WHEN DOES MID-LIFE CRISIS HIT?

Mid-life is dated not so much by age as by life experiences. Blue collar workers tend to think of mid-life as thirty-five to fifty-five, whereas professional people tend to see it as forty to sixty-five. Women think of mid-life in relationship to their family life cycle, linked to when their children enter puberty with their accompanying strong surges for independence. Unmarried women define mid-life in terms of the family that they might have had.

It was not until this century that many people lived through what we now call the middle years. In prehistoric times men lived an average of about eighteen years. Fossil remains indicate that only a few lived beyond forty. Even as recently as 1900 life expectancy was about forty-eight for a man and fifty-one for a woman. In 1900 only 10 percent of the population was middle-aged. Today our average adult person in the labor force is over forty-five. Our total population has increased almost 100 percent in the last century, but mid-lifers have increased 200 percent.[6] Today the average woman can expect to live to be seventy-five or eighty. A woman's life expectancy by 2000 will be 100.[7]

Mid-life is placed anywhere from age thirty-three to age seventy depending upon which social scientist or lay person is asked. In our research we found women experiencing mid-life crisis as early as the first half of their thirties and as late as their early fifties, but the bulk of them fell in the mid to late thirties.

Gail Sheehy points out the significance of age thirty-five as it relates to what we are calling mid-life crisis. She lists the following facts of female life that all come to focus at about age thirty-five:

Thirty-four is when the average mother sends her last child off to school.
Thirty-five begins the dangerous age of infidelity.
Thirty-five is when the average married American woman reenters the working world.
Thirty-four is the average age at which the divorced woman takes a new husband.
Thirty-five is the most common age of the runaway wife.
Thirty-five brings the biological boundary into sight.[8]

The factors that Sheehy lists, along with several other forces that we'll be discussing later in the book, all converge to bring about the woman's mid-life crisis.

REEVALUATION TIME

Bernice Neugarten records in an article entitled "The Awareness of Middle Age" that she interviewed 100 randomly selected successful men and women about middle adulthood. She and her team discovered that "reassessment of the self is a prevailing theme. Most of this group, as anticipated, were highly introspective and highly verbal persons who evidenced considerable insight into the changes that had taken place in their careers, their families, their status, and in the ways in which they dealt with both their inner and outer worlds."[9]

The mid-life woman, for perhaps the first time in life since adolescence, is becoming reflective. She is beginning to ask the *why* questions: "Why am I in this career?" "Why am I serving my children?" "Why am I married?" "Why am I a Christian?" "Why am I on the PTA Board?" Previously, she had thought that merely being involved in many activities would bring fulfillment of the dreams she had for herself in her late adolescence and early twenties. She planned to use her talents and abilities to make an impact on the world or to give satisfaction to herself. However, she attempted to fulfill those dreams through other people. "I'll get married and help my husband fulfill his dreams." "I'll raise children and help them reach their goals." "I'll take a job and help the company achieve its purposes."

All of these activities sound very noble and, in Christian terms, could be viewed as spiritual ministry. In reality, they may have been secondary goals which leave the mid-life woman emotionally and spiritually malnourished. When a person only serves and never receives, she is like a car with the headlights always on. The battery will soon be run down and it will not be able to start the engine. The car will not function—nor will the mid-life woman.

HIGHER HEIGHTS

Earlier, a woman is more concerned with *what* activities she will do. At mid-life she asks *why* she does them. There is a value shift in the mid-life woman that causes her to think of self-actualization now. Some years ago Abraham Maslow outlined a hierarchy of needs, starting from the most fundamental level. He suggested that, first, basic physiological needs have to be met. Second, there needs to be security against danger. Then there is room for the third need of love and belonging, followed by self-esteem and respect, and, finally, self-actualization.[10] By mid-life most of the lower levels are no longer an issue, and women are now ready to look again at who they are and what will actually bring about their flowering as persons.

The mid-life crisis should not be viewed as a totally negative process, although there are many hard aspects associated with it. The time can produce extremely positive results as a woman realizes that she now has one of her greatest opportunities to become alive and truly herself.

PROBLEMS IGNORED

A common response of the woman beginning mid-life crisis is one of denial. "I'm just having a bad day today. I'm feeling a little down but things will be better tomorrow. The problems that I'm having (stale marriage, kids growing independent, overload of work and commitment, growing fear of death and alarm at aging) will all pass. Tomorrow is going to be better."

Or she may claim, "I'm not at the age to have a mid-life crisis. If it weren't for my insensitive husband (or unappreciative kids, slave-driving boss, or whatever), my life would be going great. It's not my fault."

It is common for a mid-life woman to try to ignore her problems rather than realize that she is facing a major transition, that of moving from being a young adult to a mid-life adult. She needs to face that transition rather than hide from it with alcohol, TV soaps, librium or valium, excessive involvement in activities, or blaming others.

Part of the problem is that our youth-oriented society gives a lot of attention and study to childhood and youth. We also have carefully, with fear, looked at old age, but until recently mid-life has been ignored. The mid-life woman is surprised by what is happening to her, and she is unprepared. Often the result is denial or an attempt to overlook her feelings because she thinks she is alone.

NO MODELS

Where are the older women, especially Christian women, who will talk about what they went through during their thirties? Where are the older role models who will answer the questions of today's mid-life woman? "Will I be intellectually competent and have the ability to learn as I get older? Will I shrivel up and lose all interest in sex after menopause? Will I find sex repugnant, painful, or impossible? Will people find me attractive? Will I forget who I am? (Did I ever know?) How do I restore a stale marriage? How can I have it all—be a Christian, have a career, have a happy marriage and children, and be self-actualized?"

Most mid-life women "have been trained since earliest infancy to be servants. Their status in society, their worth to themselves, their joys in life, were all intended to be derived from the value, status, and achievement of other people whom they served: men."[11] But what happens if they don't have a man or children to serve? Or what happens if they lose the men or children they are serving?

Another mid-life woman observes, "The role comes upon each of us suddenly, unexpectedly. We have lived . . . structured lives, for the most part, in which we knew what we wanted and what was expected of us. And now, suddenly, with the beginnings of the middle years, we face an identity crisis for which nothing in our past has prepared us and for which nothing in our society can provide guidelines. . . .

"But even sensing the specters of the future, how could one prepare for middle age? Suddenly the guidebook is filled with blank pages, for as each of the complex parts we filled in the past ends, a vacuum appears. Our expertise, our capabilities and graces in a score of major and minor roles have equipped us for no new place. The years in which we were essential—when we found the 'I' in 'We'—are ended; our worth is no longer to *others*. . . . we witness the crumbling of all the defenses that society has provided for us—we hurtle off into nothingness."[12]

Jules Henry bluntly states the problem: "A man validates himself by working and supporting, a woman validates herself by getting a man."[13] He continues to paint the depressing picture of a mid-life woman who has centered her energies only on her family and has sought personal fulfillment only through them. He says, "As long as a woman has little to offer other than her physical person, love as obsession and idealization will fade as she gets old and as the daily collisions of marriage make living together difficult or merely routine."[14]

Henry believes the mid-life melancholia can really be solved only as we train women to live the second half of life. To him, the problem is more than an educational or institutional one, however. He thinks that it is partly the mid-life woman herself: "Yet, the victims themselves are part of its causation, because so many of them believe that all they should have to offer is youth, beauty, romantic love, and children, and because many of them have entered marriage as an escape from taking responsibility for themselves."[15]

AUTONOMY WITH INTIMACY

The mid-life woman must not continue to live in quiet desperation, hoping that tomorrow will be better. She needs to deal with some of the basic life themes that Maggie Scarf uncovered in her studies with women as reported in *Unfinished Business:* One is "to liberate the adult person from the shackles of her childhood," and the other is "to develop an independent and autonomous sense of self: . . . that inner confidence that one will be able to survive on one's own emotional resources, should it become necessary to do so."[16]

An interviewer talked to a mid-life woman named Maureen whose vivid dream revealed how she felt about herself as a person:

" 'I was in an apartment and it was a dingy, dingy place. The living room was narrow and dark. There was only one window, looking out on an airshaft. The whole place was furnished in early mother-in-law hand-me-down furniture. . . . *And I'm working here and I'm working there and nothing is showing. I'm getting so very tired.* Off the living room was a windowless room and inside were *cribs, babies' cribs, lots of them. They were all pulled apart*—headboards, rails, springs, helter-skelter. *I started trying to organize those too.* I'm working like crazy, when I'm called into an equally dingy kitchen.

" 'There I see two of my children. I start to clean up—first on top of the refrigerator—when I saw what I took to be a family pet, a little monkey. He had a collar on. He was chained on the door. He sat there, almost mummified. He was so shriveled, skeletal. Like those pictures of the Bangla Desh, starving to death.

" 'I looked at the monkey and felt awful. Oh . . . I forgot he was there. I had neglected him. I hadn't fed him. I didn't remember the last time I'd even given him water. I had this horrible sinking guilty feeling that I had forgotten. I said to my daughter: I didn't feed the monkey! . . . The poor animal just fell on the food. How could I have forgotten?

" 'When I awoke I realized that I was that mummified monkey, and that I was starving, and that it had been going on for twenty years!'

"I asked Maureen what she'd want most if she could be granted any wish in the world. She took a deep breath, stretched her arms toward the sky and replied: '. . . What I really and truly would like . . . is to achieve autonomy in intimacy. To have a loving relationship without giving myself up.' "[17]

The mid-life developmental transition is intertwined with all of a woman's life—everything she has done and thought in the past or ever will do or think or become in the future. The passage to mid-life will not go away simply by being ignored or rejected. The mid-life woman is not the same person she was at age twenty or twenty-five, nor are her cultural surroundings the same.

Instead of ignoring or rejecting the mid-life transition, it should be viewed as one of the most exciting times in life for growth. We agree with the authors who wrote, "No other decade is more intriguing, complex, interesting, and unsettled. Its characteristics are change, flux, crisis, growth and intense challenges. Other than childhood, no period has a greater impact on the balance of our lives, for at no other time is anxiety coupled with so great a possibility for fulfillment."[18]

PART **II**

TRAPPED BY ROLES

Chapter Two

THE HOMEMAKER RUNS DRY

"I never thought of being anything else but a wife and mother," Connie was saying. "The earliest thing that I can remember is that some day I would be a mother. Maybe that's because that's all I saw. I never did see much of my father. He was always off at some mysterious place called work. I never went to his office. I never really knew what he did until I became a teenager. My mother never had an outside job after she was married, so I suppose it was easy for me to fall into my mom's role of being a mother and a housewife.

"I didn't come into puberty until I was about twelve-and-a-half, but I was interested in boys before that. Again it was the same kind of thinking—I would grow up, find this good-looking guy who was going to be successful. We would get married and have kids who would all be bright achievers. We'd have a big house and a couple of cars, a cottage at the lake, and money for trips and vacations. We'd have enough money so that I could have the clothes I wanted and we could live the way we wanted to."

Most of Connie's dream had come true. She was married to a very bright, handsome lawyer who was financially successful and well respected in their city. They lived in the best part of town and had three good-looking, well-adjusted children.

She continued, "You know, it's crazy. In a couple of months I'm going to be thirty-seven, and I don't know what's happening to me. All of a sudden the things that I seem to have wanted as a girl growing up, through my teen years, through college, all those things I wanted don't seem to meet my needs now. It isn't like I grabbed just any guy in college. I was popular, but I never had sex with any guy. I wanted to make a clear-thinking choice of the best man I could find who was going to be successful, a good husband, and a good father. I carefully chose Dick, so that I could be guaranteed a good life. I've got all that now, and yet I'm still empty inside. What's wrong?"

Connie shifted in her chair and became more intense. "About now you are going to start laying all that Christian bit on me. Remember, I became a Christian when I was just a little girl. I've been raised in the church. I've learned all the verses about being submissive, following your husband's leadership, being a good mother and wife. I also know all the verses about trusting God and turning your anxieties over to him. All those things used to work very well in my life. But somehow, they don't seem to carry the impact that they used to, even just a year or two ago. And I'm sick of Christians who play 'Always Victorious' and expect me to do the same!

"Do you want to know what's *really* going on inside of me? I've got everything that I ever dreamed of. You know that we live in the most expensive area of town. We have two brand-new cars. I've got all the clothes I want. I'm the president or on the cabinet of every women's club in town. I lead a women's Bible study, and I direct the kids' choir at church. I have a husband who will give me anything. Our three kids are really neat; I couldn't ask for better kids. But they don't need me very much now that they're in school all day and sometimes I'm bored stiff when I have to be around the house alone for very long."

I started to make some neutral, empathetic comment, but she kept on pouring out her feelings.

"Do you want to know what I'm thinking inside? It's crazy—but I want to run away! I keep fantasizing about just getting in the car and leaving. Or taking a taxi out to the airport and just flying away!

"I guess there are really two directions in my fantasies. In one of my fantasies, I fly away on an airplane to one of the Caribbean islands. I spend days lying in the sun, getting golden-tan. Then one day I come in from the beach to get something cool to drink, and I'm sitting on the terrace of the hotel next to the beach when this good-looking stranger comes up to me. He begins to flirt with me, and I respond without being too obvious. I appreciate the hair on his bare chest, his muscular body, his kind, smiling face. I think to myself, 'Hey! You're a married woman!' But I enjoy it as his eyes roll over my body. I like being appreciated. I like being liked for me, not for how clean I keep the house, how well the clothes are cared for, and whether dinner is on time or not.

"The second fantasy goes in almost the opposite direction. It's a whole new area for me. The first romantic fantasy is really just a flashback of what I was experiencing as a teenager or a college girl. But in this new fantasy, I see myself going back to school, becoming a full-time student, working on a master's degree in psychology.

"When I was a sorority girl in college, we thought working women were really low class. They worked because they couldn't find a man to provide all they needed. Were we snobs! But now here I am, wanting to go to work. Not just work. I want to do something that I really care about.

"I suppose it started when I was in high school. There were kids in class with me who were really troubled. They had sort of lost control on life. They were into booze and petty crime. Part of me reached out to help them. I became a friend to some of those kids. And yet another part of me wanted to stay away from them, because they were losers. They weren't going anywhere.

"But now I want to help kids like that. I want to earn a degree and maybe be a school therapist, even a family therapist. Hey, now, that's a joke! Here I'm not even sure I want to stay in my own family, and I'm talking about being a family therapist. I told you I was mixed up.

"Where do I go from here? Which direction? Any three of the directions really scares me. If I keep on doing what I'm doing now, I'm going to go crazy. If I hop a plane and go to the beach, I'll lose everything that I have. If I go back to school, I may lose part of me and I still might lose my family. What should I do? What fits me? Who am I? It sounds all jumbled, but what I really want to say is, 'Help!' "

CAUGHT OFF GUARD

This early mid-life woman did not understand what was happening to her sexually, in her roles, in her psyche, or with the cultural pressures around her. She couldn't continue playing the Happy Suzy Homemaker games, using a few of the gifts and abilities that God had given her, while at the same time avoiding other large segments of her personality. You see, she had arrived at mid-life without having looked very far ahead. She always knew that her children would grow up and eventually leave home, but she hadn't realized how quickly it would happen. She was beginning to see a foreshadowing of the time when they would be completely independent and gone. Like many women who have functioned mainly as housewives and mothers without outside careers, she was at a loss to know what to do with herself when she reached mid-life.

You may not be one of these women; in fact, you may

not have children or even be married. In any case, this chapter may help you understand someone else who has spent several years mothering and keeping things running for her husband and is now experiencing inner or outer turmoil.

TIME TO THINK

By her late thirties a woman may be hit with a strong need to reevaluate her life. The average woman following the normal family cycle likely has been married fifteen or more years. Her last child has gone off to school for all day. In *Men in Mid-Life Crisis* this is called the time of the *quiet nest* when everyone is away from home during the day. The *empty nest,* when children move out of the home, will come later. Now she still has plenty of mother jobs, but because the rooms are finally stilled from all the noise and hubbub of preschoolers, she has opportunity to think about the meaning of her life.

Quite often the mid-life woman who has been exclusively a homemaker and mother will begin to feel that life is passing her by. Her husband generally is consumed with becoming a success in his work and her children are now launching toward their own worlds. She may feel insignificant. She may wonder if all the work of being a mother has amounted to anything. What does she do for the rest of life?

WHAT TO DO ABOUT THE CHANGES

Sometimes mid-life women experience a quiet desperation in their desire for greater usefulness, but they may not know how to bring about the necessary changes in their thinking and lifestyle to deal with the growing anxieties within them. Too often the only form of relief is an occasional social diversion. For some of these women, coming to mid-life transition is a jolting experience, much the same as taking hold of a faulty appliance cord with wet hands.

Some of the difficulty is that many women have not realized they would not always have children at home and, thus, always have the mother role. If we look at it chronologically, however, we can see that there are many years in a woman's total life span during which she is not actively caring for children. In the first ten or twelve years of life, a girl is too young to produce children. In the second ten years she chooses not to have children because she is not married. During her twenties she probably will marry and have all of her children. During her thirties, the average woman is busy raising her children, who will be entering their teens by her late thirties. The woman's forties are the launching years. The children are involved with their teen peer group, then off to college and into a career or marriage, perhaps making her a grandmother by her late forties.

As you consider an entire lifetime, a woman is really only in the direct mothering process from about age twenty-one or twenty-two through her early forties. Even during these mothering years, it is important for a mother to shift from being the mothering decision-maker to becoming a confidante and peer during the adolescent and young adult years.

We observe an interesting sidelight here. Some of the young couples who practiced "zero population growth" during the early- and mid-1970s are now starting to have children in their thirties, causing a minor baby boom. This changes the timing of the family cycle for them.

MOTHERING: THE PASSING PHASE

When her children leave home for all day at elementary school, a woman experiences a deepening sense of losing the mothering role. Up until this time she has thought of herself as a young mother with an important job to do in caring for her children. Now she begins to realize that she is in a different category.

I (Sally) remember when this strange sense of loss hit me. At an early fall meeting of the women's fellowship group at the church we were pastoring in Carol Stream, Illinois, the speaker for the evening wanted to get some idea of the kind of audience he was addressing. He asked us to raise our hands if we had children. I proudly raised my hand with most of the women there. He asked again that we raise our hands if our children still lived at home. I lifted my hand without much thought. Then he asked how many women had preschoolers. I couldn't raise my hand! Many other mothers could. Becki, our youngest, had just started kindergarten a few days earlier, and I was no longer the mother of a "little" girl. For the first time in eleven years, I didn't have at least one child at home all day.

After the matter had been so graphically called to my attention by the hand-raising activity, I couldn't get over it for a long time. I had to tell Jim about it when I got home. In fact, I probably brought it up to him several times over the next few weeks. I know I told others then and have talked about the incident through the years. Becki's entering kindergarten was definitely a demarcation time in my life.

Many a young woman has enjoyed the good, warm feeling when her children called her "Mommy." There is something special about being first in a child's vocabulary, but as her children grow older and start calling her "Mom," she may sense her role is slipping away. With the change of her name there is the unspoken question of how long will it be before she is called mother-in-law and grandmother?

By the time the average mid-life woman reaches her late thirties or early forties, she is already becoming painfully aware that her teenagers don't want to be mothered. She realizes that she is losing her grip on the mother career. If she hasn't let go and allowed her teens to begin to mature and develop independence, she probably will have a great deal of difficulty in granting freedom to her young adult children in her fifties. She likely will be labeled an interfering mother-in-law and a possessive grandmother.

MID-LIFE BABY

Sometimes the mid-life woman who is sensing that she is losing her mothering role will decide to have a baby. This may sound very exciting as a dream, but there are a lot of other factors to consider, even as simple as energy level. Can she really stand going all night without sleep? One forty-year-old mother put it, "Baby care suits a once-a-week grandmotherly schedule better than every day and every hour."

There also is a higher risk factor to the baby's health. Older mothers "produce a higher percentage of offspring with congenital defects than younger mothers. It is suggested that this has to do with the age of the ovum. Cells in the ovary start producing ova either before or shortly after a baby girl is born. By the time of menopause, an ovum is forty-five to fifty years old, and 'may well have been subjected to harmful environmental influences such as chemicals, viruses, ionizing radiation, or to spontaneous genetic accidents.' "[1]

There are some people who suggest that the risk of a mid-life baby is not very great because of the procedure called amniocentesis by which a sample of the amniotic fluid surrounding the fetus is withdrawn and analyzed to determine if the child will be normal.[2] It is true that you can discover whether or not the child is likely to be normal, but what do you do if you discover the child is abnormal? Do you opt to keep the child or go the abortion route?

There is another related problem. Assume the child you have in mid-life is normal. Your primary mothering is extended only about another twelve years. Sooner or later you have to quit having children and stop living through other peoples' lives.

THE IDEAL FAMILY

There is a common fallacy about the composition of the typical American family. We've been told for a long time that the average family is made up of a husband who is working full time and a wife who is unemployed outside the home. They are both in their first marriage and have 2.5 children. The reality is that only seven out of 100 families are like this. The more typical American family has a wife who is working at least part-time away from home. There also are vast numbers of single parent families and blended families (where two previously divorced people are now remarried, and they with their children from former marriages have established a new family unit).

The woman who was solely a homemaker and mother is an image that our nation has commonly accepted, but in reality it never has been true. In the early days of our country, women labored alongside their men, working in the fields, caring for the animals, or keeping shops. They also had the responsibility of the garden, canning, cooking, making clothes, and all that it took to create a home. They really never were unemployed.

The unemployed housewife who has been "set free" by a houseful of machinery is a rather modern innovation. Today's homemaker has shifted her energies to being a chauffeur, hostess, den mother, PTA board member, and Bible Study Fellowship leader. Some of those activities may really be in line with her personality and talents, and are fulfilling to her, but others may be just an accumulated drain on her emotional battery.

MISPLACED MEANING

Another common assumption of the woman who chooses to be a housewife and mother exclusively is that she will find satisfaction in life by living vicariously through the success of her husband and her children. A study entitled "Housewives' Self-Esteem and Their Husbands' Success: The Myth of Vicarious Involvement" revealed that "dependence on her husband for success may reduce a wife's feelings of worth, especially if she is well educated and, presumably, able to earn her own rewards. While a married woman may devise ways of converting her husband's status into her own. . . , her general powerlessness and lack of control over the course of her life may increase her level of psychological disturbance. . . . Nonworking housewives with attractive, high-status husbands felt less adequate than married professional women."[3]

The researchers also noted that the nonworking housewife may feel more inadequate if her husband is highly successful because she is contrasting herself with him.[4] We know many couples where this is so, and if the wife does enter the work world, for whatever reason, she often must take a much lower level job than her husband because she is untrained. Many women gave up college and career training for marriage when they were younger.

TRAPPED BY THE PAST

Fran wanted to work outside the home, partly to help with the family income while some of their children were attending a Christian college and partly because she "needed to get out of the house." Her husband is a highly respected professional man. Fran took a low-status, minimum-wage clerical job. She is an intelligent, relatively creative woman who is capable of much more, but she doesn't have the education or experience for other positions. She doesn't feel she can go to school at this stage in life, with three children still at home. So, although she is adding to the income and finding some outside stimulation, she feels trapped with a job beneath her abilities.

After giving fifteen years or more to making a home and caring for children, a woman often finds her skills and experience discounted and considered of little value. She may have felt very happy and considered the job the "high calling" that it is. If she were receiving satisfaction and self-esteem only from her husband's status and success, however, she was putting her eggs in the wrong basket.

Neither will she find happiness in the long run if she lives vicariously through her children's successes. All around us are examples of parents who push their kids to become what they never could be themselves. We have spent many of our adult years working with students while we pastored churches near college campuses; we have known hundreds of students with confused personal identities because of their parents' unreasonable expectations for them. Some of them have desperately tried to please their parents but have been assigned more than they can possibly do. Many have been pressured to do what will bring happiness to the parents, without regard for the child.

Elizabeth's parents had told her throughout her childhood and adolescence that she was to be a medical doctor. She was encouraged to get high grades in order to be accepted into medical school. At the same time, her parents were giving clear signals that she was to get married early in her twenties and give them the joy of being grandparents. How would it be possible for this girl to do both full-time jobs at the same time? When she came for counseling, she was nearly unable to function and this "A student" was now failing her classes.

A mother naturally will find satisfaction if her children are successful in life, but her sole source of happiness cannot rest on them. There may be times when the children will do well, but she can't take all the credit. And when they do not do well, she cannot take all the blame either.

Another common condition is the confused self-image of a woman who thinks her identity is found in her husband and children. She may have an identity through them temporarily, but in reality it is not her own. She is only assuming an incomplete identity. It is a mask that surely will be ripped off as she reaches mid-life, when her marriage may be stale, her husband doesn't need her as much, and her children are starting to leave the circle of her influence.

AN EXPLOSIVE RESENTMENT

"It hit me quite suddenly—the feeling, I mean, of what my life added up to. I can remember it exactly. I was having a second cup of coffee. The kids had gone off to school; my husband left for work. I tell you, my hands were shaking; I wanted to scream. One more set of breakfast dishes to clean up; one more dinner to worry about; one more bed to make; one more load of laundry. I had had it, I tell you. I wanted to scream. At that moment if someone had just given me a one way ticket anywhere I would have jumped. Slam the door on the whole routine.

"My husband says to me he helps. Who does the cleaning up after supper, he tells me? Well, bully for him. He puts a few dishes in the dishwasher. The kids are supposed to help. Will you tell me why a child fifteen years old won't screw on the top of the ketchup bottle after I remind him 100 times? I could do without my husband's cleaning up. All it means is I have to go back and throw cleanser into the sink to clean out stains. He won't take a sponge and scrub stains.

"You know what really gets to me? Socks! Will you please tell me why children and one adult male can't stop turning socks inside out and throwing them into the laundry? For eighteen years I have turned socks inside out and matched pairs. Underwear the same. Inside out. Shirts inside out and dumped into the laundry. That's maybe the story of my life—inside out and backwards."[5]

The analytical husband looking in from the outside probably would say, "Get hold of yourself. Organize your time. You don't have as much pressure on you as I have at work. You don't even have to go out to a job." What he is ignoring and doesn't fully understand is that this woman has sold herself on a dream—the mother/wife dream— and she finds herself unfulfilled with it. The dirty socks and the stain in the sink are simply the little straws that break the camel's back—or the woman's spirit.

ESCAPE

The temptation is to run away. Ed Goldfader, president of Tracer's Company of America, described the typical runaway wife as a thirty-five-year-old woman who was married at nineteen and had her first child within eleven months. "Since then, she has devoted her life to childrearing and housekeeping and is now at an age when she feels she no longer has time to make a meaningful change in her life-style. Often her husband has almost stopped thinking of her as an individual."[6]

The husband is asked to supply answers about his wife's personal history on a questionnaire given by the tracer's firm. The common responses are revealing:

EYE COLOR: can't remember
HAIR COLOR: dishwater blonde
HOBBY: none
HABITS: (blank)
MENTAL CONDITION: emotionally disturbed

It is startling that the runaways are economically well off. The deprivation of things is not what drives them to break out. What causes them to leave is the deprivation of meaning in life and the feeling of not being valued or even noticed by their husbands.[7]

Sometimes women do not run away. They simply explode at home. Joanne was doing her normal morning task, getting breakfast while the rest of the family was getting up. A magazine article tells her story:

" 'Mom, where're my socks?' shouted Tom from the upstairs hall.

" 'Mom, who took my blue sweater?' yelled Kevin from his bedroom.

" 'Mom,' wailed David, 'I can't find my shoes.'

" 'Honey, did you do the laundry this week? I'm all out of underwear.'

" 'Mom,' demanded Sarah from all the way up on the third floor, 'make extra coffee—I want to take a thermos to school.'

" 'Mom,' cried Jimmy, 'my baseball fell in the toilet!'

"Joanne McCarty (all names have been changed to protect the privacy of the family) . . . tried to ignore the commotion upstairs as she stirred orange juice and fed bread into the toaster. A dull ache throbbed in her left shoulder. . . .

"Five children and their father appeared in the kitchen. Framed by the doorway, their disgruntled faces made an unpleasant family portrait as they raised their voice in a loud chorus: 'Mom!'

" 'Something clicked,' Joanne says, 'I felt hypnotized— as if I had no control over my body. I took off my apron, poured the orange juice into the sink, dropped the toast in the garbage, and walked out of the kitchen. I remember announcing out loud, "I quit." ' "[8]

Joanne moved into one of the small rooms of the house and did not participate with the family. She simply cared for herself and her part-time job.

Pressures had come to a head in Joanne's life about the time that she sought a part-time job. She records:

" 'After I went to work, I learned that I had raised a

generation of incompetents. They couldn't do anything for themselves; I was mother, wife, housekeeper, cook, book-keeper—something more. I realized that I always told them what to do and when to do it. I thought being in complete command was the only way I could keep order, so I was like a full support system. . . .' "9

When Joanne was asked why she quit the family, she responded, " 'I couldn't change them . . . and I couldn't go on. I was simply worn out.' "10

Her husband and the children all wanted her to come back and assume the mothering role. The home was in chaos without her leadership, but she refused to partici-pate in the family. Her husband understood what a huge responsibility she was carrying at home and said, " 'If it's too much . . . I think you should give up the job. We've managed all these years on one paycheck. We still can.'

" 'The problem is, Dan, I don't want to.' "

Her husband and the children could not understand that Joanne wanted everyone's needs to be met, *including* her own. The family thought of her only as someone who always met their needs, but assumed that she did not have needs.

WHOSE ESTEEM POWERS YOU?

A study of self-esteem in family-oriented and career-oriented women found that "working professional women, whether married or single, by the middle adult years hold themselves in higher regard than equally gifted nonem-ployed women."12 The researchers go on to comment, "Given these striking findings, it seems we cannot in good conscience continue to raise girls to seek their *primary* personal fulfillment and self-identity within the family. If bright women seek no other sources of gratification in addition to marriage and maternity, self-esteem eventually drops and loneliness and uncertainty plague them."13

Some Christians may argue that God intended for

women to care for husbands and children and they should be happy doing so. We agree that there should be satisfaction in being a wife and mother, but a woman needs to check her motives carefully and to determine the source of her identity and self-esteem. This is true whether she is solely a homemaker, a career woman, or a combination of the two. If her occupation as wife and mother changes— she loses her husband or her children no longer need her as much—she must have a picture of herself and an identity that are based on who God has made her to be as an individual. No woman should live off the identity or accomplishments of her husband, children, employer, work colleagues, or anyone else.

Chapter Three

THE PROFESSIONAL SHIFTS DREAMS

Lois is a single woman who is chairman of her department in a large state university. Her major book, along with her journal writings, has given her national and international standing in her field. She is one of a half dozen specialists in her area of expertise in this country. When we got together to talk about what was bothering her, her story poured out as from a little girl who, through her tears, was telling of a devastating nightmare.

"I don't know what's happening to me. I just can't do anything. Even simple tasks. I don't want to clean my house, make meals. I don't even want to get dressed. Even the little things that I used to like to do, like sew and play tennis—I don't want to do those things.

"And my job! I'm supposed to be a teacher, and yet here we are, a month into the semester, and I don't even have a syllabus for the class. I don't know where I'm going in the course. I'm just totally unprepared. I know what I should do, but I just can't do it. What's wrong with me?

"It's as if I'm totally rejecting who I am and what's happening in my life. I keep saying to myself, 'You know, you chose this life.'

"When I was a college girl, I didn't want to get married. I

wanted to be a career woman. I wanted to be successful in my field. I wanted to make a name for myself, to achieve something. I didn't want marriage and family to get in the way of my career success. Now, here I am, with all the things I wanted when I was a college student—knowledge, skills, success, respect. Yet somehow they seem insignificant to me now.

"Maybe what I'm really saying is that I'm going to be forty and I wonder if I've been a fool to give up the chance to get married and to have children? The idea of such a change in me is scary, and I'm not even sure I'd know how to be a good wife and mother if I had the chance. But, I really don't want to grow old alone."

SOMETHING GAINED, SOMETHING LOST

The wrestlings of this mid-life woman emphasize that our lives are always changing. We are not static and fixed. Choices we made earlier in life need to be continually updated and modified to meet our ever-changing value system.

Carl Jung's words in *Modern Man in Search of a Soul* reinforce this idea: "We cannot live the afternoon of life according to the program of life's morning, for what was great in the morning will be little at evening, and what in the morning was true, will at evening have become a lie. I have given psychological treatment to too many people of advanced years, and have looked into the secret chambers of their souls, not to be moved by this fundamental truth."[1]

There are many women who have chosen the career-only direction and who later struggle with the implications of their choice. They ask, "What have I missed? Or what will I miss?" As we consider the ramifications involved when a woman has made a career the dominant part of her life, we must remember that life changes. Points when choices have to be made are factors to be reckoned with, especially by mid-life and after.

A third-year Harvard Medical School student says, "I'm going to be a surgeon. I'll never be a trapped housewife like my mother. But I would like to get married and have children, I think. They say we can have it all. But how? I work thirty-six hours in the hospital, twelve hours off. How am I going to have a relationship, much less kids, with hours like that? I'm not sure I can be a superwoman. I'm frightened that I may be kidding myself. Maybe I can't have it all. Either I won't be able to have the kind of marriage I dream of or the kind of medical career I want."[2]

THE TIME GAMBLE

A mid-life woman in her thirties says, "I'm up against the clock, you might say. If I don't have a child now, it will be too late. But it's an agonizing choice. I've been supporting my husband while he gets his Ph.D. We don't know what kind of job he'll be able to get. There's no pay when you take off to have a baby in my company. They don't guarantee you'll get your job back. If I don't have a baby, will I miss out on life somehow? Will I really be fulfilled as a woman?"[3]

Because of the absolute biological time limit on a woman's child-bearing years, women in their late twenties and thirties often feel they have to start having their family in spite of where they are with career goals or family economics.

Janet, who is married and nearing thirty, told us that she wants to be certain she has completed her lengthy, demanding education and has had a solid start in her career (to which she strongly feels God has called her) before becoming a mother. She intends to be a good mother when she does have her children, so she wants to be sure she is ready. She and her husband both want her career to be at a point where it is rather self-sustaining so that she can devote time and energy to doing a very good job of mothering. But there is that biological time limit. Janet said, "I feel like I'm being forced to choose, and with either choice, I'm losing."

UNSUNG HEROINES

We in the twentieth century have not been very aware that many women in other centuries chose to remain single—or if married, childless—to devote themselves to service for God and fellow humans. The important work done by these women has not often been included in church history or secular history, but their biographies can be found in libraries. As we have read some of these, we have been stimulated to an appreciation of their dedication to God's call and to a questioning of our own commitment and priorities.

One example is Marcella, a Roman woman who lived in the fourth century at the time Jerome was translating the Bible into the important Latin version, which was the Bible used for a thousand years. Marcella persuaded Jerome to teach Bible classes to some of Rome's leading women. At his urging, Marcella studied the Old Testament in the original Hebrew text. She became an excellent scholar of the Bible and established a center for study, prayer, and charity. After Jerome left, he used Marcella as the one to whom others could go for Bible materials and once asked her to settle a dispute over Scripture.

There have been many dedicated women down through the years right up to Henrietta Mears, Mother Teresa, Corrie ten Boom, and others in our time. *Women at the Crossroads*, by Kari Torjesen Malcolm, gives synopses of the lives of some of the inspiring women in history and also gives the bibliographical information so that you may locate the complete works.[4] An accurate study of women in

Scripture also reveals that God gave them varied gifts and opportunities for service. He called them to do many different kinds of work, and we are impressed by their faithfulness.

The subject of a woman's dedication to a career, whether "Christian" or "secular," is still a matter of motives and perspective. First of all, for a Christ-centered woman, her life's work should not be categorized as either Christian or secular. When we are doing whatever is right for us, it is "Christian," although it may not be funded by a Christian institution. A woman may have a "secular" employer, but she is in "full time Christian service" if her motivation is in line with God's.

Second, a woman's identity and self-worth should not be based solely on what she does. A woman needs a whole life perspective which is founded on who she *is* as the individual God has made her to be, with her unique background and experiences, gifts and qualities, and opportunities for expressing them.

The important key is that at every life stage a woman should be evaluating who she is and where she is to go with her life, so that she doesn't reach mid-life with major adjustments to be made when so much else is happening. Since life is always changing, we continually need to fine-tune our goals and motives.

A BIGGER PIECE OF THE PIE

As we've mentioned earlier, women have always worked at more than keeping house and caring for children. The number of American women who leave home to do that other work, however, is growing. Prior to the Second World War, women were not highly involved outside the home, but the war drew women out of their homes to run the factories and other businesses while the men had gone to fight. In a sense, women never went back home after the war. By the end of the 1940s, however, only about 20 percent of the women age sixteen and older worked. In the '80s the number is nearly 50 percent.[5]

The *Journal of the American Medical Association* reports that almost one-third of the first-year students in U.S. medical schools in 1981 were women, more than a 300 percent increase since 1969. The report goes on to say that women now comprise 25 percent of the M.D. graduates and 27 percent of the overall medical student enrollment.[6]

Even though half of our women are employed outside the home, it is strange that males do not believe that women really want to be employed. Men often feel that a woman is working only until she can find a husband and then she will be glad, as one author says, "to buy sheer negligees for her trousseau, and cheerfully abandon her career."[7]

DOUBLE BIND

The mid-life woman who does not work because her husband does not want her to, or her religious culture will not allow her to, may be put in the emotionally dehumanizing position of having to justify her existence on the basis of hobbies or "busy work." On the other hand, the woman who has chosen the career-only role may have done so because she has bought into our work ethic, which implies that one is not a person unless one gets paid for work.

We are not suggesting that people ought not to work nor that they should not be fulfilled in that work. We do believe, however, that the motivation for work should not be an uncontrollable workaholism or an unfulfilled need to justify one's existence. Neither should it be, as it is for some women, an all-out, I-can-do-it-no-matter-what-you-say effort to prove a point. Rather, we ought to work with an understanding of the abilities God has given us and with his guidance about how these gifts are to be used to support ourselves and to serve others. When work loses its connection to God and a ministry orientation to people, we become inhuman robots.

By mid-life, the Christian woman may find herself in a double bind. If she has chosen the career-only role, she may find herself unfulfilled as a woman and at the same time criticized by the religious community. If, on the other hand, she chose the housewife/mother role, she may find herself out of a job in the middle years and have to fill empty hours with rather meaningless activities if she is not to have an outside career.

THE IMPACT OF FEMINISM

The Women's Movement has had both positive and negative influences on our society, including our Christian subculture. This movement has been a help in alerting us to the needs of women and their rights to equal pay, job advancement, and educational opportunities. The movement also has had a positive effect in helping marriages return to a more biblical and egalitarian style.

Some of the negative effects are that some women who neither wanted to nor had to work outside their homes were caused to feel foolish and wrong for finding fulfillment as homemakers and mothers.

Some women also have mistaken equal opportunities and rights to mean that they were to become like men. In *The Gift of Feeling*,[8] Paul Tournier, that wise Swiss psychiatrist whose books and lectures have so significantly helped us understand ourselves, reminds us that the world needs both feminine and masculine attributes. Our society as a whole and we as individuals need the sensitivities and perspectives of both sexes. Some feminists have made the error of trying to erase all lines and make one sex. Reading *The Gift of Feeling* makes you glad you were born female and helps you realize that you have equally important contributions to make to the world.

FEMINISM RECONSIDERED

Betty Friedan, author of *The Feminine Mystique* and one of the most important women behind the modern thrust for feminism, now says in *The Second Stage:* "I sense something *off*, out of focus, going wrong, in the terms by which these young people [of today] are trying to live the equality we in the women's movement fought for. . . .

"I've begun to sense undertones of pain and puzzlement, a queasiness, and uneasiness, almost a bitterness that they hardly dare admit. Despite all the opportunities we won for them, and for which we envy them, they seem afraid to ask certain questions. And they continue to be troubled by those old needs which shaped our lives and trapped us, those needs against which we rebelled."[9]

Friedan is suggesting that women may have exchanged roles—that is, believing the feminism message and surrendering some or all of the marriage, mothering, homemaking roles to accept the career-only role. Now these women are expressing a sense of frustration over being trapped in this newly-constructed feminist cage.

Betty Friedan goes on to discuss the fears of the feminist movement even to consider that perhaps the older values of motherhood and homemaking are really important for women. She says: "If we suddenly suggest that old experiences supposedly irrelevant or distracting to new women are, in fact, more important than we wanted to admit— experiences like motherhood, which the old feminine mystique and the new enemies of equality claim are the only important experiences for women—do we thereby deny the importance of the gains won in the women's movement? Would we want to go back?

"That is the fear, of course. That is why we do not want to face new questions, new tests. But if we go on parroting or denouncing or defending the clichés of women's liberation in the same old terms until they harden into a new mystique, denying the realities of our personal experience and the new problems, *then* we are in real danger of going back. *Then,* we invite a real backlash of disillusioned, bitter women—and outraged, beleaguered men."[10]

SOMETIMES SINGLE

Now, more than ever before, women have a choice whether to marry at all and whether or not to remarry after divorce or their husband's death.

In the early 1950s the reasons women gave for being unmarried were "hostility toward marriage or members of the opposite sex, lack of interest in heterosexual partners, emotional involvement with parents, poor health, feelings of physical unattractiveness, unwillingness to assume responsibility, inability to find one's 'true love,' a sense of social inadequacy, the perception of marriage as a threat to career goals, economic problems, and geographic, educational, or occupational isolation that limited the chances of meeting an eligible mate."[11]

By the mid-seventies, however, reasons for remaining single were more positive: "increased freedom and enjoyment of life, opportunities to meet people and develop friendships, economic independence, more and better social experiences, and opportunities for personal development."[12]

Being single does provide the opportunity to more easily carry out a career, but the career also provides the capacity to remain single. Lifestyles in earlier times caused women to be dependent upon marriage for support.

Singleness is important for every woman to consider because at some point in her adult life every woman is likely to be single for a time because of the high divorce rate and the different life-spans of men and women. The woman who has followed the career-only direction will likely not have to worry about support if she is never married or becomes single after marriage. The woman who has had no career or work experience, however, may have serious support problems if she becomes single.

CHOICE FOR CHILDLESSNESS

On what basis does a married woman decide to have or not to have a child? A *Ladies Home Journal* poll in 1961 of young women aged sixteen to twenty-one found that " 'most' wanted four children, and 'many' wanted five."[13] Today the desired number is most often two.

The authors of *For Her Own Good* condemn childlessness by saying, "The moral excuse of childlessness was the 'population explosion' discovered by demographers and futurists in the mid-sixties, but the real reason for most young couples, was that children just didn't fit into the lifestyle they had become accustomed to as singles. For every idealist, like the Mills College valedictorian of 1969, who declared, 'Our days as a race on this planet are numbered . . . *I am terribly saddened by the fact that the most humane thing for me to do is to have no children at all,'* there were dozens of women who saw no reason to defend their childlessness in anything but personal terms."[14]

New York magazine presented some self-indulgent arguments against parenthood:

"We [her husband and herself] treasure the freedom to pick up and disappear for a weekend or a month or even a year, to sleep odd hours, to breakfast at three A.M. or three P.M., to hang out the DO NOT DISTURB sign, to slam a door and be alone, or alone together, to indulge in foolish extravagances, to get out of bed at seven A.M. and to horseback ride in the park before work . . . to have champagne with dinner for no special reason at all, to tease and love anywhere, any hour, without a nagging guilt that a child is being neglected."[15]

Some women and their husbands are unable to have children, so have no choice. Others choose not to have children for health reasons or because their careers or ministries are such that it would be difficult to care properly for children.

SHIFTING VALUES

The decision to enjoy personal freedom or to pursue a career in place of having children may prove to be wrong and unfulfilling, however. As people move into the latter half of mid-life (an era we call the "mellow age"), they feel a need to become "generative," as Erikson has said.[16] A characteristic of generativity is a strong urgency to pass something on to another generation, to leave part of yourself behind, to prepare a younger generation for leadership. The authors of *The Indelible Family* found in their research that there is within us the "dynastic imperative"—the drive to reproduce ourselves and our family of origin.[17]

The career-only woman who deliberately chooses childlessness will be setting herself up for a potentially exacerbated mid-life crisis and for increased stress in later years. Women may fulfill the need for generativity through surrogate children, but childless mid-life women have reported to us a desire to nurture their own children after it was too late.

Increasing numbers of single women adopt children and some single mid-life women deliberately choose to bear a child outside of marriage in order to have the mothering experience. Nancy Petersen is one who, around age forty, elected to do this, and she reports in her book that there are many others.[18] We do not condone this, but it points up the fact that a parenting desire hits most women sooner or later.

Each couple and their circumstances are unique. There can be no pat mold for everyone regarding the choice to have children. Each couple needs to communicate openly and often with each other and to seek God's guidance about his plan for children in their lives. He is, after all, the only one wise enough to know future circumstances, feelings, and needs.

CAREER AND MARRIAGE

As we think about the working wife, it's important to realize that there is a difference between working for money that is used to pay bills and working in a career. A career not only brings the money rewards but may also bring the satisfaction of "I know who I am. I understand the gifts and abilities that God has given to me, and my career is in line with those talents." Too many working wives have had to take any available job. They have not been able to consider seriously the match of their gifts with the job requirement.

The career woman who is married needs to think through a whole set of questions as she matches career with marriage. Does she keep her salary for herself, put it into the household, or divide it in some way? Will her job require her to be gone from her home many hours when her husband is there? Does the situation of the job and the glamour of meeting new people lead her to seek inappropriate pleasures outside her marriage and perhaps threaten her marriage? Does her working constitute a threat to her husband's ego and add to his self-doubt?

Each of these factors needs to be evaluated for the career involvement of both husband and wife. They should look at their overall career goals, keeping them in line with their individual gifts and abilities and making sure that their marriage is enriched by each one's career involvement.

The November 1982 issue of *Psychology Today* reported the impact of the wife's earning more than her husband: "If the man's job is beneath his potential, while his wife not only makes more money but also has a prestigious job, he is 11 times more likely to die of heart disease in middle age." The author also observed: "In egalitarian marriage, when both husband and wife held professional, typically male jobs, the chance of divorce was twice as high as (those) in which the wife held a typically female job—33 percent versus 15 percent." If the wife has a higher paying or higher status job than her husband, it is more acceptable if it is a typical woman's job such as nursing or teaching. Among the husbands whose wives earn more than they do there also is insecurity about whether their wives really love them. Other studies show there is a lessening in frequency of sexual intercourse.[19]

It is crucial, therefore, that both the wife and the husband take a serious look at their careers and their marriage relationship. Later in the book we will explore this in more detail and will make some suggestions from our own experience as we have worked together in rearing a family and in dual careers.

PROPER QUESTIONING

A young woman needs to evaluate properly the career-only approach to living, especially if that career-only direction leads her into isolation from meaningful relationships. Remember, as a person ages and reaches mid-life, quality relationships become more significant.

It would be important to listen to those cautions we noted earlier from Betty Friedan and the concerns she had heard from women who are questioning what they'll miss by going solely for a career.

A woman will be wise to consider her total personality and, as much as possible, try to understand what her needs and feelings will be as she ages.

Counselors, therapists, and other people-helpers are noting, along with our own observations over the last twenty-five years, that many who "sold themselves to the company store" when they were young are now disillusioned or resentful at mid-life. The company store does not meet many of their emotional needs as their values change; in fact, the company often threatens to discard them because they are aging.

Chapter Four

WONDER WOMAN TRIES IT ALL

Nine out of ten women work outside the home at some time in life. For most it is a necessity and not a choice. By 1976 only 40 percent of the jobs in the country paid enough to support a family. Instead of children being the reason for women to stay at home, their expenses were the reason mothers had to go to work. Demographers estimate that by 1990, 55 percent of all women over age sixteen will be working, including half of the mothers of young children. They also forecast that sometime in the '80s the number of women will surpass the number of men in the work force.[1]

At some time in life most women marry, and most of those have children. Until recently, it was exceptional for a woman to combine marriage, family, and a paid career entirely different from her husband's occupation. Since World War II, however, it has not been abnormal for a woman to work at a "job" to help pay the family bills, and it has never been exceptional for some women to carry out an unpaid mission along with housekeeping.

We have said that a woman should not find her identity or life satisfaction solely through a career nor in being a housewife/mother only. Today, however, many women are trying to juggle all three roles of housewife, mother, and career woman, and a new breed of "Super Woman" has evolved. It is just as faulty for a woman to race along in this lifestyle as in the career-only or homemaker-only roles. The sheer demands of time and energy mean a headlong race with little time for reflection or evaluation. A woman may keep this up for a time, but when she reaches mid-life, she is a prime candidate for a crisis because many forces converge upon her.

THREE-THIRDS ARE MORE THAN A WHOLE

One of the problems is that each of the three jobs is more than a one-third-time job. This is true emotionally as well as in the demands on her time. Women who are trying to handle all three at once often wrestle with a lot of guilt. They also must live with the actual consequences of not doing one or all of them as well as they could be done if there were only one role.

The authors of *The Working Mother's Complete Handbook* report that a survey of women all over the country revealed that mothers with outside occupations "care more about their families than about any other area of their lives."[2] This study also found that because the mothers are not at home all day, they worry about not giving enough attention to their families.

Another problem is how the career is affected by family demands. Usually the mother, not the father, is the one who stays home from work when a child is sick. Schools traditionally call the mother first if a child is injured or becomes sick at school. Many employers who hire mothers are tolerant of this; others are not. Some occupations are more easily adapted to unexpected absences than others.

In trying to meet all the family needs, or what we think

they need, some women wear out themselves and their families. They put a strain on everyone around, attempting to prove that they are not neglecting their family duties because they work.

GRINDING AND GNASHING

Eleanor was an efficient but uptight Super Woman with a lot of guilt about being a working mother. She actually enjoyed her work a great deal, but she also wanted to make sure no one could accuse her of slacking up on caring for her family. Her children were in their early and middle teen years, and most of their classmates ate lunch at school. Eleanor, however, insisted that her children come home so that they could be together over the lunch hour. By the time she got home from work and the kids got in the door from school, they had about twenty-five minutes to make lunch, eat, clean up, and have *togetherness*. The kids got back to school feeling they had missed out on all the fun their friends were having, and Eleanor raced back to work through the traffic to get to her desk before 1:00, breathless and short of patience with her co-workers. We can imagine that in that tense situation during lunch at home, little of value happened.

We have to be realistic about how much we can handle in a day or a week. We hear about many successful professional women, especially now that the opportunities for women are becoming more prevalent. There is a price to pay, however, the same as successful men must pay a price when a decision is made for one option over another. For every direction we choose, we have to turn our backs on other directions.

One poll of women executives shows they are well paid and enjoy their affluence. But 63 percent said that to achieve their successes they had had to give up their marriages, family plans, time with their families and friends, travel, and cultural activities.[3]

DOUBLE DUTY OR DOUBLE PLEASURE

Dual-career couples have some special issues to work out. One is the attitude of the husband toward the wife's outside employment. Many men are still very traditional about providing the income while the wife makes sure that the homefront is running smoothly so his career is unhindered.

Some men are threatened with the possibility that their wives may become too independent from them in everything from use of money to making decisions and having outside stimulation. The need to be strengthening the marriage relationship is always present whether both are working or only the husband is. In either situation it takes time to communicate, to have fun together, and to be relaxed for sexual experiences.

One author points out: "To 'succeed' within the framework of a double-career marriage—that is, to enjoy satisfaction and growth in both the career and the relationship—couples must call into play those skills which have proven effective in the marketplace: communication, teamwork, preplanning, goal-directed activities, etc. This is difficult because a personal relationship brings with it emotional triggers that usually are absent in a career. Efficient and skilled workers often find themselves totally unprofessional when dealing with their partners. While no careerist would enter into a job interview without first preparing a detailed resume and anticipating questions that might be raised, many enter into their marriage relationship merely trusting to love, luck, and the Lord."[4]

One study of 1,089 dual-career marriages shows that a higher probability for success in both the marriage and the careers exists if both spouses have "androgynous gender identities." That means that the traditional sex stratification is less important to the couple, and they "would be comfortable with either spouse having superior occupational attainments."[5]

The author of The Two-Paycheck Marriage, after analyzing polls, surveys, biographies, and conversations with hundreds of men and women, suggests the following eight types of dual-career marriages:

"*Traditional homemakers* agree with their husbands that a wife should stay at home.

"*Defiant homemakers* insist on staying at home, even though their husbands want them to work.

"*Submissive homemakers* want to work, but their husbands want them to stay at home.

"*Reluctant homemakers* want to work and their husbands agree, but a family problem or lack of training holds them back.

"*Reluctant working wives* wish they didn't have to work, but their financial situation demands it.

"*Submissive working wives* want to keep house, but their husbands want them to work.

"*Defiant working wives* work because they want to, although their husbands don't like it.

"*Contemporary working wives* are working, and that's what both they and their husbands want."[6]

You probably see yourself in one or more of these categories. If you are not happy with the type you are, perhaps you see another one you would rather be. You and your husband should discuss the various aspects of your working and make some agreements and compromises that will help you work out an arrangement that will be comfortable for both of you.

MINE, YOURS, OR OURS

Use of the wife's salary is another issue. Women who go to work to pay the family bills have little question about how their salary will be used, but those who are following a profession for reasons other than making ends meet may have different uses for their money. Some dual-career couples have specific divisions for their salaries: he pays the mortgage and utilities; she buys the food and clothes. Others use the wife's salary strictly for luxuries they would not otherwise have. Some couples use only the husband's salary for all living expenses, and the wife uses hers totally on herself. However it's done, both mates need to agree.

Probably one of the biggest hassles for the working wife and mother is simply keeping the household running. Household tasks do not carry any prestige, but they still have to be done. In most cases, the woman is the one charged with the responsibility. Even if she can find ways to cut corners and let some things slide, her family may complain. In other cases, the family may not mind if things are not done perfectly around the house, but the woman insists upon it because of her guilt and Super Woman complex.

Caroline Bird reports from her research that some men help with the housework, but they pick only the jobs they like to do. She also says it appears that some husbands deliberately bungle their help in order to get out of it: "I asked him to vacuum the bedroom, and he did—all around the edges of the furniture, but not under the dresser or the bed!"[7]

We have noticed that men are glad to do special projects, such as barbecueing the meat for guests or making a special dish. These activities may get counted as hours contributed to housework in a month, but the average husband does very little in a month to help with the routine necessities that may be unpleasant.

If the wife complains about too much to do, she is offered the option of quitting work. Besides, she—and her husband—keep hearing glorious tales of Wonder Women who do it all with grace and ease. These women not only give their children focused attention and meet every emotional and physical need, they do the same for their husbands, keep the house clean and charmingly decorated, plan and execute gourmet meals every day, keep up the unceasing laundry, carry on the family correspondence, make the runs to doctors and teachers, take adult education classes, stay on a diet and exercise program, and— sew their own pinch-pleat drapes and their husband's sport coats! All the while, they are efficiently managing their careers. And let's not forget keeping up with all the community, school, and church activities either. These Wonder Women probably also lead a meaningful Bible study or direct the annual Vacation Bible School program.

END OF THE ROPE

Many women cope well with running three jobs at once— at least for a few years. Most of them that we have met, however, have to make some compromises and decide to do less than a magnificent job in every area. The ones who don't compromise come to a time, sooner or later, when they have some kind of crash. When the mid-life transition time arrives with its many forces of aging, innumerable change events, accumulation of children's and husband's needs, and urgent desire to reevaluate, the Super Woman is likely to have the biggest mid-life crisis of all.

Burn-out, whether given that label or not, is a common phenomenon of the woman who blindly tries to do it all. Judy was a well-meaning wife and mother who was also carrying on a ministry-related career. She had been so busy that she had not had time to do much reflecting or reorienting of her values for several years. When a family emergency hit, she was unable and unwilling to be the same strong one who always pulled things through. "I'm burned out. This time I'm not going to carry the load," she said as she withdrew from every aspect of her old life. At the time we're writing this, no one knows if she will ever return to her ministry, her husband, or her three children.

WHOSE DRUM BEAT?

When we try to find an answer to the dilemma of roles, experiencing fulfillment and meaning in life, and meeting financial and family needs, we could get confused by all the voices we hear. At one extreme are secular, impious advocates who propose that a woman can have it all (including multiple sex partners and a guilt-free conscience).[8] Just as extreme are those who give scriptural justification for women to be nothing more than keepers of home, husband, and children.

Somehow evangelical Christians have come to believe that the unemployed homemaker has always been the norm—God's only will for women. In early marriage she is to care for her children, but from age thirty-five or so, she is to be contented with hobbies or volunteer work. What about the woman who *never* marries? And what about the woman who *must* contribute to the family finances?

We have heard many Christian speakers denounce working wives and mothers without taking into account that sitting in the audience were women who had to work outside the home because of the husband's physical disability, his low earning power, or unusual financial needs due to medical or other expenses. These women were not working to provide luxuries or frivolities.

It is true that our standard of living keeps rising and what was once considered an extravagance is now a necessity, but we must be realistic and realize that there are certain minimums for the average American family. Possessing a working refrigerator would be outrageous for the African bush woman, but it is standard equipment in an American home. As we noted earlier, more than half the jobs in our country do not provide enough income for a family, so many women *must* work. Others choose to work for a variety of reasons, including feeling a calling for a particular ministry or profession.

FROM THE BEGINNING

As we look at Scripture and history, we see that women always have been involved in much more than housework and child care. In the Creation story we note, "Man and maid did he make them. And God blessed them and told them, 'Multiply and fill the earth and subdue it; you are masters of the fish and birds and all the animals' " (Genesis 1:27b-28). It is clear that from the beginning God was not anticipating a passive role on the part of the wife. Along with helping to multiply, she was also given co-responsibility of managing all aspects of the earth.

Other female examples in Scripture include women who made national impacts, such as Deborah, who was the chief executive officer of the Nation of Israel (Judges 4:4—5:31) and Esther, whose wisdom and assertiveness saved her people from destruction (Esther 2:5—9:32). In the New Testament there are examples, such as Priscilla, who worked alongside her husband in ministry in the early church, contributed to the spiritual development of the apostle Paul and Apollos, and was probably the stronger of the two (Acts 18, Romans 16:3, 1 Cor. 16:19, 2 Tim. 4:19), and Phoebe, whose leadership Paul places on a par with his own (Romans 16:1).

The authors of *Christian Women at Work* point out, "The Old and New Testaments provide enough exceptions to the portraits of women as wives and mothers to suggest that a woman's work should be related first to who she is as a person before God and then to the norms of society."[9]

Only in recent years have women wondered where they belong. The Industrial Revolution and modern technology have taken over many of women's tasks. These jobs have been moved into the marketplace, and at the same time women are told, "Stay home where you belong." The authors of *For Her Own Good* point out that formerly "the skills and work of women [were] indispensable to survival. . . . She could hardly think of herself as a 'misfit' in a world which depended so heavily on her."[10]

IN HER TIME

When I (Sally) think of models to follow, I have to think of my own mother. I always loved and appreciated her, but only in recent years with all the controversy over "woman's place" have I realized that it was not just because she was my mother that she was an outstanding woman.

As a young woman Mother was a school teacher. She lost her money when the banks failed during the Depression, so she did not get to have much college training, but she had more than nearly any other woman—or man, for that matter—in our entire neighborhood. ("Neighborhood," meaning a ten-mile radius surrounding and including a small rural town of 710 population.) Many had not even finished high school, which was not uncommon in the '20s. Mother continued teaching after marrying my father, who was a farmer. She was probably the only farm woman in that area who had an outside career after marriage. But she was needed and she was qualified, so she did it.

She was a full-time housewife and mother for the years that my brother and I were home, but that is by no means all that she did. She was important to my father in helping with the farm—caring for livestock, milking cows, feeding pigs, lambs, and calves, raising chickens, tending the garden, and preserving the food. She helped with special projects in the field too, such as stacking hay and combining grain. She also did a lot of preparing and serving huge meals at times when the other farmers came to help with work that neighbors did together in those days.

Mother was church treasurer, a Sunday school teacher, an officer in the women's missionary group, school board member, local newspaper columnist, and the one who took the time to solicit funds for every worthy cause. She also cared for the sick and needy of the community. Among many other things, I remember going with her to deliver May baskets filled with canned and baked goodies to elderly shut-ins. I'm probably forgetting many of the extra things she did, but the point is that things needed to be done, Mother could do them, and she did them. There was no worry about whether it was her place or not. My dad, brother, and I never felt slighted; in fact, we felt involved in whatever she did. We knew we were in first place with her anyway.

After my brother and I left home, my parents moved from our Nebraska farm to Denver. In addition to helping manage apartment buildings, my mother went back to her original profession of school teaching. She also continued her unpaid career of people-helping in her new location. When my parents moved to Texas, Mother began a new profession in the large county library where she worked for eighteen years until her retirement. She may be retired from paid outside employment now, but she is still ministering to people in many ways—and her husband, children and their mates, grandchildren and their mates, and great grandchildren are still first in her life.

You see, besides being able and willing, Mother accomplished so much in her lifetime because she did it according to seasons. She didn't do everything at one time. When we are young, we tend to think that we have to get everything done at once and that career choices we make at one point are binding until death. Not many of us realized when we were young women that we were going to have as many or more years of marriage with the children grown and gone from home as when they were in the home. In general, there is time for a career for a few years before children are born and for many years after they no longer need our care. It is a waste of God-given potential not to plan for the best use of those times.

A TIME TO BE. . . .

Ideally, then, for the wife and mother there seem to be two good seasons for an outside profession—one before children are born and the long period after children leave home. The advantage in the post-child era is that a woman now has more life experience, wisdom, and assertiveness than she had as a young woman. But some women have professions they wish to maintain, at least to a certain degree, during the child-rearing years. Others need to be employed for economic reasons. Even if a woman is employed or carrying out a ministry during her years of caring for children, the "seasons" concept is a good one to remember.

Eda LeShan tells about a friend of hers who, although highly trained, chose to remain home as a mother and invest her energies in her children. Eda chose to combine her career with mothering. From her late mid-life years Eda writes:

"Helen was wiser than I: she paid no attention (to predictions that her well-trained mind would be lost by staying at home), stayed home to have three children, enjoyed it thoroughly, and felt she got more out of it than she gave, and then, about ten years ago, when her brood was well on the way to independent lives of their own, she went back to school herself and is now happily fulfilling herself as one of those 'born teachers,' working in one of the toughest and saddest ghettos in the country. I envy her those years at home; I envy the unhurried, contented time of fulltime mothering. Not romanticizing it—of course, she had days of despair and disaster, like every other mother—but she also was allowing life to happen, was nourishing the young and savoring it. And I confessed seeing this as profoundly feminine."[11]

HER SEASONS

The Proverbs 31 Woman is an example of a woman using her gifts and abilities wisely and in season. She has been wrongly accused of being a Super Woman, an ideal that none of us can expect to attain, nor would we want to. She has been misunderstood, and we have missed a source of strength if we have tossed out her model. Nowhere are we told that she accomplished all those feats in a day or even in a year. She did it in her seasons and according to needs and her gifts and energies. She had herself, her family, her roles, and her spiritual life in good balance. Her life is exciting, and I (Sally) am inspired to pattern mine after hers.

Patricia Gundry's *Complete Woman* is based on the Proverbs woman and, out of the dozens of Christian womanhood books on the market, is one of the most outstanding. We highly recommend that you read it.[12]

WHY COMBINE ROLES?

Many studies show that working women are physically and emotionally healthier than women who are not employed outside the home. They also show that they live longer, have more self-confidence, and more fun. Some of these studies are discussed in detail in *The Two-Paycheck Marriage*.[13] The Metropolitan Life Insurance Company Statistical Bureau also reports, "The sense of personal satisfaction and accomplishment derived from success in your vocation does more to contribute to morale and a sense of well-being than any other single factor. And research has shown that such satisfaction has a direct bearing on how long you are likely to live."[14]

Most people have known for some time that housewives have a high depression rate. One study that validates this found that "a woman who has to get up and go to a job is more apt to carry on through a serious depression than a housewife who has no one around to help pull her out of it."[15]

We see evidence that women who are housewives-only regress intellectually. One study was done on men and women four years after high school graduation. The women who had married and done only housework for the next four years "scored lower on intellectual measures, . . . were less curious about the world around them, less open-minded, less interested in new experiences, less able to cope with ambiguity and less autonomous."[16]

Physical and emotional well-being, longer life expectancy, less depression, and intellectual stimulation are a few of the benefits of keeping up with an outside career or ministry. Homemakers and mothers also have certain advantages, as we have discussed throughout the earlier chapters.

A study done to determine the effect of childlessness on the well-being of older women concluded that "widowed childless older women had lower psychological well-being than did widowed mothers."[17] In spite of stresses caused by the marriage relationship and children, most women want both.

HOW TO BLEND

If combining career, homemaking, and mothering is desirable, how do we bring it about? There are no one-size-fits-all patterns. There are too many individual variations to hand out a pat answer. There are careers and there are "jobs," paid and unpaid careers, and full-time and part-time careers. Add to that the many kinds of homemaking and mothering situations, and we can see that one prescription won't work for all.

We can make some generalized hints, however. *First of all, evaluate.* Take stock of who you are, what your abilities and interests are, and what your particular situation is as to family needs and career opportunities.

Second, realize that your life has various seasons. Wherever you are on the spectrum, you can fit your various roles to match your time of life. Whatever you want to do doesn't have to be done all at one time. And one woman doesn't have to be on the same time schedule as another woman.

Third, do dream dreams and make plans. Set goals. You don't have to get everything done at once, but neither will you get much of anything done without plans. "A wise [woman] thinks ahead. . . . It is pleasant to see plans develop" (Proverbs 13:16a, 19a).

A part of goal-setting is realizing your limits. Don't try the Wonder Woman stuff. In the long run it will crush you, or something important to you. Be realistic about the number of hours in a day and about your physical and emotional strength.

Fourth, enlist your husband and children to share with household tasks. If they can't help, arrange for some paid help. Jim told me (Sally) several years ago that I had scrubbed enough johns in my lifetime, so I didn't continue to need the experience to build my character. He said my time was worth more in other areas. (Isn't that great!) He is the one who has urged me to get a "cleaning lady," which I often do.

GENEROUS MEN

There *is* a trend toward husbands sharing more with household tasks, even though most experts find that it usually hasn't reached equal proportions yet. Kindly and gently present the need to your husband. Of course, you'll have more trouble getting his willing help if he is still viewing housework as woman's work and if he is not in agreement with your working. You'd better work that out too.

Our three sons-in-law are examples of the changing husband. They willingly share in household tasks (I have seen one son-in-law do more ironing than his wife), and Marc, who is a father, has done as much parenting of Nathan as his mother has. Mike, Marc, and Craig all encourage our daughters to keep developing as the women God made them to be. As we write this, Barbara is doing graduate work for a counseling degree, Becki is finishing her undergraduate work and doing part-time work in her career, and Brenda is mothering and continuing her drama profession through her local church. All are homemakers. Their actual housework hours vary, depending upon their situation. And all three couples spend more time doing things to enrich their marriage relationship than we or anyone in our generation seemed to do.

YOUR RESOURCES

If your children are still at home, encourage your husband to get more involved with the parenting. He may be getting a late start, but he can do a good job. It's been interesting to see new research prove that fathers make good nurturers.

If your circumstances don't allow for an outside occupation, look for creative ways to use your gifts and abilities at home. Our daughter Brenda wants to be at home with Nathan during these years, but she is continuing to use her degree in communication and theater arts by acting in church dramatic productions, writing a play, and organizing an improvisational group of other Christian women interested in drama. She also has time to make Christmas and birthday gifts, so even though she is not earning money, she is saving it.

You are a unique woman and God has a plan for you. You can help head off a mid-life crisis or pull out of it a little faster if you will search out your resources and make plans for using them. And remember that there are seasons for you to produce various kinds of fruit.

MY SEASONS

We have now lived long enough that we can look back over our many years together and see the different times I (Sally) have had for various kinds of roles and activities. Before we were married I was a student, an executive secretary, and an elementary school teacher. Following our marriage I worked again as a secretary before our first daughter was born. I also audited the first semester of seminary classes the year Jim began his Master of Divinity studies, and I've been forever grateful for that experience.

I worked closely with Jim in pastoring a small mountain church and in helping to manage an apartment building in order to earn our rent during seminary days.

Following our move to our first full-time church, I was a very busy mother and pastor's wife. I also was my husband's secretary. The same was true when we moved to our second church six years later. At this time, however, I started to work part-time in order to help with some medical bills and the increased cost of living in the new area. I enjoyed my work because it was with a mission organization and I felt it was a ministry. The job allowed me to be home whenever the girls were—before and after school and during vacations. When we moved to our third church another six years later, I thought it would be great to be home all day, keep house exactly as it should be, and attend Christian women's daytime meetings. But that's when I moved into the most difficult time in my personal life—early mid-life.

I eventually found some ministry-related activities, such as discipling some university students and teaching adult Christian education classes as well as returning to school. These added fulfillment to my life. When our oldest daughter started attending a private Christian college, God provided me with a part-time teaching position as a remedial reading specialist. Helping those students improve in language skills was very rewarding to me. Our second daughter also chose the same Christian college, so I continued to teach until I resigned to help Jim through his mid-life crisis and with writing projects. By the time our youngest daughter was a senior in high school, I was receiving several speaking opportunities, locally and away at conferences with Jim. God gradually increased my opportunities for writing and traveling to speak after our daughters were grown and gone. Now I am also an adjunct instructor at a seminary, sharing my knowledge and experience with graduate students and in turn being stimulated by their bright, enthusiastic lives.

My full-time career at this time in life is possible because I now have no direct mothering responsibilities and
Jim shares in the housework. There are certain areas that
are very much my domain, such as the laundry, and areas
that are his, such as the lawn. But we share many of the
other tasks. We also enjoy a simpler eating style when we
are alone. Jim does not want big, elaborate meals, so that
frees me to use my time elsewhere. And he is as apt to
make the meal and to clean up afterward as I am. He has
always helped more with the child-raising and special
household tasks than most men, but as I have moved to a
full-time career, our housework has become even more
egalitarian. He is as busy as he ever was with his professional obligations, but he makes time to enable me to have
my career.

So, I have had some years of full-time career, then many
years of full-time housewife and mother, followed by
most-of-the-time housewife-mother and part-time career,
and gradually moving to less time as a mother and more
time in a career. As God allows, I look forward to having
another twenty or twenty-five years of active participation
in a career, mixed with my roles as wife, mother-friend,
and grandmother. I am excited about the fruit that God
still wants to produce through me, and I am honored that
he has made me a part of his plan.

"They [the godly] are like trees [transplanted] along a
river bank bearing luscious fruit *each season* without fail.
Their leaves shall never wither, and all they do shall pros-
per" (Psalm 1:3). [Italics ours]

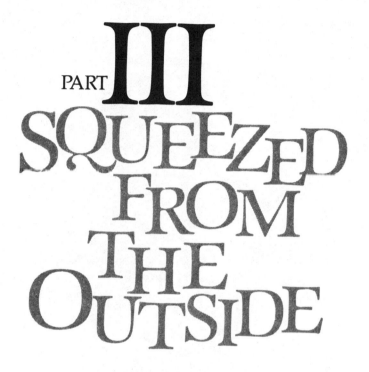

PART III
SQUEEZED
FROM
THE
OUTSIDE

Chapter Five

CULTURE'S CREATION

Dianne said, "I don't know why I've become such a mess. I can't understand my emotions or what is going on around me. I feel as if I'm no good to myself or anyone else. I'm making my family miserable."

Tragically, many women feel guilty for having a mid-life crisis, as if they voluntarily brought it on themselves. To make matters worse, critics are jeering on the sidelines, like those in the Roman Coliseum who were glad to see the Christians being devoured by the lions. Those antagonists, however, are not observers of how our changing culture has created the Twentieth Century mid-life woman.

Prior to the Industrial Revolution, before corporations and industry took over woman's tasks and knowledge in certain areas, she had a position of worth and value alongside her husband. She practiced the skills of sewing, handcrafts, medicine, nursing the sick, raising a garden, canning, smoking meat, cooking meals, and educating her children. She also worked beside her husband in constructing their home or other farm buildings. She helped in the fields and cared for the livestock, or she worked with her husband in their little place of business or small industry. Strangely, in that era, men did not find these co-laborers to be a threat but were glad to have a wife who joined with them. They worked and cared together about their livelihood and their family.

Women who were homemakers had a respected position in our culture through the First World War. For example, in a *Ladies' Home Journal* of 1919, the pictures are of mid-life women with matronly bodies. They are not skinny young fashion models poured into Jordache jeans. The fashion sections of the magazine suggest that "the plain country woman finds it absurd to dress up in finery to give the illusion of youth."[1]

In an Ivory Soap advertisement in the same magazine, a young mother is giving her baby a bath with her own mother looking over her shoulder. The ad reads, "A quarter-century ago Grandma's mother told her how to bathe a new baby girl . . . today she in turn passes on the same instructions to that girl, now a mother herself."[2] That magazine also encourages women not to send their children to school until they are ten years old and tells how mothers can teach their children at home.

The pre-1920s woman not only was devoted to her husband and family, but she also was interested in adventure and in personhood. She read magazine articles about mountain climbing, the first woman born in the West, politics, and religion. The woman in those early decades seemed to know that she fit into the scheme of life. How very different from the mid-life homemaker of today who has had her jobs taken away and is told by some not to go into the marketplace where those jobs are now.

GIRL OR WOMAN

During the '20s there started a shift in the image of women. The models were now the flappers—young, skinny, dizzy air heads. Women abandoned all of the mature role models that had previously marked them and they now followed a brainless, giddy approach to life.

This change in women coincided with a revolution within the home. Machinery began to take a woman's tasks and skills away from her. Her value would now be found in being a sex symbol without commitment. It was the beginning of woman's struggle to find her identity after her role at home was diminished.

Other important events took place which made an impact on the role of women. First came the Great Depression, which, interestingly, returned her to her earlier position as a helper. The frivolous flapper girl of the '20s was replaced by the serious woman helping her husband and family to survive the economic chaos of the early '30s.

Then we entered the Second World War in the '40s. "Rosie the Riveter" became the image as women manned the home front in industry and business. Women not only produced the guns, bullets, planes, and tanks, but they were entrusted with the quality of the material which would protect their men's lives. "For the four years of the war, America was a woman's country, and the woman was a grown-up."[3]

Women had gone to work by the millions and when their husbands and brothers came home from war, the women continued in jobs outside the home. In the '50s their work was directed toward putting their husbands through school and later supported a suburban lifestyle. Only recently, in the '70s and '80s, have women's careers moved more toward personal fulfillment.

THE BOMBS

The atomic bomb in 1945 caused another cultural impact with universal destruction becoming a frightening possibility. The population bomb also began to explode after the Second World War. The first members of this large group of people making up the "Baby Boom" began to enter mid-life as we started the '80s.

Another explosive development of the 1950s and 1960s was the massive involvement in higher education. Knowledge became the avenue for success and upward mobility. Women entered the educational system in record numbers.

Then came the Viet Nam War, which created a tremendous division within our country, pitting youth against "establishment." We also developed a heightened awareness of civil rights of all kinds, including equal rights for women, which brought struggles, misunderstandings, and a wide spectrum of beliefs and philosophies of womanhood.

In the '50s and early '60s the focus was on childhood; in the late '60s through early '80s the emphasis was on the youth movement. Because of the Baby Boom population reaching mid-life, the focus of our culture in the late '80s and '90s will likely be on mid-life.

ROOTS

Another strong influence on women is that we are now basically urban rather than rural. In 1900 approximately 90 percent of our population lived in rural or small town settings. Today less than 10 percent do.[4] That rural setting was marked by a great deal of stability. Today the average family moves once every five years.[5]

I (Sally) grew up in a farming community in Nebraska where all of my grandparents, aunts, uncles, and my own parents were known by everyone. These relatives had lived in the community all their lives before I arrived on the scene. When I started attending the one-room Riverside School for the first eight grades of my education, I already had history there with two previous generations. My grandmother and my mother (as well as their brothers and sisters) had been pupils in the school, and my mother had taught there. Some of my teachers had been my mother's students ten or fifteen years earlier.

My brother and I graduated from the same small Ewing High School that both of our parents and their brothers and sisters had. In fact, when I later attended a summer school session at a teacher's college ninety miles from home, one of my professors had been a high school teacher and principal at Ewing High School during the days of my parents and their brothers and sisters. Her class that summer was highly seasoned with illustrations furnished by my relatives of the earlier generation.

WHO CARES

My last name, Christon, gave me immediate identification as coming from a family of hard-working, thrifty, highly moral people. The community knew that my mother's family, the Larsons, were of the same caliber. I grew up knowing that I would never want to bring dishonor to our families. I also knew that there were a host of people in the community who cared for me and to whom I could turn in times of need. I think that today, mail addressed to me at that location would find me, because there is still a network of ties in that community, although my parents and I have moved from there.

About two years ago, Jim and I, along with our three daughters, two sons-in-law, and one grandson, moved to Southern California. We know the names of our immediate neighbors, but they know me only in my current role, and that a very limited one of adjunct instructor at Talbot Seminary, conference speaker, and writer. (I know less than that about some of them.) They know nothing of my background, and I know nothing of theirs.

The problem with mobility is that when a woman needs someone with whom to talk over the crucial issues of life, she finds herself with casual friends or impersonal counselors. Often our linkages to other people have been lost. We, as a nation, have become a caravan of U-Haul trucks passing in opposite directions on the interstates, stopping only for gas and a Big Mac.

TECHNOLOGY AND KNOWLEDGE EXPLOSIONS

Technological advances have done two things to women. One is to take away the jobs that they used to do in the home. The second is to cause them to be quickly outdated if they are out of the work force for three or four years.

When we were growing up, Monday was always "wash day" at our houses. The clotheslines at Jim's house in Cleveland were strung from the back of the house to several different hooks on the detached garage. On Sally's farm there was room for the clotheslines to be permanently erected. Load after load of clothes would be washed in the tub with the agitator and hand-fed through the wringer. Jim's mother was more fortunate than Sally's; she had an automatic hot water heater. Sally's mom had to pump her water, carry it to a "boiler" on a wood cook stove to heat, and then carry it to the washer. In early years she had to hand crank the agitator and the wringer. After the clothes were finally washed, the baskets of soggy clothes were carried out of the house and individually pinned to the clotheslines. It always seemed strange to Jim that his mom hung the sheets on one side of the yard, the towels on the other side, and the unmentionables in between, where the neighbors could not see them!

What happened in winter? The clothes were hung out anyway. They often were stiff as a board when we took them down because they had frozen before drying. Because of the frequent nasty weather in Cleveland, Jim's mother would hang the clothes in the basement, and then the whole house would feel damp and clammy.

"THIS IS THE WAY WE IRON OUR CLOTHES. . . ."

The next day was "ironing day"—all day and all evening
—shirts, sheets, tablecloths, dish towels. Sally's grandmother even ironed her husband's and sons' socks. Both of
our moms had to cook up buckets of starch into which the
clothes were dipped before drying and ironing. Wow!
What a mess! Washing and ironing took two full days out
of the week.

Remember, there weren't any "wash and wear" materials. How very different to do the laundry now with automatic washers and dryers, and permanent press fabrics
that need little or no ironing. Most of Jim's dress shirts are
just snatched out of the dryer and given a quick spray of
starch and touchup with an iron on the collars.

Besides laundry, our mothers had to mend, darn, and
sew new clothes. Yes, it was hard work, but at the same
time, the women had a sense of identity and purpose. So
while technology has taken away some of the drudgery, it
also has taken away some of the women's identity.

WHAT'S A FLOPPY DISC?

If Jan decides to drop out of her job as a secretary to have
a child, she may find when she returns to the office that
technology has passed her by. If she quit a secretarial job
just three years ago, she would return now to find that
IBM's dancing ball on the typewriter is out-of-date. Her
new typewriter is electronic with a daisy wheel and a
memory for several pages of material.

As Jan applies for the job, the personnel officer will ask
how much experience she has had with word processors.
Her response is likely to be, "None." Yet, in three years
word processors have become common equipment in of-
fices. The personnel person will ask her other questions
about computer experience. Is she familiar with floppy

discs and key punching? She may find herself very intimi-
dated by only a short absence from the working world.

Let's jump to the situation of Carolyn, who decides to
drop out of work, raise three children, and then return to
work after all three of them are in school full time. That's
about a fifteen-year period. The knowledge in her field
would have doubled three times. Suppose that her field
was medicine. When she graduated fifteen years ago, fifty
books would have contained the core of the information
she needed to know. Five years later it would take one
hundred books, ten years later it would require two hundred books, and fifteen years down the road she would
need to know the information in four hundred books. The
reality is that she probably has not even kept up with the
original fifty books, so when she steps into the office of a
hospital personnel administrator, she feels like a kinder-
gartner going to school for the first time.

TRAPPED IN THE YOUTH CULT

When the Declaration of Independence was written in
1776, half of the nation's population was under sixteen
and three-quarters was under twenty-five.[6] We have not
been able to overcome that youth orientation in our culture, even though America is graying.

When someone asks your age in China, he will likely
offer you sympathy if you are young. The older you are,
the more enthusiastic will be the congratulations. The Chi-
nese equate age with wisdom, and they esteem both.
Americans tend to value what you do more than what you
are.[7]

We have a strange situation. No one over forty really
enjoys the demands of the youth culture, in terms of the
time, energy, and money required to try to stay young. We
may hear a woman of forty complain about the youth cult,
but, at the same time, she wears the clothes of the youth

cult. Her hair is in a youthful style. She believes the advertisements for younger-looking skin, a wrinkleless face, and
no telltale gray in her hair. "The trend which nobody really
wants seems to be inexorable, the suction of the whirlpool
ever more powerful,"[8] drawing mid-life women into the
vacuum of the youth cult.

If a woman in her late twenties discovers a few strands
of gray in her hair, she probably will not be bothered by
them. But a few strands of gray hair discovered by the
mid-life woman who, for the first time, is confronting her
aging in the mirror may have an enormously shocking
impact. These are not just strands of gray hair. They spell
O-L-D!

CAUGHT IN THE MIDDLE

Research reported in a doctoral dissertation, "Effects of a
Youth Culture on Feelings and Attitudes of the Middle
Woman," showed that mid-life women felt that the young
adult had the greatest advantage in the life cycle. Mid-life
women, on the one hand, wanted to tie into that strength
and gain youthful recognition, but at the same time, they
resented the youth-oriented phenomenon in our culture.[9]

The mid-life woman is really caught between two
worlds. As a child she was probably brought up to respect
older people and to believe they had much wisdom to
offer her by their experience. But she is living now in an
age that primarily values youth. It used to be that white
hair, a lined face, and a bent body earned respect because
of a life of hard work. Today, however, the highest compliment that can be given to someone is, "You don't look your
age!"

Some of the fatigue that is experienced by the mid-life
woman is from the cultural stress that assaults her from
many directions. The mid-life generation is a tired generation, not only because of pressures, but because they often

don't know who they are or where they are going. "At 20, you can't wait for tomorrow to come. After 40, you never quite finish with the day before yesterday."[10]

NEW PRODUCTIVE YEARS

At the turn of the century, families were larger than they are now. A woman also became pregnant more often and was likely to bear children until her early forties.

Normally, her nest would be emptying out when she was in her mid-fifties. By the time she reached her mid-forties, however, she was already considered an old woman. To understand a forty-five-year-old woman of 1900, we would have to compare her physical condition with the health and vigor of a modern woman in her mid-seventies.

At the beginning of the century, the married woman in mid-life often had very young children in the home. Today, however, because the childbirth years are usually compressed into her twenties, the mother at thirty-five experiences more freedom than the woman of 1900. At the time the average mid-life woman passes forty, she will have sent her first child off to college or into a career.

Not only are all the children launched when the mother is younger today, but women have a much longer life expectancy and vastly improved physical health. The woman of forty today can easily expect thirty more productive years. This mid-life era has essentially been unknown before in history. It is a phenomenon of our present culture and medical science. With the loss of her traditional jobs and her extended years of freedom and health, people ask, "Now what do we do with women?"

MARITAL DISSATISFACTION

Marriage expectations have changed drastically during this century. Before 1900, a suitable wife was one who was able to bear and rear children and was strong enough to help run a farm, grow, preserve, and cook the food, and make the clothing. A desirable husband was ambitious, an able provider, and in good physical condition. Now our expectations of marriage center around psychological dimensions such as intimacy, companionship, caring, and the capacity to meet each other's needs through exhilarating sexual experiences.

In a later chapter we will consider in more detail the modern marriage situation and its pressures on the mid-life woman. At this point we will simply point out that numerous studies show the mid-life years to have the lowest level of satisfaction at any time in a couple's experience together.[11]

In addition to the low level of marriage satisfaction at mid-life, we are confronted with strong demands for role redefinition. The inexorable move in our society toward egalitarian marriages is a difficult transition, not only for many husbands but also for wives.

Insecurity within a marriage is transmitted to the children who, realizing that things are not going well with their parents, sometimes begin to look outside the family for sources of strength, sometimes causing increased competition and family fragmentation.

SEXUAL LIBERATION

The new sexual freedom in our culture has allowed the wife to become an active partner in the sexual experience. She can be not only a willing participant but also an initiator and stimulator, helping the sexual experience to be creative and fulfilling for both her husband and herself.

Some Christian movements down through history have been antisexual, but God created sexuality and the Bible promotes sexual relationships in marriage. The dialogue in the Song of Solomon is an entrancing picture of a man and a woman in love with each other, each an equal partner in a loving physical relationship.

The girl in the account says, "Kiss me again and again, for your love is sweeter than wine. . . . The king lies on his bed, enchanted by the fragrance of my perfume. My beloved one is a sachet of myrrh lying between my breasts" (SS 1:2, 12, 13). This is not the picture of an inactive, passive woman who does not enjoy sex. She is an initiator and an equal with her partner. The woman and man mutually enjoy the physical relationship.

Sexual liberation has had positive benefits by helping us return to a more biblical view of sex, but it also has negative dimensions. In some cases it has turned sexual partners into competing contenders in the sexual relationship. Neither seeks to build the other's pleasure, but exploits the other in order to arrive at the full sexual experience that seems due.

WHEN IS ENOUGH ENOUGH?

Sexual liberation also has given us some distorted images of sex with the heavy emphasis on the various vaginal orgasms. Books such as *The G Spot* focus on technique and nerve endings rather than on the psychological and spiritual dimensions of caring, building one another, and providing stability for one another. The sexual revolution has portrayed love as the sexual experience instead of *love as a commitment* that results in a sexual experience. Many women experience total marital dissatisfaction because they feel they're being cheated in life if the sky rockets don't go off when they have sex with their husbands.

A pastor friend of ours tells of a woman in his church who left her husband, saying that she was going to keep on looking until she found a man that "really turned her on, even if he was bad in every other way, because 'I won't go on living with less than a total sex life.' " She left behind a crushed husband and two young daughters. The tragedy, this pastor goes on to recount, is that for most of her adult life she has envied her sister, who is a misfit and who has bounced from bed to bed, from one bad man to another. The sexual liberation movement has created unrealistic expectations that cause many women to become sexual vagabonds, testing their attractiveness and sexual finesse with man after man.

LIBERATION—FROM WHAT TO WHAT?

As in many other movements in the past, exaggerated extremes arise which, a careful look at history will show, were not the original intent of the movement. The Women's Liberation Movement, for example, has sometimes confused women's rights with being a woman. An early advocate of the movement, thoughtfully reflecting on this problem, says, "I am convinced that in the process of minimizing differences women will lose touch with the deepest and most important resources within themselves. We need to differentiate between women's *rights* and women's *liberation*. The first seems just and necessary, but the second seems too often to be associated with the rejection of the enjoyment of being female."[12]

As we have said, women need equal rights, but they should not lose their special feminine insights. If that is gone, all of humanity suffers. Sometimes extreme liberationists have pushed for women to be like men in every possible area. The problem is that women sacrifice their unique identities when they become like someone else.

Adolescent girls often wear the clothes, hairstyles, and bras or no bras, to imitate the currently popular female members of the hottest musical groups. The sad thing is that every time one individual duplicates another, the world has lost a person. When women try to duplicate men, simply for the sake of proving they can be like them, they never quite pull off the job, and in the process they lose their own identity and their unique contribution to the world. It's as it was when we were little kids, dressing up in our parents' clothes—the clothes didn't fit, but we really thought we were like our parents because we had on their clothes.

SMELL LIFE'S ROSES

Some of the price of believing all of the Liberation Movement information is verbalized by Eda LeShan, a proponent of women's liberation:

"I think I am eminently qualified to make some judgments about the price one may pay for liberation. My mother was a liberated woman, long before that term was used; so were most of my other female relations. I grew up in a milieu in which all the important men and women in my life assumed that I could and should do 'far more important things' with my life than 'only' stay at home and take care of babies and a household. . . .

"I am delighted that I was encouraged to use whatever capacities I had, and I am deeply grateful for the fact that I *did* live and work in a time when I could fulfill myself as a person. My regrets have to do with what I did *not* do: that in my struggle to achieve, to be an intellectual, I often lost touch with the woman in me. When my daughter was a baby, I spent so much time worrying about the possible atrophying of my brilliant mind while changing diapers that I rarely allowed myself the privilege and the joy of *just plain reveling* in motherhood. When we went to the playground, instead of permitting myself to enjoy the wonders of growing, allowing myself to experience the miracle of looking at the world through her eyes, all new and fresh and full of curiosity, I would bury myself in the latest child psychology book. Instead of building sand castles, or walking in puddles or smelling a flower with her, I made notes for my next lecture or article on raising children. Instead of really listening to the growing sounds of her, and joyously responding to what she had to teach me about just *Being,* just watching and looking and listening to life happening, I was agitating about wasting my time. I was an idiot, and I deeply regret the times I missed out on quiet moments of loving.

"In order to focus so much of my attention on my career, I became the world's best manager—always planning, organizing, running things. I was so efficient that it never occurred to me then, as it does now, that my chronic backaches at that time had more to do with trying to carry too many burdens, too many roles, than with any organic or anatomical difficulty. In recent years I have been discovering that I paid a price for my efficiency, that in the process of directing the traffic of my life so well I lost touch with myself and with the people I loved the most."[13]

MISSING MORALITY

Coupled with all of these changes in our culture, there has been a declining morality, dramatized by Watergate, the scandal of white collar crime, the billions of dollars in merchandise lost through shoplifting and employees stealing items at their jobs. Every kind and degree of crime is increasing, including terror reigning in public school systems. This was illustrated in our daughters' high school where the students had so vandalized the washrooms that they were unusable and the school system simply refused to repair them.

In a permissive society with declining morality, a woman who is questioning her values in life finds it easy to get lost in the fog of shifting values. A woman's moral scruples need to be her own, but at a time when she is resorting values, it helps if there also are some solid standards on the outside.

During the Depression of the thirties, American women had a strong female model in Eleanor Roosevelt, a woman of stability and vision, a tough woman with commitment in spite of her husband's sickness and his infidelity. She was a heroine who, by her manner of living, said to other women, "You can make it, no matter what you're experiencing."

Today the incessant flow of soap operas from TV reinforces the Peyton Place morality. The proliferation of cable television, offering optional adult-viewing packages, brings X-rated material directly into a woman's living quarters. Most women wouldn't think of going to an adult-only, X-rated movie by themselves in a public place, but many feed themselves on such material in their own homes. The Bible says very simply that as a person "thinks within [herself], so [she] is" (Prov. 23:7, NASB).

ME-ISM

At first glance the Human Potential Movement helped people to understand who they were and what they could accomplish in life. As the movement gathered strength, however, it began to move toward its logical conclusion: "I'm the most important thing in the universe and all else circulates around me." The name of the new game was "Don't Give Yourself to Anybody, Even in the Marriage Relationship." All people enter marriage to meet their own needs; therefore, logically, when their needs aren't being met, they are free to leave.

This me-ism (or plain old selfishness) was to be thought of in a different way. "You don't have to live up to anyone's expectations." Selfishness is not a dirty word; it is an "expression of the law of self-preservation."[14]

The "Gestalt Prayer" which appears on thousands of posters, greeting cards, and coffee mugs expresses the philosophy of me-ism:

I do my thing, and you do your thing.
I am not in this world to live up to
your expectations

And you are not in this world to live
  up to mine.
You are you and I am I, and if by chance
  we find each other, it's beautiful.
If not, it can't be helped.[15]

This me-ism also had the impact of putting all of time in the reference of *now.* "Reality exists only in the present. A person's memory of the past (despite his sincere denials of this fact) is a collection of obsolete distortions and misperceptions."[16]

The new me-ism was especially destructive for women, because human relationships were now portrayed as unimportant. At the same time, several studies showed that women were still gaining much of their identity through their relationships with other people.[17]

So the woman is caught in another cultural box. If she goes with the Human Potential Movement to its logical conclusion, she thinks she is getting a better grip on who she is, but in reality she is cutting herself off from people and thus destroying a large section of her self-identity.

CULTURE'S IMPACT

Whenever a great number of cultural changes occur in a short time, you will find it difficult to adapt. If you are in a personal transition at the same time, you will have even more stress. "Crisis precipitated by aging will be more difficult when shifts in cultural values increase people's uncertainty about their own values, make them indecisive about their future goals and ambivalent about their best choices."[18]

As a mid-life woman, you come to this time in your life comparatively highly educated and self-aware, sometimes assertive, and working toward self-fulfillment. At the same time, everything around you seems to be coming unglued and you have no models or road maps.

You are a child of the Bomb, the Viet Nam War, inflation, and recession. Some voices encourage you to develop yourself. Other voices tell you to be contented to be "barefoot, pregnant, and in the kitchen."

We have found from our national research that women possess a great deal of uncertainty that lies just under the surface. A large portion of this uncertainty comes because of the impact of culture and the community, both secular and spiritual, giving you mixed signals.

Chapter Six

A STALE MARRIAGE

The mid-life woman may experience several negative change events taking place at one time in her life which in combination will cause a crisis. The events that will cause the most stress are people-related. She can put up with the washer breaking down, a leaky bathroom faucet, an old car—but loss of a close relationship—especially with her husband because their marriage has grown stale—will produce the greatest stress.

How do you tell when a marriage has gone stale? It happens so gradually, over many years. At what point do you say, "Yesterday it was fresh; today it is stale"? It's like walking on a country road. After a while you notice there's a small stone in your shoe. At first you just keep walking because it's not very big and the pain isn't that great. After a bit you start tapping your toe, hoping to slide the stone to a different position. You keep on walking, moving the stone around from place to place. Finally your foot becomes so painful that you have to sit down and take the stone out. The question is, at what point did the stone become painful? A stale marriage takes years to develop, but finally it is painful enough to force you to do something about it.

LIFETIME LOW

The authors of a journal article, "Marital Satisfaction Over the Family Life Cycle: A Reevaluation," summarize several different studies in which events in the family life cycle are correlated with marriage satisfaction. All of the studies showed that the lowest point of marriage satisfaction came at the time when there were teenagers in the home.[1] Having teens in the home usually means that the husband and wife are in their mid-life years. Therefore, the lowest marriage satisfaction time in the marriage is at mid-life.

Before marriage there are forces that tend to draw a couple together. When we don't fully understand a person and yet we are attracted to him, we want to know more about him. During the courtship days we experience a drawing together for mutual understanding. There is a testing of one's social expertise—how well can I get along with another person? Can I cause that person to like me? Can I deepen his interest in me?

We also experience the magnetism of the unexplored sexual relationship. What is this person like sexually? At first, the question is, what would it be like to be held in this person's arms? Then, what would it be like to be kissed? Each progressive stage has its questions and magnetism that draws the couple toward each other. The wedding, honeymoon, setting up housekeeping, and coming of the first child are all forces that draw the couple toward each other.

CENTRIPETAL TO CENTRIFUGAL

After the coming of the first child, life tends to become repetitive and settles down to a routine. At the same time strong forces pull people away from the couple relationship. The career experience for either husband or wife provides stimulation, adventure, and advancement. They find new and challenging people to work with.

For most husbands, and for the wife who is heavily career-oriented, the strong outward pull of the career starts to produce a dullness in the marriage relationship. The centripetal forces that drew them toward each other in the courting relationship have now given way to a centrifugal force that is pushing them apart.

THAT'S ENOUGH

Another mid-life force that produces a dull marriage is the vast increase in the responsibility caused by children. When you are first pregnant, it's an adventure. Yes, it may be nauseating, but it's an adventure. It's going to be fun. When the baby is born there's a sense of victory. I've done it! I've endured the pain and the pressure; I've become a mother. Hurray for me! But the birth is only the beginning. Ahead of you lies a whole lifetime of relationships, both positive and negative.

After you've had the baby a couple of years, you begin to say, "Wouldn't it be nice for our child to have a brother or sister?" You think it wouldn't be very much more work or expense. You remember some of the warm, cuddly times. That sort of cuddly reasoning and limited insight causes young couples to make decisions that many mid-life women wish they didn't have to put up with twelve or fifteen years later.

Our studies have repeatedly proved the old saying, "I wouldn't take a million dollars for any of my kids, but I wouldn't give a nickel for another one!" Women in our studies love their children, but the agony and stress of raising them has taken a toll on their own personal lives and on their marriages. There was a deep sense of relief, an audible gasp, and a sigh of freedom as the women entered the "launching" and the "empty nest" stages.

WINDS OF CHANGE

Another pressure on the mid-life marriage is the lack of understanding of each other by both the husband and the wife. By mid-life they've lived with each other about twelve to fifteen years. They think they have each other all figured out—but they're shocked with the amount and intensity of change at mid-life.

The husband becomes a hard-driving, selfishly preoccupied career person, who repeatedly puts off everything—except his career. Later in mid-life he abruptly changes and becomes angry, frustrated, confused, and disoriented. He may start to verbalize some of the feelings and insecurities that he has never before mentioned.

His wife is yo-yoed. At first he seems to be going on in his career without the family. Then, surprisingly, he begins to express "feminine feelings" of tenderness and intimacy.

The wife previously had committed herself to one of several roles—homemaker-only, career-only, or some combination of the two. Now, as she comes to mid-life, she becomes more assertive, outspoken, sometimes almost obnoxious. She begins to say, "I'm tired of this. It's time for me. It's time for my dreams to be fulfilled." Her husband is shocked by this sudden switch in her personal direction. "What about all of the things we have together?" he asks. What he may be trying to do is keep her quiet, keep things in order, so he can continue his own career. All of these dramatic changes take a toll on the marriage.

THE THREE DEADLY B'S

Many dull marriages at mid-life are characterized by being busy, battered, or bored.

BUSY

A common response when a couple begins to recognize that their marriage is getting dull is to try to keep busy. In the early years their marriage worked fine, because the children kept them preoccupied. They were able to focus on the things they were buying together—blankets, diapers, tricycles, and the condo.

Sometimes a mid-life couple with a dull marriage try to recreate the courtship days. They spend excessive amounts of time with each other, believing that the total source of their emotional nourishment should come from each other. This does not usually result in happiness, because their lives are thrown out of balance with too much togetherness.

One of the major problems in a dull mid-life marriage is a lack of intimacy—lack of understanding and sharing with each other. Intimacy is a quality of life, not the quantity of time that a couple spends together. Intimacy demands that each person be continually growing so that new areas of discovery are continually offered to the mate.

The dull marriage-busy compensation syndrome is illustrated by John and Grace. "At first, things looked better than ever; with extra money and time, Grace and John finally began to make plans to realize their long-time dream of building a country house and leaving the city behind. During the next two years, they seemed busy, happy, excited, and deeply involved in planning, building, and furnishing their house. Finally, the last bedspread was selected, the painting hung, and they moved in. Two weeks later, Grace packed her bags, took a cab to the train station, and headed for New York; she checked into a hotel and, before she even unpacked her bags, contacted the divorce lawyer.

"All of Grace and John's friends were shocked; there had been no clues—or none that we had been able to see, no hints of infidelity, some awful wrong, or any long standing grievance that had never been resolved. What had happened was not uncommon; left alone together, without the children and the stimulation of the city, Grace and John had nothing to say to each other, and even worse than that, they seemed constantly to get on each other's nerves. Neither one could make a move that wasn't irritating to the other.

"As Grace told us much later, she and John had never been particularly happy with each other, but they had not come to grips with the problem. At first, they hadn't even been aware of the emptiness of their relationship because they were so distracted by problems of mere survival with very little money and two children to raise. Later, they were both absorbed by and held together by their severe problems with their older child; in addition, their warm interaction with friends and families in the neighborhood kept them socially busy and cheerful most of the time. They weren't even aware of how little time they ever spent alone together.

"When the children grew up and left, and the great silence descended upon them, it was much more agreeable to throw themselves into the dream-house project than to face the truth. For two years, they worked side by side solving the problems of the house—but when the house was finished, they were out of business. They finally saw the sad truth—that they could collaborate only on external problems, but could never begin to solve the internal ones of their marital relationship, which was without any emotional or intellectual validity, and no longer had any reason for being. And therefore ended."[2]

BATTERED

An ineffective mid-life marriage is one where people are rapidly changing, do not understand each other, and are overloaded with responsibilities. This marriage will quite often turn into a battering marriage relationship in which either the wife or the husband physically or emotionally attacks the other.

Recently at UCLA, a group gathered to discuss domestic violence. "Domestic violence . . . knows no racial, ethnic or socioeconomic boundaries. One-fourth of all murders in the United States occur within the family setting. As many as 60% of American couples report that violence is a part of their marriages."[3]

The panelists went on to say, "You are more likely to be killed in your own home, and by someone you love, than by a stranger on the street.

"Your bedroom is the most dangerous place in your world."[4]

The reasons for domestic violence are many, but some believe it is perpetuated when a husband feels that he has the authority to punish his wife for any failures as he would punish a child.

We also see a startling correlation between wife beating and child incest. A high incidence of girl/child incest occurs in families where there is violence.[5]

Sociologists also observe frightening overtones to the pattern of being battered or molested as a child. Abuse is likely to change the direction of the child's life. One study found that 70 percent of all young prostitutes and 80 percent of female drug users in the U.S. had been molested by a family member. It was found that in the Los Angeles juvenile hall, 80 percent of the children had been molested.[6]

The pattern seems to be that a child who is battered or molested is more apt to follow an antisocial pattern for his or her life. If that person marries, he or she will likely batter or molest a family member. If a wife is being physically abused, a child is also probably being sexually abused.

If the dull mid-life marriage has degenerated into a battering marriage, this indicates more than marital dissatisfaction. Both of the marriage partners are in deep psychological trouble and need therapy so that their problems do not spread to the children and thus cause reverberations for generations to come.

In his short story "A Far Country" Jack London writes: "Two neophytes entered the Yukon to find their fortune in gold. Undisciplined, they overextended themselves and were forced to winter on the Arctic Coast. Immature, their relationship quickly deteriorated into hatred and violence.

"Each lived alone, refusing to talk, gloating over the marks of death growing upon his adversary as the elements gradually took their toll. While frostbite blackened their faces, scurvy ravished them from within, turning gums, tongue, and lips a creamy white. Each relished in the demise of the other, failing to realize he was staring at his own reflection.

"One day, while searching for firewood, unbeknownst to each other they entered a thicket from opposite directions. Suddenly the nakedness of reality was exposed as '. . . two peering death-heads confronted each other. Shrieking with terror (they) dashed away on their mangled stumps. . . .' "7

In the battered mid-life marriage the combatants fail to see the destruction of themselves as they batter or put up with battering.

BORED

Perhaps the most common expression of the dangerous three B's of the stale mid-life marriage is being bored. We observe boredom in the subtle situation where a husband and wife live together but are never stimulated by anything in the life of the other. They eat together, sleep together, watch TV together, go to movies together, play golf together, attend church together, entertain friends and play bridge together, but the truth is that they could do all of these same activities with any of a thousand different people and find it 1000 percent more stimulating.

It isn't that they hate each other; it isn't that they don't love each other. They are just apathetic. They are bored, bored, bored. They are trapped in roles of marriage by obligations and commitments. They are like two prisoners of war unable to escape, gradually living out their lives while they watch each other age. Their hair grays but there is not enough nourishment or stimulation to make life anything more than the deadening, debasing experience of prison life.

The difficulty with boredom is that it creates its own vacuum. The more boring the marriage, the greater the vacuum. Sooner or later something must rush in to fill the vacuum. That something or someone may also cause the breaking of the marriage.

A boring marriage is like the extra pounds that you put on year after year. The pounds go on gradually, but one day you realize that you think of yourself differently. "I am fat!" You notice that men look at you differently—as if you are no longer an attractive woman. A marriage may get boring slowly, but at some point you realize it has become terribly dull.

A boring marriage causes each partner to think the other is not worthwhile. The commitment to stay in a boring marriage decreases year by year. Soon there is no commitment to the marriage, there is commitment only to the children, to the church, to other relatives, but not to the person to whom you are married.

RESULTS OF THE BIG BAD THREE

We have already alluded to some of the results of a stale marriage—busyness, battering, or boredom. It is also important to see that quite often other problems such as a lack of communication, conflict over money, repeated affairs, lack of intimacy, and continual dehumanizing and fatiguing of each other may also contribute to a stale midlife marriage.

One woman in our study said, "I found myself getting angry because I kept thinking, 'What about me?' I decided I just don't have it in me any longer to be the loving, supportive wife, and yet I hate to see this marriage go down the drain. We live in such a 'disposable' society, but I really don't want this marriage to become a discard. I turned forty this past summer, I work part-time and try to keep up with the family, my faith is weak, and my cup is empty."

Some of the following suggestions may help your tired, stale marriage to recover.

QUALITIES FOR A STRONG MARRIAGE

A journal article entitled "Healthy Family Functioning: What Therapists Say and What Families Want" points out that healthy families have three basic qualities: cohesion, adaptability, and communication.

Cohesion is the bonding or belonging of each family member to the unit and to each other. Some of the aspects of cohesion are emotional attraction, mature dependency, supportiveness, loyalty, psychological safety, reliability, family identification, and physical caretaking.

Adaptability means that the family is able to change its rules and change the responsibilities that people carry out during different eras of the family's experience. Some of the qualities of adaptability are flexibility, assertiveness, negotiation, and feedback.

Communication was viewed by these families and therapists as a means to enable the family to adapt and to be cohesive. Communication skills were divided into three areas: listener, sender, and general skills.

Listener skills included attentive listening, indicating that messages were heard, paraphrasing, and checking out what the listener thought the sender was saying.

Sender skills included speaking for oneself, being specific, expressing thoughts as well as feelings and intentions.

The *general communication skills* included being spontaneous, providing feedback, and encouraging others to speak.[8]

Virginia Satir in her book *People-Making* said that she discovered healthy families have the following four general characteristics:

1. High self-image for each person in the family.
2. Direct, clear, specific, and honest communication.
3. Flexible, human, and appropriate rules.
4. Open and hopeful linking to society; that is, unafraid to relate to society.[9]

If you're living in a dull mid-life marriage, probably some of these values that family researchers have identified are missing in your relationship or are not functioning properly. To improve a marriage does not require that everything that is wrong with the marriage be changed at once. Each small improvement causes your whole relationship to improve.

If you're making stew and have not put in any salt, onion, or bay leaves, the stew will be rather bland, dull, and tasteless. But as you add each of these small ingredients, the meat and all of the vegetables take on a richer taste. Small improvements in your marriage will make the whole marriage taste better.

THE MEANING AND FUNCTIONING OF LOVE

What is love? How can we get it back? Mid-life married people repeatedly ask these questions.

Whatever love is in a marriage relationship, it must function at several different levels to be truly effective. The spouses need intellectual understanding of each other as well as an emotional understanding of each other's needs. Intellectually, we say, "Yes, I understand that you have a need." Emotionally, however, we should begin to feel that need of the other person. We must try to see life through the other person's eyes.

Love is also expressed in physical dimensions by touching, hugging, a back rub, a leg massage, or a deeply exhilarating experience of sexual intercourse. Love cannot exist as a concept—love must be expressed through intellectual and psychological understanding as well as with physical contact.

Another dimension of love often overlooked is the spiritual caring for each other. In the same way that we reach out physically and touch each other, we also touch each other spiritually, through prayer, by encouraging each other's spiritual gifts, and by reminding each other of the unity that we have because of God living in our lives.

MATURITY, VULNERABILITY, ACCOUNTABILITY, INTIMACY

Qualities of love also must include dimensions of maturity. We have come to know and accept ourselves. We have learned how to be interdependent with other people. We have learned how to give ourselves for the well-being of other people.

Another characteristic of love is vulnerability, or allowing ourselves to be open and exposed to our mates. Through vulnerability we allow our mates to know who we are—our weaknesses as well as our strengths.

A quality of love often overlooked is accountability to each other. Sometimes it's easier to be accountable *for* someone than *to* someone. It's easier to take care of someone than to allow that one to take care of you. It's easier to ask someone to account to you for his actions than it is for you to account to him for your actions. Accountability is closely linked with vulnerability. If we are willing to be open and emotionally exposed to another person, we can usually take the short step toward implementing accountability.

Flowing out of this will be intimacy. One cannot truly be spiritually, intellectually, psychologically intimate with a person without maturity, vulnerability, and accountability. Intimacy means you are aware of another person's innermost feelings and attitudes, that is, the core of the person. Intimacy also assumes an equality in the knowledge of the other person and the exposure of your life to that person.

The motivating force that causes all of the rest of these attributes of love to be expressed in a relationship is our will. Somewhere along the line, a person wills to expose himself or herself—to be accountable—to be intimate. Somewhere, one makes a choice to be involved with a person or not to be involved. The dull mid-life marriage, tragically, is the expression of repeated choices not to demonstrate the qualities of love to each other. A dull mid-life marriage is in reality a nonrelating relationship.

A MUTUAL MARRIAGE

Marriage styles have changed down through history. There have been sad times when men treated women as owned possessions much like items of livestock. In some eras women were viewed as just the carrier of the husband's baby. Not long ago people didn't believe that the woman even contributed to the formation of the child. She was just the nest.

But in other periods in history, women have been highly respected and revered as equal partners in the marriage relationship. Our pioneer forefathers practiced this kind of equality in marriage. It was very different from the European type of marriage they had previously known. The equal marriage in the United States was born out of hardship and necessity. Each person had to pull his or her own weight. Each person's ideas and contributions were significant and valuable.

The mutual marriage is built on the scriptural principles that each member of the body of Christ is gifted by Christ (Ephesians 4:7). Each member is to exercise those gifts and abilities on behalf of the whole body so that the entire body grows and becomes complete (Ephesians 4:16, 13).

The concepts of our interrelatedness, our mutual dependence on each other, and our mutual contributions to each other are clearly foundational stones in the New Testament. The Scripture teaches us that we can't say to each other, "I don't need you" (1 Corinthians 12:21). In fact, the Scripture says that the weaker, insignificant parts are vital to us (1 Corinthians 12:22-24). The Scripture also teaches that we grow or experience loss as a group, not as individuals (1 Corinthians 12:26).

When people get married, they do not drop out of the body of Christ. Since Scripture teaches us that in Christ we are all equal (Galatians 3:28) and we all have gifts (Ephesians 4:7), we must incorporate the scriptural principles of interpersonal relationships in our marriages. The family should be run by concepts that show our equality in Christ. The mutual marriage will be the more fulfilling type for both the husband and the wife as they move through the middle years.

A mutual marriage means that each partner practices mutual submission in the following important areas:

1. Mutual valuing of each other and ourselves. If each of us has been given gifts by God which we are obligated to exercise on behalf of the other, then each of us possesses something that the other one doesn't have, and the other's life is going to be incomplete without our contribution. I then have importance in your life and you have importance in my life. Both partners value the other's contribution to their lives. We each supply, we are each valuable— we are *crucial* to each other.

2. Mutual responsibility for the growth of the mate. Marriage is a heavy responsibility where each person is obligated to enrich the other. At times one is stronger than the other and must allow the other to lean on him or her for emotional strength and spiritual direction. We are compared to stones in a building, each one supporting the other and yet resting on the other. And our stones together produce a building that is an honor to God (Ephesians 2:20-22).

3. Mutual serving and being served. In the Upper Room, Jesus clearly set the pattern that we are to serve

each other (John 13). I am to let you serve me without responding to you, "OK, first you rub my back; then I'll rub yours." Being served means that you allow the other person to contribute to your life without your earning it. Marriage is a grace relationship. Our relationship in the body of Christ is a grace relationship. We didn't earn it; we don't deserve it; we can never pay it back. Mutual submission means that we are mutually serving each other. Serving is also a grace expression. It is not something that the other person earned or for which we expect a return. It is an expression of care for that other person and wanting the best for that one's life.

4. Mutual forgiveness. In the early sixties, Eric Berne wrote *Games People Play*. He pointed out that people relate to each other through predictable patterns, predictable manipulations, predictable leverage. We know how to get what we want. Most marriage relationships are filled with repeated game processes.

Mutual forgiveness means that we give up the game-playing process. We stop the one-upmanship. We are willing, as the Bible teaches, to put up with one another in love (Ephesians 4:2). Forgiveness means I know that my mate may fail, but I dare not manipulate him.

Forgiveness means that I relinquish punishment and correction to God. I yield to him the redirection of my mate's life. Forgiveness means that I will no longer hold my mate accountable for something that happened in the past, but I will turn him loose from that bondage. I will allow him to straighten the matter out with God; I will allow him to continue to flower under God's leadership.

TRUE MUTUAL SUBMISSION

"True submission does not deny my own value or negate our differences. It *offers* my ideas, opinions, and strengths to you with the motive of adding something to you that only I can give; but this is an *offer*, not a command; a sharing, not a takeover; a giving of myself, not a power play.

"In submitting to you I do not give up my true self; rather I give *out of myself,* not denying who I am but offering who I am as an act of love and trust. True submission cannot take place if I deny my true self because I then have nothing of substance to offer you—not a real person, only an empty shell."[10]

Following is a beautiful statement of a mutual marriage from the book *Choosing to Love* by Jerry and Barbara Cook:

If I am the object of your love
  and you are the object of my love,
    then we are each free
      to be ourselves.
When secure in your love
  I need not control you,
    manipulate you,
      compete with you
        or remake you in my image.
I admire you,
  accept you totally,
    respect and trust you.
But I do not feel I must apologize
  for not being like you,
    for thinking different thoughts,
      feeling different emotions,
        enjoying something you don't
          or being excited about
            something
              that bores you.
If I deny who I am,
  I have nothing to give you
    but a mindless china doll;
      an empty shell who is not a
      real woman,
        but a toy you've outgrown.
When I share what I think

It is not to coerce—or
   demand that you agree.
I offer myself
   to persuade—
      encourage—
But—
   not to dominate.
Whatever I share
   is a gift of my love
      an act of trust that you'll accept me
         and understand that
            I'm making an offer,
               an honest disclosure;
                  not a power play.
Love is not possible between superiors and inferiors
   since the superior can only condescend
      and the inferior only admire.
Mutual respect means I do not exploit
   either your strengths
      or your weaknesses,
         but enjoy you
            a unique friend.
To believe we can have a marriage of
   sustained mutual respect
      can only mean
         we believe in forgiveness!
So when I ask, in the pattern of Jesus,
   "What do you want?"
      "What are your needs?"
I am not being subservient
   nor am I giving my will to you
      (handing over the lordship of my life . . .
         even God will not take over my will)
I am rather
   making a choice
      a decision to love
         to truly give—for the joy of it
            because of your value to me.[11]

122

Chapter Seven

HER HUSBAND'S OWN CRISIS*

We were going out the door to catch a flight to Denver. The phone rang, and we had mixed feelings. Probably someone in trouble was calling. Every day we were receiving about five hours of long distance phone calls from women whose husbands were in mid-life crisis. If we answered this call, we might be late for our plane. I (Jim) picked up the phone anyway.

The crying woman on the other end said, "You don't know me, but I've read your book, *Men in Mid-Life Crisis*, and I need to talk to you about my husband." I asked who she was and where she was calling from, but she said, "I can't give you that information, because my husband would be very angry. He doesn't want anyone to know. He is the minister of a large church in our denomination and well known in our state. If he comes into the house, I will have to hang up quickly." The story had barely started to spill out when she abruptly hung up the phone.

During the following days Sally and I prayed often for this unknown woman and her husband. She finally called back about two weeks later, gave me only her first name, and began to tell this story:

* Certain concepts in this chapter can be found in *Men in Mid-Life Crisis* (Jim Conway; David C. Cook Publishing Co., 1978) and are used by permission.

"My husband has been acting very differently. He was always very careful of his behavior around women. He would never give women of the church a ride home in his car, even if it were raining and they had no other way, because he wanted to avoid all appearances of sin. But now he has changed drastically.

"Recently we have been helping a divorcée," she explained. "We've helped many individuals and families over our years of ministry. This young woman and her children were spending a lot of time with our family as she went through the recovery process following her husband's abandonment.

"One day," the pastor's wife continued, "I came home from work unexpectedly. The divorcée's car was at the house which was not unusual. But when I entered the house, it was strangely quiet. Our two youngest children were playing in their room, but my husband and this woman could not be found anywhere. I went from room to room, looking for them. With a growing dread in the pit of my stomach, I moved toward the last room in the house—our bedroom. I got there to find the door closed and locked. In frantic desperation, I beat on the door and called out my husband's name! He came to the door, embarrassed and hurriedly dressing, profusely apologizing for what was happening.

"What would cause my husband, a straight-laced Christian, to go in such a strange direction? It seems that the things he thought clearly black or white—right or wrong—have become fuzzy gray or have changed colors. The most confusing part is that he doesn't even realize that his values have switched."

WHY THE CHANGE?

On that flight to Denver we picked up the *Flightime* Magazine and found a synopsis of Avery Corman's book *The Old Neighborhood*, which describes some of the changes that take place in men as they experience mid-life crisis:

"As a young man, Steve Robbins left his neighborhood to be a success. He has become one of the best advertising copywriters in the field; he has a beautiful, successful wife and two lovely daughters. He has achieved everything he thought he wanted.

"Yet, at forty-five, Steve Robbins finds that the life he had so desperately wanted is meaningless. His relationship with his career-minded wife is less a marriage than a corporation. His children are independent and growing away from him. His career has turned into a monotonous game of being clever. Where once he would have given anything to create an award-winning advertising campaign, he would now trade all his success for an egg cream at Fisher's candy store."[1]

What is it that causes a hard-driving, moral, clearly-focused man suddenly to be diverted into a different direction, a direction that seems counter to his previous lifestyle and thinking?

THE LAST STRAW

Martha Lear summarizes some of the stress of a man in mid-life crisis: "The hormone-producing levels are dropping, the sexual vigor is diminishing . . . the children are leaving, the parents are dying, the job horizons are narrowing, the friends are having the first heart attacks; the past floods by in a fog of hopes unrealized, opportunities not grasped, potential not fulfilled, and the future is a confrontation with one's own mortality."[2]

Bergler, a psychoanalyst and author of *Revolt of the Middle-Aged Man*, calls this time in a man's life an "emotional second adolescence."[3] Fried says that this can be a very dangerous time, not only for the one in crisis but for other people as well: "He (or she) has a great deal of social expertise, power, and freedom—considerably more than either an adolescent or an older person; he is old enough to know and young enough to do, so that *his* hostility, *her* rebellion, *their* love affairs are potentially hazardous to others as well as to themselves."[4]

The mid-life woman is not only dealing with her role identification as a wife, mother, and possibly career person; she is also handling the stresses that are produced from our culture, her children, a marriage that is probably at its lowest level of satisfaction, physical aging, and perhaps other losses in her life. On top of this, her husband may be going through his own mid-life crisis.

Anyone who is going through a major developmental life transition, such as passing from young adulthood to mid-life, needs to have supportive people around him or her to give perspective and encouragement to make the transition. If both the husband and the wife are going through mid-life crisis at the same time, they will find themselves unable to help their mate and probably will be very critical of each other. Their marriage is likely to experience serious stress.

A woman in mid-life crisis must realize that as the amount of stress increases in and around her life, she needs an enlarged support group that can provide the stability and emotional and spiritual support that she needs. Both she and her husband need friends of the same sex who will help each of them during this hard time when they are less able to help each other.

FREQUENTLY ASKED QUESTIONS

TRANSITION OR CRISIS?
Some people ask what the difference is between mid-life transition and a crisis. A transition means that a person moves from one era or stage of life to another. These transitions take place several times during life, such as when moving from being a child to an adolescent to a young adult to a mid-life adult to a mellow adult to a retiring adult to an aged adult. Each of these movements, if properly understood and planned for, can take place without an overwhelming amount of stress. However, if

several stress factors converge at the same time that the transition is taking place, a crisis can be produced.

For example, if your kitchen is like many American homes, you probably have too many appliances running off your electrical outlets. If you would turn all the appliances on at the same time, and they were appliances that drew a lot of power, you would probably blow a fuse. The same thing is true in us emotionally.

It's not terribly difficult for most people to handle one or two stresses in their lives. If you are a healthy person, you should be able to handle the normal stress of the mid-life transition. However, if your children are going through a rough transition from childhood to adolescence or adolescence to young adulthood; if you are having a difficult career adjustment; if your husband is having a horrible mid-life crisis and wants to resign from his job, divorce you, split up the estate, and sail around the world with his secretary; and if your father has just died of a heart attack, you are likely to have a crisis.

HOW MANY MEN?
Another common question is, "How many men have a mid-life crisis?" Our field studies and evaluation show that somewhere around 75 to 80 percent of the men age thirty-five to fifty-five experience a moderate to severe mid-life crisis. This means that for a period of time they do not function as usual. They eventually make an extensive evaluation of their life's direction that causes shifts in their values and pursuits.

Daniel Levinson and his Yale research team who studied forty men from several occupations over a ten-year period of time found that 80 percent of the men experienced a mid-life crisis.[5]

CAN'T CHRISTIANS AVOID IT?
People often ask, "Will mid-life crisis happen if you are a Christian?" Every person will go through the developmental transitions, and yes, many Christians will experience a

not stop life's processes by being a
ot say to a ten-year-old, "Look, if
n, you'll never have to be a teen-
childhood to adulthood without the
adolescence." Skipping adolescence is not
desirable, because there are so many things that adolescents need to learn as they go through those years that
will prepare them for living the life of a Christian young
adult. Being a Christian should help to sort out values at
mid-life, and a vital relationship with God will provide
stability and perspective, but the mid-life issues cannot be
avoided. It is not even desirable to skip this time of value
redefinition.

WHAT ARE THE SYMPTOMS?

Many wives ask, "If my husband goes into mid-life crisis,
how will he act?" Each man is unique, of course, and his
reactions to mid-life crisis will be different from any other
man's. Some experience a very quiet withdrawal and in-
trospection. Others exhibit drastic outward lifestyle
changes.

Some of the early indications of mid-life crisis are personality changes. A man may become unusually grumpy
and irritable. He will feel that everyone else is wrong and
can't do anything right. He is extremely critical of the
world around him while he feels that he alone is right.

Often there are lifestyle changes. My (Jim's) father, who
was a hard-driving workaholic, suddenly bought an airplane and began taking off from work in the middle of the
day to go flying. Other men become preoccupied with
their bodies, take up new hobbies or sports, and perhaps
trade in the old, family-style brown Buick for a nice, bright
red Porsche.

WILL IT EVER END?

"How long will my husband's mid-life crisis last?" The
most honest answer is, "Until the transition is completed.
Until all of his values can be sorted out and his life reor-

iented now as a mid-life person instead of a young
Generally, it takes three to five years. During the first
or so, there probably will be a gradual increase in tens
and anxiety, and maybe some lifestyle changes. The mid
dle phase can be quite traumatic, including depression,
running away, or a drastic job change. After many of the
values are sorted out and realigned, there is a gradual
coming-down from anxiety and a return, surprisingly
enough, to life structures quite similar to the previous
ones, only now more refined and effective.

Sometimes the value readjustment at one transition in
life is delayed or suppressed, only to bubble up later in
life. We have known some men who seemed to have almost no stress at mid-life. They deliberately threw themselves heavily into work to forget their aging and to keep
from reflecting on the values in their lives from the new
perspective of mid-life. They pressed on as if nothing had
changed in their lives since they were young adults. However, as they came to retirement, they went through a giant
internal revolution. They had compressed two transition
times into one and experienced a serious crisis.

A difficult factor about the mid-life developmental transition is that until recently, our culture did not realize there
were changes in the middle years. We believed that after
age twenty-one the adult life was very stable until retirement. It was common in educational circles to use phrases
such as, "You can't teach old dogs new tricks."

In the middle sixties when I (Jim) was working on a
master's degree in psychology, it was a common clinical
perspective that anybody over thirty-five was essentially
hopeless for change. We were to work with them from the
viewpoint of making things as tolerable as possible as they
lived out the rest of their lives.

HOW ARE MEN'S AND WOMEN'S
MID-LIFE CRISES DIFFERENT?

With regard to mid-life crisis, men and women are very
similar in a number of areas.

1. Both are influenced by the youth culture.
2. Both are aware of their changing bodies.
3. Both are affected by the generations on each side—adolescents and aging parents.
4. Both are influenced by the disposable society that doesn't seem to need them as much as before.
5. Both are experiencing a lowered self-image.
6. Both are aware of their personal aging.
7. Both are feeling unfulfilled in their marriage.

They are distinctly different in a number of areas, however.

One area is career. The man at mid-life is asking, "Why should I work? What have I accomplished with my life? How can I slow down or redirect my energies into career experiences that are more meaningful?" The mid-life woman, however, is asking, "When can I start to work? How can I develop my career?" She is wondering about returning to school, finishing a degree. She considers going to seminars. In short, she is really starting to blossom in her career aspirations.

The wife is taking off like a rocket while her husband is fizzling like a balloon with a slow leak. The woman at age forty-one is like a man at age thirty-one. He knew then where he wanted to go and he committed himself wholly to it until he finally burned out. She is just seeing where she wants to go and is willing to put great effort to get there, as he did earlier.

A second area of difference is intimacy. The man became intimate in his early marriage in order to get the marriage established, but then his concentration shifted toward career, which has been the focus of his life through most of the years while the children were home. As he enters mid-life crisis, however, he is beginning to think about the interpersonal relationships he lost, especially in relationship to his children. He also wants his wife to be a girl friend and lover, not just a mother and household manager.

The mid-life woman quite often trades intimacy for assertiveness. She sees clearly where she wants to go and sets out to accomplish her goals. Sometimes the goal-oriented mid-life woman sacrifices some of her earlier qualities of intimacy in order to accomplish her life goals. She may be back in school as a full-time student. It's catch-up time, and if she is pooped out at the end of the day and can't talk—well, then, talking will just have to wait for another day.

A third area of difference is assertiveness. The mid-life man who has been a driver and pusher through most of his married life now begins the mellowing-out process. He begins kicking back, putting his feet up, starting to enjoy some of the things he has accomplished. He suggests a few more vacations. "Let's get away for an extended weekend." "Let's slow down."

The mid-life woman is going the other direction. She says, "I want to go back to school. I'm eager to get going. Things are finally coming to the place where I'm able to move. Let's get moving." He wants to go out of town for a few days and she says, "I can't go out of town; I'll miss classes or that special seminar." He says, "Let's spend a quiet evening at home or go to a movie." She says, "I have to work overtime at the office. They're considering me for a new position."

A fourth area of difference is their view of family. Earlier the mid-life man ignored his family while he focused on his career. Now he is dealing with remorse and guilt, wishing he could relive some of those years. Pete said, "I'm really a success in business, but in the process I lost my kids."

The mid-life woman has spent most of her time with the family. She's ready for a new challenge in life. It doesn't mean that she doesn't care for her family, but they are taking a less predominant place in her life. In a sense, he is moving toward the family and she is moving parallel to the family, but with a focus on her career.

A fifth area of noticeable difference between men and women at mid-life is their view of death. During the forties, there is a sharp rise in the number of men who die suddenly from such problems as heart attacks. A man wonders about life and death—wonders how long he will live— how much time he has yet to accomplish things—what really is important in life. He is confronting his own mortality.

The mid-life woman, however, is not thinking much about death. Women tend to live longer and the incidence of sudden death from heart attacks and other diseases usually will not take place in a woman's experience until after she passes menopause. So, in a sense, the man is looking at death and wondering when his life will end, while his wife is saying, "Life is just beginning for me."

JIM'S MID-LIFE CRISIS

Mid-life crisis was not supposed to happen to me (Jim). I was informed about the problem and had helped other men work through this era of their lives. I had a very secure family relationship with my wife and daughters who loved me very much. I was soaked with education, with master's degrees in theology and psychology and a doctoral degree underway. I had a successful ministry at Twin City Bible Church in Urbana, Illinois, and enjoyed a very positive relationship with people there. Each week I would receive several notes telling of the helpful contributions of my ministry in individuals' lives. I had ministered overseas on several occasions and had had many articles published in national magazines.

I did not anticipate a mid-life crisis. But then I turned forty-five, which seemed to me like stepping off the edge of the world. At the same time, I received word that one of my close friends, Gaston Singh, had died of a massive heart attack at age thirty-six. In a few months Gaston and

I were to have gone to India to start a training program for southeast Asians.

I began to ask, "What is life all about? What is life, if only to die?" I was experiencing an ever-deepening depression. I would ask Sally, "Why did my parents have the right to bring me into the world? Why didn't they just skip over me, wherever I was, and bring somebody else into the world?" I would stare out the living room window for long hours at a time and say, "You know, living life is the biggest waste of time that there is."

As I went through an extended depression, I was angry at society, at life itself, at God for creating life. I had irrational fears of losing my job, that I was useless in life, and that anyone my age was fit only to be buried.

Sections from Psalm 102 verbalized my thinking. I was encouraged to see that people from other generations had wrestled with some of the same concerns that I was experiencing. The Psalmist talked about the breakdown in his physical and emotional life as he experienced mid-life stress. He wrestled with the conflict of God's becoming ever more famous from one generation to another while he was getting weaker and going down the tubes! I found it helpful to read Psalms 102 and 103 together. Psalm 102 presents the problem; Psalm 103 presents God as ever-caring and involved in our lives.

CAUSES

Many cultural impacts intensify the mid-life transition and help cause it to become a crisis for men. Some of these problems are very similar to forces that impact women.

1. We live in a youth-oriented society. When we are young adults, we enjoy being "in"; however, when we reach mid-life, we feel "out."

2. We live in a throw-away society. When I (Jim) was at a men's retreat with a number of men who worked for electronic companies, they said their competitive industry

has a systematic evaluation program to wash men out as they come into the mid years. When they started with the company as young men, they were given lots of affirmation and positive strokes, but when they turned forty, the company started evaluating them more often. These men at the retreat said, "You can always tell the mid-life guys who have just been evaluated. They don't show up for work the next couple of days; sometimes they're gone a whole week. They are so devastated." After awhile the older men quit. Their leaving makes room for the new, young turkeys coming up the line. Those twenty-seven-year-olds don't realize they are being put on a human conveyor belt that is going to chew them up and spit them out the other end before they are fifty.

3. We have two other generations to care for. We in the middle generation have to care for our children, and we may have to begin parenting our parents. Our parents have provided backup, support, counsel, sometimes even financial assistance, but now it's the other way around. Many parents are needing guidance and direction, emotional support, and perhaps some financial assistance.

4. Marriage satisfaction is low at mid-life. A man in his thirties is so directed toward the single goal of achieving in his career that he is willing to sacrifice almost everything else. The marriage in the forties becomes marked with the husband's mid-life crisis, when he is feeling a combination of guilt because he has neglected his marriage, and hopelessness because he feels the marriage is dull and dead. Why should he even try to revive it?

5. There is a new awareness of the potential of death. A twenty-five-year-old looks back and sees that twenty-five years have passed since he was born. A forty-five-year-old realizes that he may have only twenty-five years left.

The young man does not look at the obituary page on his way to read the sports; the mid-life man, however, takes a glance and when he sees that someone died at age forty-two, he calls out to his wife, "Hey, Honey, did you see this in the paper? This guy was only forty-two, and he died of a heart attack!" He begins to feel his chest and he wonders about that pain that he has been having. The mid-life man suddenly feels that death isn't far off, especially if he has lost one or more of his parents or close friends. He feels that he is the next one in line.

6. The knowledge explosion is intense. Actually two forces are working in opposite directions. The one is the explosion of knowledge, and the second is the expanding responsibility at work, which demands time and energy. Both of these factors work in opposition to an aging body that doesn't have the bounce and spring it had at twenty-five.

7. The body is aging. One morning as he shaves, he looks at his face and sees a really old man, with wrinkles around his mouth and eyes, graying hair on the temples, a receding hairline, and the growing bald spot on top. He looks at where his magnificent chest used to be. He thinks back to his college days when he had muscles there. And then, horror of horrors, he looks at his waist. So, that's where his chest went! Oh, what an ugly glob of fat. That's where all those doughnuts have gone: straight to his middle. He turns sideways, sucks in his stomach, and sticks out his chest. He almost looks like a man again. He holds his position for a long, glorious moment, but finally he has to breathe. As he lets it all out, his "chest" flops down over his pajamas again. What a disgusting sight!

He mumbles to himself, "I'm not keeping up at work, I'm repeatedly told that youth is the only good age. My marriage is in trouble. My kids think they don't need me. My parents are needing my attention. I'm getting nearer to death. What does it all mean, anyway?" At this point, we have a man who is entering mid-life crisis. He begins to feel that he has too many problems. There is a circuit overload. Too many things are keeping him from accomplishing what he wants to do. He has spent all of these years, all of the vigor of his youth, and what has it done for him? He feels crummier than ever before in his life.

ENEMIES

He decides that he has some enemies.* If he could get rid of these, life might be better.

The first enemy is his *body*—this sagging blob of flesh standing before the mirror. If he could get it back in shape, he'd feel better about himself. He remembers recently when he was playing racquet ball with a younger guy from the office that his mind said to his arm, "Go, get that ball! Stretch! Reach!" But his body just stood there and said, "You've gotta be kidding!" He has to do something about this body that opposes his mind.

A second enemy is his *work.* He feels trapped because he needs the dollars to pay for piano lessons, orthodontic braces, and college educations. He also knows that if he drops out of work now or tries to shift to a job he might like better, he'll not only take a cut in salary and lose other benefits, but he might not even find another job. And he wonders what he could do for work that would give him satisfaction and, at the same time, help him meet his obligations.

During the mid-life years a family needs the biggest house and the greatest number of cars, and probably will have the highest expenses of all time. A man in mid-life crisis can easily identify his *wife and family* as the third enemy. He sees them as the reason he is trapped at work and limited from doing what he'd really like to do. He has too many obligations to just drop out, walk along the beach, pick up odd jobs, paint pictures, or sail.

God is identified as the fourth enemy, because the mid-life man sees God as the ultimate culprit. He pictures God grinning fiendishly and pointing a long, bony finger as he says, "You despicable, disgraceful Christian! You are the worst possible example of a mature man. You are selfish.

---

* These enemies were first identified by Jim Conway in 1977 as he worked with other men in mid-life crisis and after going through his own crisis. He discusses them in more detail in *Men in Mid-Life Crisis.* These ideas have since been used by several other writers.

You are filled with lust. You are lazy. You are so disgusting that I want to spew you out of my mouth!"[6]

The mid-life man sees God not only as an accuser but as unfair. The man says to God, "You are the one that made me this way. You gave me these drives for achievement. You gave me strong sexual urges. You designed me as a disposable human being who would grow old and die. Now, God, you come along and say 'Adjust to it. Live with it. If you step out of line or think bad thoughts, I'm going to squash you like a bug.' That's unfair!"

The man in mid-life crisis becomes engaged in what is called projection. He is not owning his problems as his own, whether with his body, his work, his wife and family, or his relationship with God. He is projecting all of the internal value struggle onto other people, situations, or objects. This process is a dead-end road and will only cause him to be more angry and feel like a victim. He must take charge, think through his values, and reorder his life according to his adjusted values.

REACTIONS

The average mid-life man will try some short-range solutions that he hopes will enable him to escape from these enemies. Unfortunately, they are not the real answers.

WITHDRAWAL

One of the things that a mid-life man may do to try to relieve his stress is to withdraw. It may take the form of alcohol: "Just a couple of beers after work to take the edge off so I don't have to think." Or he may escape by sleeping: "When I'm asleep, I'm not thinking about my problems." Endless hours of watching TV may also provide diversion from needed reflection. Depression, that personal pity party, is the result of feeling a victim in life's circumstances as well as a choice to become a martyr: "Perhaps if I'm seen in a desperate situation, someone will love me." Depression, along with alcohol, TV, sleep, and other escape mechanisms may appear to provide relief, but they are only temporary.

ANGER

A mid-life man may think he'll feel better if he can punch something. His anger is almost aimless. He is not sure what he is angry at, but he is angry at everything—himself, society, individual people, and God. He goes around with a chip on his shoulder. He is grumpy and irritable. He cannot stand the imperfections and the distractions of life. There is a great deal of turmoil going on inside him, and the slightest incident may trigger an almost unaccountable explosion.

NEW IMAGE

Another escape that a mid-life man quite often tries is that of the new look. He is the macho man with a suntanned body. He works out regularly at the local fitness center. When he's around women, he tends to stand so that he can show off his muscles. He wears tight shirts or shirts that can be unbuttoned down to his belt. A gold chain on his chest finishes off the image. But what can he do about the clump of gray chest hair showing out of his open shirt?

A man with a brand-new yellow Toyota Celica picked me (Jim) up in front of my hotel to go to a speaking engagement. As I got into the car, I noticed a well-worn copy of *Men in Mid-Life Crisis* on the console between our two seats. He put the car into first gear and about snapped my head off as we took off from the curb. We came to the first corner; he down-shifted—rum, rum, rum! Three different gears. We whipped around the corner and he went through the shifting process again. We came to another corner—and the same thing. It wasn't a matter of just stepping on the brakes. He down-shifted all the way. I thought for a while that I was in a Grand Prix race. Finally, after we had gone around every corner in the whole city, or so it seemed, we were out on the freeway. When he finally got it into fifth gear, he looked sheepishly at me and said, "I really wanted to buy a Porsche, but I couldn't afford it!"

The mid-life man in the old brown Buick gets a small, sexy sports car and tells his friends it's because it gets good gas mileage. The truth is, it's the image. "If I can change my lifestyle," he thinks, "maybe it'll solve this turmoil."

DROP OUT

Many men try dropping out of work. They think of taking an early retirement. Retiring at age forty-three sounds funny, but the thought occurs to many men. One of our friends in his late thirties thinks of retiring to a small farm where he and his family can be totally self-sufficient. They want to raise their own animals and vegetables; grow a corn crop in order to convert it into gasohol, which would provide the fuel they need for vehicles and electricity; design an energy-efficient house; drill their own well. But all of these dreams are really escape dreams. He actually is saying, "Life is too much to handle. Stop the world; I want to get off for awhile." The problem is—and this is what's so frustrating at mid-life—you can't stop the world and you can't get off for awhile, and the grinding reality is that you can't cope either.

NEW LOVE

Of all the possible escape solutions that the mid-life man in crisis may try, the affair is the most disturbing to the wife and the most played up by the media. A wife can probably handle job changes, a different car, his working out at the gym, and his new wardrobe. She can even handle his withdrawal and anger, but the specter of the other woman cuts deep into the wife's self-image. She has a sense of being rejected. "I have been evaluated, compared with another woman, and I've been given low marks by my husband." The sanctity and specialness between the two of them—the sacredness of something given by God—is broken by the affair.

If your husband has been or is in an affair, you may be pushed into your own mid-life crisis. It is important to remember not to moralize at this point but to understand the dynamics inside the man and in your marriage relationship. Focus your thoughts and energy on resolving the affair, understanding each other, and meeting each other's needs.

Questions always come. Will the affair last? Will he marry the younger woman? The statistics show that only about 2.9 percent of men aged forty-five to fifty-four are married to women under thirty-four.[7] The younger woman quite often sees the older man as a father figure and the relationship can be very rewarding at first, but sooner or later, most young women want more than a father figure and most mid-life men want more than a daughter.

HEALING FROM THE MID-LIFE AFFAIR

As dreadful as your husband's affair might be and as damaging to your self-image as it has been, perhaps you can turn it into new growth and insight for your life. Following is one woman's story:

"That image of the other woman sliced (me) and became a nagging obsession. What did she look like? Was she tall? Slender? Young? (I) imagined her as someone he worked with at the college—someone intelligent, informed, and involved in the world. Saturday afternoons were probably the only times she was free so they could meet.

"Where did they go? To a motel? (I) tried to picture them together—how they made love. Did he *love* her? What were the things they talked about? Science? World affairs? How long had they known each other? Were they *still* together? What really were his plans for the future? . . .

"Suddenly, (I) knew no fear. I exist too. I think I've

earned the right. . . . I know this must sound funny, but the woman my husband was involved with changed my image of myself—of what a woman should be. That old image of me was pretty much destroyed. I felt worthless; my pride hurt and my ego sagged. I went out and bought a completely new wardrobe. Don't misunderstand, I don't mean that as a surface thing. I suddenly *cared enough about myself* to want to take care of myself. No more skimping. No more tattered sweaters. I'd lost fifteen pounds because I'd been upset, but it was becoming. I didn't want to be a gray-haired lady anymore either. So I went red!

"I got shocked out of my complacency in many ways. She did me a service. I wanted to be the woman I imagined him with. An involved, independent woman. Maybe it was the kind of woman I wanted to be all along, but never dared be. . . ."[8]

Try to keep your perspective and realize that you have history on your side. If you have done some growing and eliminating of friction areas, your husband may find it a pleasure to be with you once again and to continue what he has had with you for all these years.

Dr. Bernice Neugarten, professor of human development at the University of Chicago, has said, "Intimacy can be quickly attained, but it somehow doesn't suffice if it is without length. . . . You can go to bed with someone, but that somehow doesn't dismiss the need for the long-standing relationship; you *still* want to go home to someone who has known you for twenty-five years.[9]

HELPING THE MAN
THROUGH HIS MID-LIFE CRISIS

Your husband's mid-life crisis is one of those additional loads on your circuit that may cause your own crisis to become more difficult or perhaps start you into mid-life crisis. If you know how to reduce your husband's crisis and help him through this time, it will help to lessen the pressure on both of you and your marriage relationship.

First, *understand the problem* of mid-life crisis. You have accomplished some of that by reading through this chapter. Perhaps you need to extend your reading a bit further by reading other books under "Suggested Reading" at the end of the book.

Second, *listen to him.* Listen as a friend. Listen nonjudgmentally. Yes, there may be some things that he is doing or thinking that are wrong, but let him sort those values out. If you impose your values on him at this point, the crisis is only prolonged. He needs to evaluate and establish his own values.

Also, listen to him without yielding to the urge to set him straight. He may be thinking of irrational or impetuous moves in his career or marriage. Your role is one of caution, providing the courage to investigate, to explore what these options might mean.

Draw him out. Encourage him to talk about his wishes and hopes and dreams. What are the things that he always wanted to accomplish but is afraid he's not going to get done before he dies? Your willingness to participate in this will help him as he wrestles with his heavy problems.

As our friend Dale came to mid-life, he decided to quit his secure position in a state job and to start his own business. This would mean reduced income and longer work hours for a time. It would require his wife's assistance in the work. When Dale shared his dream with his wife, Evelyn, they discussed it cautiously, but with the affirmation from her that she was willing to make the necessary sacrifices in order to see Dale's dream come true. His wife was a good sounding board for him as he weighed the advantages and disadvantages of going with his dream. She got caught up in the dream too. Today they have a happy marriage and a shared career.

Third, *"be with him."* Don't hover and mother, but be available. When I (Jim) was going through my mid-life crisis, Sally was teaching school Monday through Friday. My day off was Monday. In order to be available to be with me, Sally resigned from teaching so that we could get away more frequently for the recuperation and reflection time that I needed.

There will be crucial times when you need to be with him. At other times he needs to be alone. Be sensitive to the times when he is lonely, unsure of himself, would like to yell, "Help!" but because he is a man he feels he is not allowed to. Be with him in those moments.

Fourth, *commit yourself to friendship with him.* What your husband needs at this time in life is not a mother, but a girl friend. Think of the two words: girl, carrying the idea of spontaneity and freedom; and friend, someone who is willing to be a peer, a companion.

Think back to when you were dating. How did you act then? What were the things you did to attract him? Do you remember how you made a study of him? Do that now. Friendship grows through understanding each other and meeting each other's needs.

Commit yourself to being his friend, no matter what— even when his values are not your values and when he does things that you don't like. Commit yourself to him with an unconditional love. "I'll love you no matter what. I'll be your friend no matter what."

Fifth, *be reflective* when he is ready. Be a mirror to him. A time will come in your relationship when he begins to ask, "What do you think?" Reflect, but don't direct. A mirror does not show anything by itself, but only reflects the image that is presented to it.

He is asking what you think, but he doesn't want a domineering opinion. He wants more of a discussion. Your response should be, "Well, what have you been thinking? What are some of the options? Let's talk about it." After the discussion progresses, perhaps you can insert comments, such as, "Seems to me there's another option." or "Maybe this is a spinoff of what you suggested."

Ask questions in response to his questions. If he says, "I've been thinking about quitting work," your response might be, "What does that mean to you?" He can go on to explain some of his feelings, some of his anxieties and frustrations. When he comes to a stopping point, he is stopping to see how you react. He is deciding whether to go farther because you are listening and understanding or whether he should shut up because you are being threatened.

When he stops, pick up on his last ideas and reflect them back to him, "John, what I hear you saying is that you've worked for twenty years for Widget, Inc., and now you want to go on your own. But you have a mixture of fear and enthusiasm." When you respond this way, you give him the permission to continue to talk and share his feelings with you.

When all the feelings get out on the table, along with all the options, give him a chance to verbalize the directions toward which he is leaning. At this point, because you have been a good listener, he probably will want more input from you. Begin to share with him some of your thoughts, feelings, reasons, anxieties, or joys.

Together you have begun to solve a major problem. Instead of your husband's handling this in isolation or with another woman, you have worked on it together and the process will reduce tension in your husband and will also tend to draw you closer together in your marriage.

Chapter Eight

THE PAIN OF PARENTING

It's no secret that children add stress to our lives. Along with the joys, fun, and fulfillment, they produce problems we wouldn't otherwise have. Many studies show that women who have children will have a lower life satisfaction and a lower marriage satisfaction.[1] Yet most women experience a strong urge to have children, and those who haven't had any feel they've missed something. Apparently, it's the years of living with children after they're born that takes away the joy!

It's strange, isn't it, that children seem to cause more dissatisfaction for the present mid-life generation than for earlier generations, yet this one has concentrated more on their children. One authority observes, "We were the first crop of parents to take our children's failures and limitations as an indication of *our* inadequacy, not theirs; the first to believe, even briefly, that one could aspire to being a perfect parent. We were the first parents in the era of the child-centered family."[2]

MOTHERS AT ALL AGES

Mid-life mothers could have children whose ages range from newborn to college. Some women in our survey started families while they were yet in their teens, with childbearing completed by age twenty-three. Other women delayed having children, choosing to have a career first, so their childbearing didn't start until the mid-thirties.

In recent decades the standard childbearing era was during a woman's twenties, but that is no longer true. Not many years ago if a woman had a child in her mid-thirties, everyone was convinced that something went wrong. Quite often there was a nosy person around who would ask what everyone else was also wondering, "What happened?" Today a mid-life pregnancy is not uncommon and may be planned.

"From 1975 to 1978, there was a 37 percent rate of increase in the number of women from age thirty to thirty-four who had their first child, . . . For women age thirty-five to thirty-nine, the increase was 22 percent."[3] As we think through the impact of children on the mid-life woman, therefore, we will have to look at several different age groups of children.

MUTUAL SHAPING

The apartment, condo, or house that you live in is not only an expression of you, but your home also tends to form you. The same is true with the coming of a child. Building a nest and filling it with a child says something about you as a person and the things that you value, and that child also forms you.

When you were married, you surrendered some of your independence, but you looked at your gains in intimacy and companionship as more than equal to your losses. The same reshaping of you by gains and losses happens with the coming of children. You form your life around them; in effect, they mold you.

Sometimes the younger woman experiences a sense of her special life dream being put on hold when her first child comes. She begins to wait, biding her time until her children become sufficiently independent for her to again pick up her dream. The unthoughtful woman, who quickly lays aside her career dream or has her dream shoved aside by an unwanted pregnancy, may at mid-life find herself ventilating years of suppressed anger. Her innocent child may then be the focus of this woman's resentment and anger because she feels "bent out of shape" and unfulfilled.

Most women who want to have children plan to raise them in an atmosphere of love and marital strength. But, ready or not, the coming of children causes a redefinition in your life as a "woman" at each step along your life.

FROM PAMPERS TO PUBERTY

When our oldest daughter went off to kindergarten, we realized that we were no longer newlyweds, even though we had three children by that time and should have realized the fact earlier. Jim had graduated from seminary and we were pastoring a church. Yet, in our minds, we thought of ourselves as just beginning married life. At each milestone for our daughters, we experienced a startling need for updating ourselves.

Do you remember the first time that you saw pubic hair on your children? Did it make you feel old? One woman told about taking her son to the hospital emergency room. They stripped off his clothes to attend to him and she said, "It was a shock to me to find out he already had pubic hair. I felt about a hundred years old."[4]

If a mother has found her identity and self-fulfillment only in her children, she will lose part of herself when they grow up and leave. If, on the other hand, she has raised her children from the beginning to become gradually independent, then adolescence and young adulthood are simply the capstone of her involvement with her children.

NEW FRIENDS

As a couple we are enjoying our new identity since our daughters and their husbands relate to us as equals, friends, peers. We have three daughters—Barbara, Brenda, and Becki. Barbara and her husband Mike spent two years in Switzerland, working with high school kids under the auspices of Youth for Christ and doing postgraduate work in architecture. We were in frequent contact, but we were surprised by their call from Switzerland one day. When we asked if everything was all right, they said, "Yes, we just wanted to call and tell you that we really love you, and of all the people in the world, you are our closest friends."

We are excited as we watch the three young couples launch out into the world and take on various challenges to which God has called them. And we find it very pleasant to have a growing, trusting, open, true friendship with each of these couples.

EVEN GRANDCHILDREN SHAPE US

We also notice that our self-images have been changed by the coming of our first grandson, Nathan. Except for Barbara and Mike in Switzerland, we were all at the mobile home during the last day of Brenda's pregnancy. She had been in labor several hours, and Marc was caring for all of us, including his parents, as we waited for the birth of this child.

But there were identity questions. For Sally, the transition to being a grandmother was easy and joyful. It was fun for her. But for me (Jim) it was different. I didn't want to be called "Grandpa" because the media characterize grandfathers as gray-haired, deaf, decrepit, and rather senile old codgers who smilingly rock in their chairs. I didn't feel like that kind of man. I felt as if I were thirty-two years old, in the prime of life, with a world of things ahead of me that I wanted to accomplish for God. The family kept pressing me, "What should Nathan call you?" I said, "Have him call me 'Jim.' That's my name." They all laughed and said, "No, we can't do that! You've got to have a different name. What do you want to be called, if you don't want to be called 'Grandpa'?" After a lot of family discussion, it was finally decided that I would be called, "Jimpa!" Isn't that wonderful! I'm not really Grandpa. I'm a Jimpa with my own unique identity.

As the life cycle progresses, our children are going to continue to define us and to influence who we are as people. By mid-life this can be both negative and positive. Knowing how to raise your children and lead them to maturity will help make your mid-life transition go more smoothly as well as help them define themselves.

ADOLESCENCE—A RECENT IDENTIFICATION

The strong, devoted focus on children is a recent development. "In the twelfth century, there was no concept of childhood. It is difficult, in this child adoring world, to think what it might mean never to have been a child, but in the society of the Middle Ages an infant was nursed in his swaddling clothes until the age of six or seven and then became a small adult, living the same life as his elders, gaming, eating, dressing as they did, marrying at twelve or fourteen. When Jesus suffers little children to come unto Him, the Medieval painter portrays Christ surrounded by eight little men. . . ."[5]

Only in the sixteenth and seventeenth centuries did children begin to acquire special clothes which set them apart from adults. In the eighteenth century, pressure from the church for child education helped to define childhood more clearly. Not until this century did the adolescent era become one of the ages of man. Previously, children were considered miniature adults who stepped right into full adulthood. Now we have further refined the developmental stages so that we clearly see stages for children, adolescents, young adults, mid-life adults, and aging adults, and each has several subsections.

MATURITY THE GOAL

We pass from each of these stages to the next with no effort on our part—that is, we get older without trying. The task is to bring about the greatest maturity and reach the fullest possible potential. As we've indicated, a mid-life woman may be at a crucial time in her own development at the same time she is needing to help her children in their growth.

ACCEPTANCE AND APPRECIATION

Maturity has many dimensions, but qualities that we definitely ought to help our children attain are an acceptance and appreciation of themselves as individual persons. Your role as a mother is to help your children define who they are. What are some of the insights that you have into your child's life? What gifts and abilities do you see that God has given to your child? What are his or her strengths and weaknesses? Almost all of the definition of self in the early years of life comes from the significant people around the child. As a mother, you perhaps have the most strategic input because of your closeness and the amount of time that you spend with your child.

Here is where the catch comes. If you don't think much of yourself as a person, you will generally pass a low sense of worth on to your children. The Bible says the sins of the parents will be visited on the third and the fourth generations (Exodus 34:6, 7). In self-image terms, that means if a mother has a low self-image, she influences her children to have low self-images. They then influence their children, and the cycle keeps on going until someone or something intervenes.

LOVE

A mother needs to help her children learn to love other people. Loving is a two-way street. One side of love is to understand people and their needs, and then to take energy from our lives and give it to enrich them.

The other side of love is learning to accept love from others, not earning it but receiving it as a gift. Sometimes children are "good" and do kind things in order to *earn* our approval and our love. They need to feel that they are loved unconditionally, whether they are good or bad, whether they do kind things or not. Genuine love is *not* something that we earn, but is offered unconditionally from one person to another.

Loving your children unconditionally helps them to understand that God loves them the same way, so they are not caught in the trap of thinking that God loves them only when they are good. Otherwise, they may end up with a "works" religion and think they must earn their salvation.

VALUES

A mother needs to help her children establish their own values. Have you ever said to your children, "We don't do that in our family"? That's an appropriate way to teach children values and how your family is different from other families, but unless those values become their own, they may not follow your definitions and values when they become adolescents.

When our daughters began to move into their teenage years, we realized that there was no way we could control all of their lives all of the time. We couldn't go with them to school and make sure they didn't cheat, tell dirty jokes, get involved in drugs or sexual activities. Nor could we force them to become witnesses for Christ on the secular junior high and high school campuses. All of these values had to be their values, or they would never live them out as they entered the teen years.

It's important to help children think *why?* What are the

reasons behind the statement, "Our family doesn't do that"? When they get into school, someone is going to ask them the why questions.

"Our family doesn't drink."

"Why not?"

"Well, I don't know; my parents just don't drink."

"Well, why don't you?"

"My parents told me that I shouldn't."

"What's wrong with drinking? Have you ever tried it? How do you know it's not OK? Who says your parents are right when all the rest of our parents say it's all right? Maybe you just have odd parents. Tell me, how many parents do you know who don't drink?"

Unless the *why* questions have been handled earlier in life and your children have had a chance to reflect thoughtfully and make them their own values, they'll never be able to stand the growing pressure during the teen years.

Remember that the teen years are characterized by a separation from the parental home and an alignment with the teen peers. If children have been living off parental or church values that are not their own, they probably will reject those values as they associate with peers during their teen years.

HOW TO DEVELOP A VALUE SYSTEM

To develop your children's own value system, let us suggest that you think about ways to accomplish some of the following:

First of all, your children need to be *confronted with authority-based information*. The source of values is the Bible. Your children need to have value concepts to work with. What are the scriptural bases for deciding such issues as lying, stealing, and sexual sin?

Your children also need an opportunity to *reflect on those concepts*. Provide opportunities to meditate and encourage your children to do quiet reflecting about life. It's OK to sit on the roof or behind a tree. Maybe those are good places for them just to sit and listen to a bird, watch a sunset, count the clouds. Hold up the value of meditating. Let them see you spending some quiet, reflective times.

Your children need an opportunity to *discuss values*, a free time of give and take where they can verbalize their questions and their doubts. It has to be a time when you are not going to shut them up with the famous old line, "Just do it because I said so!" You may be able temporarily to silence your children and make them do or think what you want them to, but that old line certainly won't work during the teen years.

Your children *need life experience* in order to establish their own values. Use incidents around them or in the community as learning experiences to help them develop their value system. Talk about the kids who are cheating in school. They are getting ahead and are getting better grades than they deserve now, but what does the Bible say? Cheating is only a short-term gain. Help them think about what happens to people who keep on cheating. Point out some of the examples of white collar crime, of people who have become dependent on cheating and finally have been caught. Life experience, coupled with the other three factors of value information, meditation time, and free discussion, will help bring about value growth in your children.

An important dimension of life experience is to avoid protecting your children from all the results of their own wrongdoing. For example, if one of your children is caught cheating in school, let the child experience the natural consequences without your interference so that the life experience can bring about change and growth in your child.

SERVING

Another quality of maturity is learning to serve other people. Jesus did not come "to be served but to serve" (Matthew 20:28). When he was with the disciples in the Upper Room during the last hours before his crucifixion, he took the role of a servant boy. If you have read the account in John 13, you know that the disciples were humbled to have Christ take off his outer robe, wrap a towel around his waist, and go from disciple to disciple, washing their feet. Jesus was Master and Lord. He was their leader, and yet he was down on his knees, washing their feet as a servant. Peter finally exclaimed, "You shall never wash my feet!" (13:8). (Peter had not yet quite learned how to receive love.) Jesus said, "If I don't [wash your feet] you can't be my partner. . . ."

Jesus' act made an indelible impression on their minds, one they would never shake. He reinforced his action by saying, "You call me 'Master' and 'Lord.' . . for it is true. And since I, the Lord and Teacher, have washed your feet, you ought to wash each other's feet. I have given you an example to follow . . ." (John 13:13-15a).

Your children need to learn to serve other people including their family, not simply for your convenience, but for their growth. They need to serve as their special ministry to people. Without ministry, we become self-centered people and we buy into the "me-ism" that has grossly distorted our culture.

LIVING WITH LIMITATIONS

An additional quality of maturity for your child is to learn to live with stress and the inadequacies or imperfections of life. Nothing in life is perfect, nor does anything in this existence last forever, other than our relationship with God.

Our youngest daughter, Becki, is in the process of writing a book about limitations. Becki knows from experience. She was only a sixteen-year-old high school junior, winning track meets, when she had to have her left leg removed about mid-thigh because of cancer.

Becki can share about how it is to live life with a twenty-four-hour-a-day reminder that life is imperfect. Help your child to learn that losses hurt but that life has both gains and losses. When disappointments come, remind them that God loves them and that stress helps them to become mature.

THOSE TERRIFIC AND TRYING TEENS

The majority of you women in your late thirties and early forties have children who are in adolescence. Adolescence generally is not a quiet, smooth period of development! Emotional upheavals are frequent as the teen at times leaps toward adulthood and at other times falls backward to childhood. The teen years are a normal but painful period, filled with stressful inconsistencies and a testing of limits, of oneself, and of others. It's a time filled with frustration, conflict, and growth. Even under the best of circumstances with the best integrated parents and children, it can be a time of considerable family strain.

During the teen years *both* the mother and the child are going through very important developmental times. The teen is emerging from childhood into young adulthood while the mother is emerging from young adulthood into mid-life. Probably there will be a great deal of misunderstanding of each other. In a sense, they both need each other, but both are preoccupied with their own needs and may not be able to help.

Anna Freud describes what is happening in the adolescent, but her description may also describe what is happening in the mother of the adolescent:

"It is normal for an adolescent to behave in an inconsistent and unpredictable manner, to fight his impulses, and to accept them; to love his parents and to hate them; to be deeply ashamed to acknowledge his mother before others, and unexpectedly to desire heart-to-heart talks with her; to thrive on imitation and identify with others, while searching unceasingly for his identity; to be more idealistic, artistic, generous, and unselfish than he ever will be again, but also the opposite: self-centered, egotistic, calculating."[6]

CATCH UP!

Sometimes the stresses during the teen years become so great that communication breaks down between parent and teen. You may feel a great urgency to take advantage of these last years of training, but your teen is moving away from your authority. You may feel very rejected and hopelessly cut out of his life. And, you may feel a deep sense of guilt: "Look what's happening to him! I've failed as a mother." During this era you are probably wrestling with your own self-identity and the conflict with your teen may reinforce your low self-image.

Sometimes the problems you see in your teens will create tension within you because you find yourself reexperiencing some of the same issues that were not fully resolved when you were an adolescent. These old problems revisiting your personality may, in fact, make your mid-life transition more difficult and cause you to be angry at your teens when you see some of the same issues in them. It is common for a mother either to put down her teenage children or to live through them.

Dorothy would visibly light up when her daughters had teenage boys around the house. She would stand up straighter, freshen her hair with a quick comb. She tended to wear tighter clothes when the boys were around and was constantly pulling her sweater down tighter. She became noticeably more witty, positive, and outgoing when these young males were around.

Dorothy had no idea what she was doing, but unconsciously she was living through her teenage daughters and vicariously identifying with their roles. If she were confronted, I'm sure that she would deny that she was trying to win the approval of these young males, but her actions clearly indicated that there were some needs in her life that were being filled by these experiences.

We have also watched the other problem take place when mothers put their children down, belittle them in front of friends or family, or constantly harass them. These all diminish their self-image.

Both of these expressions—living vicariously or putting your teen down—indicate some incompleteness in yourself that you might want to think through as you make your own transition in life.

BOTH NEED LOVE

The dynamics are challenging in a family where both the adolescents and one or more of the mid-life parents are going through a transition at the same time. Each needs to help and love the other, but neither can muster the energy to do so.

Most people need to know that they are unconditionally loved as they go through life transitions. A grabbing line from *A Woman of No Importance* says, "Children begin by loving their parents; after a time they judge them; rarely, if ever, do they forgive them."[7]

Bertrand Russell in *The Conquest of Happiness* says: "The value of parental affection lies largely in the fact that it is more reliable than any other affection. One's friends like one for one's merits; one's lovers for one's charms. If the merits or the charms diminish, the friends and lovers may vanish. . . . Our parents love us because we are their children, and this is unalterable fact."[8]

Providing your teens with a base of unconditional love that they don't have to earn will reduce some of the tension in the home and make your own mid-life transition a bit easier.

LEAVING THE NEST

Mothers report strongly mixed feelings in the child-launching era of life. On the one hand, they would be glad to have the adolescent/young adult move out, go to college, get into a career, or get married. It would mean a reduction in tension in the home, some space to breathe, perhaps an opportunity for the mothers to launch into a new phase of their careers. Perhaps they can now work on their marriages or reestablish some friendships other than with their children.

On the other hand, women report a strong desire to replay some of the earlier childhood years. Mothers aren't saying to their adolescents or young adults, "Give me the present time with you," but they are saying, "Give me the past with you." It can't be done.

When you as a mother confront that reality, sometimes there is a sense of loss, of wishing to replay those early childhood years to make the necessary changes that would produce more growth, less tension, and reduce this gnawing sense of guilt and failure.

One parent said, "For years I've been in mourning and not for my dead, it's for this boy, or for whatever corner in my heart died when his childhood slid out of my arms."[9]

This is a hard time in your life. Your husband may be moving away from you as he madly dashes to use these last few years to achieve all his career goals. Your children probably are moving away from you, trying to establish their independence. You know they have to, but it causes you to feel very lonely and isolated.

You may feel a desperate need to be needed—a need that is frustrated by your husband's career and your children's independence. A woman "offers love, support, guidance, help to others—and the significant people in her life counter with hostility and the desire to escape from her nurturing."[10]

Your marriage may be at a low ebb of satisfaction. You

may be questioning your worth and value as a person because you feel less needed and important in life. If you are caught in this vise-grip of life, you may find yourself leaning almost dependently upon your children.

NO CHANCE TO GROW UP

A few years ago when we surveyed University of Illinois students whose parents had been divorced within the last five years, we heard a story repeated many times. Parents who were unsuccessful in their marriage relationships and were experiencing separation or divorce tended to become dependent on their children. One girl sadly related to us how she would hold her mother in her arms and rock her while her mother wept. Another graduate student reported that he was the intermediary between his first family and the second. He had to be a sort of messenger and mediator between his father and his mother, even though they were divorced and each had remarried. Another girl, recounting incident after incident of parental dependency, said, "You know, I need parents too!"

When your adolescents/young adults come to the point of leaving home, you must let them leave, physically and emotionally. They should not be given the responsibility of parenting you at this age in their lives. Later on, when you have reached old age, they will probably parent you. But at this stage in their lives, they need to establish independence and their own identity. They should have the opportunity to flower as people without prematurely having to carry the role of parent-caretaker.

NEW ROLES

A rather new phenomenon is taking place now as young adults leave the nest to go into career, start their own marriages, or go for higher education. They are returning to the nest in great numbers because they need financial,

...upport. When they reenter the
... boundaries between parent
... different places than before. This
... communication, understanding, and
...eryone.

...life woman must search for a new identity in
...ship to her grown children. You cannot be a dicta-
... or a domineering mother. You must not be a meddling
mother-in-law, but you can have an extremely fulfilling
role as a counselor, mentor, and peer.

As a counselor, mentor, and peer, you can continue to
have an intimate relationship with your young adults, and
they will welcome your input when it is offered rather
than imposed on them. These identity roles of counselor,
mentor, and peer also will allow you to put your experience to good use. Your relationship with your young
adults is not terminated when they leave the home; it is
just changed to a new kind of relationship. You will not
always be "mothering," but you will always be a mother.

Chapter Nine
TOO MUCH TOO FAST

The four Bradleys were having a normal breakfast. The two kids were partially dressed for school. As they ate their breakfast, they were reading the backs of the cereal boxes and exchanging their usual competitive verbal jabs. Mom was playing her role of referee. Dad was trying to read the morning paper. Just the evening before he had finished a week of heavy seminars.

Mom finally hustled the kids away from the table, supervised their last preparations for school, and sent them out the door. She returned to the table where she and her husband David leisurely enjoyed another cup of coffee together.

Without warning, David suddenly fell off his chair, grabbed his chest, and cried out in pain. He had great trouble breathing. Everything in his throat seemed to have closed off. His body jerked and convulsed. Donna didn't know what to do. She felt a sense of frustration, terror, and panic. She kept calling his name, asking if he was all right. Then he gave a shudder and his body lay still.

It was only then that she thought to get help. She frantically called the police, and they called a paramedic ambulance team to go to the home. It was a full eight minutes before the team arrived. No, it wasn't eight minutes, it was a lifetime—an eternity of feeling helpless, of praying desperately, "Please, God, don't let this happen," of thinking that surely this nightmare would be over shortly and she would awaken to find David alive and well.

But it was no dream. The rescue team rushed through the front door, began to pound on David's chest, and inserted IVs. They ripped open his shirt and applied the heart defibrillator while Donna watched helplessly. David's body convulsed repeatedly. Miracle of miracles, his heart started to beat! David was alive. He was going to be OK.

Quickly he was put on a stretcher. But before they could get him out the door, his heart stopped again. Again the team jumped into action. Again the heart responded. In moments the ambulance was screaming down the quiet little residential street toward the hospital. The hospital team had been alerted. In five minutes David would be in the cardiac unit of the hospital, but during those five minutes his heart would stop two more times.

He was wheeled into the hospital and people in green gowns swarmed all around him. Orders were snapped by specialists. Machines sprang into life, monitoring David's vital signs. Tubes were running everywhere. The urgent work to control his condition went on for more than an hour.

Finally he was stablilized. He was under an oxygen tent and his condition was listed as extremely critical. The head physician came to the waiting room and talked to Donna. He explained that David's brain had been without oxygen for probably more than ten minutes. The likelihood of his surviving was extremely remote. If he did survive, he would be nothing more than a vegetable.

What does a woman with two children do when her husband is gravely ill? In a few short minutes, she went from being the wife of a successful Christian leader to becoming either a widow or—even more dreadful—a wife with a husband who would be living but as good as dead.

A woman in mid-life may be experiencing the normal routine of life, coping with the transition from young adulthood to being a mid-life adult without any great stress. If, however, an unexpected or traumatic loss occurs, everything in her life may become too much to handle. She would experience the domino effect—an overload of the circuitry—too many straws on the camel's back.

Many things can happen at mid-life that can become traumatic losses:

- The early death of her husband, parents, children, or a friend
- The birth of an unplanned child
- An early empty nest or early grandparenthood
- Forced retirement
- Major illness or injury
- Financial loss
- A major decision that causes loss

CHANGE EVENTS

Each incident that happens to us is called a change event. Every change event of life has some effect on us as persons. Obviously, the more major the event, the more significance it has in our lives. Some of these major change events will cause us to spring into action. Perhaps we will seek more education, the counsel of a friend, a spiritual growth activity, or some other positive adjustment.

A study by Aslanian and Brickel reported in *Americans in Transition* found that adults do not learn and grow simply because they have the opportunity but because a life event triggers them into action. Eighty-three percent of those learning experiences are related to family and/or career change events.[1] A traumatic event in your life may become part of the impetus that will bring about a great deal of growth.

Major change events can bring about a negative direction in your life, however. This generally happens when the event is so large and so significant that it overwhelms you or when it causes a chain reaction of disasters in your life. The death of one of your parents at the same time your teen gets into trouble with the law may cause you to go into deep depression and fail to function normally, which could then result in the loss of your job.

Through our surveys we found many women who had experienced traumatic losses, such as death, divorce, illness, or financial loss, at mid-life. They felt these jarring events were a crucial part of their personal mid-life crisis.

THE DOMINO EFFECT

Gail's divorce was so shattering to her that she was unable to cope with life. As a result, she was hospitalized under psychiatric care for a period of time. She lost her job and her husband was given custody of their children. The event of divorce started the toppling of the dominoes. After losing her ability to function, her job, and her children, she was severely depressed. Her self-image previously had been built on her relationship to her husband and her children. When these were gone she said, "I feel like nothing, as if I don't exist."

All through life you will experience hundreds of major change events. At any time, illness, death, family stress, financial loss, or a number of other traumatic events might happen to you. When a large number of change events take place in a short period of time, you will experience a greater stress level, even if all the change events are not negative. There are key times in life when the accumulation of change events is more likely.

IN THE BEGINNING

One crucial time for many changes is during the transition from adolescence to young adulthood. Adolescents are trying to develop their own identity and independence. They are learning how to relate to other people and how to give and receive love appropriately. They are trying to establish career directions and to decide if they should marry, and whom.

In about a five-year period of time, during the late teens and early twenties, average young adults move from their parental homes to their own homes. They probably will finish college, and/or will choose a career direction, will establish friendships, probably will choose their marital partner, and perhaps also start a family. In that five year span of time they should go from being inexperienced adolescents to responsible young adults.

From the mid-twenties to the mid-thirties, people usually experience career advancement and move to a larger house or apartment. If they are married, the last of their children usually are born during this time and those children start school. At this time adults get settled into the community and life in general. Their change events are spread out over a longer period of time than during the late-teen/early-twenty era.

At retirement a large number of change events also accumulate rapidly. Many of the events relate to the career change of the husband and/or wife. The cessation of the job which controlled daily routine often is accompanied by a loss of self-image and identity. They may also experience a reduction in income and loss of other benefits such as medical plans, paid vacations, use of a company car and company facilities, and free continuing education. The home life and schedule will be readjusted. Sometimes they must search for a part-time job with all the associated anxieties of penetrating a new career. Usually they move to smaller housing and perhaps a smaller car. They may even relocate in a totally different part of the country.

The change events in moving from adolescence to young adulthood are viewed by most people as positive even though they may be stressful. The change events at retirement, however, are generally viewed as losses and still carry stress with them.

IN THE MIDDLE

The people involved in mid-life change events view them as a mixture of negative and positive, but mostly negative. The positive change events are usually expected by mid-life women. They feel they have earned the benefits of success and it's time to collect. The negative change events are what really throw the mid-life woman for a loss.

At mid-life you have a huge number of change events. Your children are probably moving into adolescence, with all the dynamic changes in their lives and their urges to break free. You also are wrestling with the change events related to your husband's last wild dash to make it big in his career. Reawakenings within you may cause you to want to reenter school or go back to work, change to full time in your part-time career, or begin thinking of work as a career instead of just a job.

Added to all of these change events, you now have the change events of your parents and parents-in-law who are retiring and coping with aging. At mid-life you are impacted by the change events of a younger generation, your own mid-life transition, and the adjustments of the older generation. These three different developmental eras contain dozens of potentially traumatic events that could cause your own mid-life transition to become a mid-life crisis.

ON TIME/OFF TIME

Bernice Neugarten suggests that predictable, on-time events are not unsettling when they arrive because "the events are anticipated and rehearsed, the grief work completed, the reconciliation accomplished without shattering the sense of continuity to the life cycle."[2] Her point is that major stresses are caused when events in our lives do not arrive "on time." She says that when the rhythm of life is broken—such as by the early death of a parent, a child born too early or too late, the unforeseen empty nest, unexpected grandparenthood, untimely retirement, major illness, or widowhood coming at an unexpected time—a major crisis is produced. She does not believe that the ordinary problems of living through change events produce crisis.

Other researchers, such as Roger Gould, would disagree. In "Phases of Adult Life," Gould shows eighteen sample curves portraying degrees of satisfaction associated with the major, normal experiences of the adult life span. Fifteen of these research items show that men and women experience discomfort and stress during the mid-life years.[3]

From our observations during more than twenty-five years of counseling, stress is not caused simply by the events of the mid-life years coming out of sequence or "off time" but by the change events themselves, whether on schedule or unanticipated. For example, the mid-life woman knows the inevitability of her body's aging, but simply knowing it will happen does not eliminate the stress, since our society places so much value on being young.

The mid-life woman also may know that her husband is going to experience his own mid-life transition. Having that process appear on-time does not reduce the trauma of his failing leadership in the home, personal depression, criticism and rejection of her as a mate, or any other actions or attitudes he displays during his mid-life transition. The empty nest may appear on schedule but the woman who has placed all of her energies and interest in her children still will experience trauma. The timing of the event is not the most important element, although it does bear impact.

Another factor is the sheer number of events taking place at one time in her life and in the lives of significant people around her. But perhaps the most important factor that will determine the degree of stress is the value she assigns to each of the change events.

GROWTH OR COLLAPSE

One woman may look at the independence of her children as very exciting and the fulfillment of all that she has been trying to accomplish. She may view the event as providing additional time for her to pursue her own career and educational directions. Another woman may look at the same event and feel that she has lost some essential part of her self-identity.

Some women have rebounded positively from a husband's involvement in an affair and have gone back to school, become engrossed in a career, taken up some hobbies, or lost some weight. Even though their husbands' affairs were traumatic experiences initially, they would place a positive value on the experience overall.

Other women that we have known have gone into deep and prolonged depression that caused them to become nonfunctional. The first kind of women had personal worth apart from their husbands and were able to stand on their own. The other women's life values were centered in their husbands and when they lost that, they lost everything.

Why is it that some women seem to be able to handle more stress than others? We think that in addition to the value they assign to each problem, it has something to do with the worth and security they feel within themselves.

Some women who place little value on themselves tend to assign high stress values to events that take place in their lives. A few stressful events for them can produce a high cumulative stress level. Other women feel quite secure within themselves. The world can be swirling around them, but their assignment of stress levels will be much lower. These women seem to be able to go through a torrent of trouble and still not get sucked under.

INTERNAL WORTH

You need to consider what causes you to think yourself worthwhile. Do you personally appreciate yourself, or do you have worth only as you feel significant to other people? If you feel that you are worthwhile because your parents, husband, and children love you, what will you do if this support is missing?

Your children will become increasingly independent and you may interpret that as rejection of your value as a person. If one or both of your parents die, you may not only lose a parent, but you may lose a part of your own value. If your husband has a traumatic mid-life transition and begins to criticize and reject you, you may find that you have lost more than a deep relationship; you have lost some of your identity.

It is true that our worth is initially established by the value assigned to us from significant others, such as our parents. As we mature we need to shift so that we come to value ourselves apart from what others think. Otherwise, we are vulnerable to being manipulated by others' opinions of us or to living vicariously through others.

MID-LIFE PEPPERONI

From our research, women were experiencing stress from many sources. Some was from husbands and their attitudes or from lifestyle changes. Unhappy situations with children, family illnesses or injuries, death of a loved one, or divorce were other problems that greatly compounded the mid-life issues.

Decisions made by the husband often greatly affect the wife and cause some traumatic losses. For example, if the husband decides to reduce work, take more vacations, and start slowing down, his wife may view this as a personal threat to her goals. If her husband wants to take more breaks from work, how is she going to expand her career now? She may want to go back to school but that would require that they be in town most of the time. Or, she may have full time employment and be trying to climb the employment ladder by putting in extra time and energy. Her husband has made a decision, and he either assumes his wife wants the same thing or he doesn't care.

At mid-life Ron decided to change careers. Instead of staying in his position with a pharmaceutical firm, where he was making about $60,000 a year, he decided to open a pizza parlor. This meant he had to invest all the family savings, mortgage their home, and start working from dawn until midnight. The business was not a success. They suffered heavy financial loss. Millie, who had wanted to go back to college to pick up her degree in special education, was forced instead to take a mundane job just to earn money. She had to support the family while her husband muddled along through the collapse and chaos of his decision. "It wasn't just that the business failed," she said, "but I realized that now I was never going to be able to accomplish the things I had hoped to achieve."

SKIM OR WHOLE MILK

A mid-life mother also experiences traumatic loss if a child leaves home under messy circumstances. Carol had assumed that there would be the normal chain of events with their son Rich—childhood, adolescence, going off to college, visiting home on breaks, getting married, starting his own family—and there would always be close ties.

But when Rich turned fifteen, he had a strong urge to establish his own independence. At the same time, John, his father, was in the depths of his own mid-life crisis. Everything seemed to irritate John. One evening the three of them were shopping for just a few items in the grocery store. Carol put two different kinds of milk in the cart, skim milk for the parents and whole milk for Rich. The aisle was jammed with people, but to John it was as if they were alone. In a loud, angry voice he roared, "What're you doing, buying two kinds of milk?"

"One for you and me, and the other one for Rich," Carol answered.

Then there gushed forth a surge of anger and obscenities. "Why do we have to spend extra money on that kid? Why is he a privileged character?"

Rich quickly disappeared and went to the car. Carol tried to slink out of the store, but all the way through the check-out John was talking in a loud voice and continuing to express his anger. You see, it wasn't the ten cents a gallon difference in price; it was a deep-seated dissatisfaction with himself and an unresolved relationship with his son.

When they reached home, John was still angry. Dinner had just barely started when John and Rich were at each other. John's eruption of anger now was even more violent than in the store. Rich fought back. Finally his father said, "Go to your room. Pack your things and get out!"

The fifteen-year-old boy went past his mother as he left the room. Her mouth was open in disbelief. She followed him to his room. Rich jammed some clothes and personal belongings into a duffle bag. He grabbed his sleeping bag, and in spite of his mother's protests and pleadings he pushed her aside, slammed out the door, hopped on his bike, and was gone into the night.

All of the dreams that she had held of the gradual growth and transition from childhood to manhood were gone. What would happen now? Maybe it would blow over. Maybe there would be forgiveness and reconciliation between John and Rich.

Two days went by. There was no softening or bending on either side. Two weeks, two months passed.

More than two years have gone by since Rich moved out. He lived with a friend for a while and took a part-time job. He finally moved into an apartment with some other guys and has been living an independent life. His mother never planned on this sudden, tragic emptying of the nest. The sorrow and loss have left her depressed even when she speaks of it now.

LIFE RAINS ON EVERYBODY

We know that bad things happen to good people. We know the Bible says the rain falls on the just and the unjust. But somehow we never really believe that bad things are going to happen to us and to our family. For some reason we are never really prepared to handle the unexplained and unexpected tragedies of life.

At age fifteen our daughter Becki had recurring pains in her knee. Doctors assured us that her problem was just growing pains and the stress from being a cheerleader and gymnast.

One Friday as she was being treated for displacement of her tailbone, the doctor noticed that she was limping. He was concerned when she told him her knee had frequently troubled her for a couple of years and sometimes caused her to stay home and keep it elevated. When he x-rayed her knee, he discovered there was a massive enlargement of the bone just above the knee. "I want you to see an orthopedic surgeon immediately," he announced.

On the next Monday, we had an emergency appointment with an orthopedist, a Christian who attended our church. His x-rays also showed the enlargement in the bone, and he began to explain how serious this problem might be. A biopsy would be performed to take samples which would be sent to several labs around the United States. There might be nothing to worry about, or perhaps the bone would need only to be replaced. There might, however, need to be an amputation and there might even be the possibility of death.

Within days, the biopsy was performed and samples of the growth were sent to labs specializing in rare tumors.

The reports indicated an uncertainty about the type of tumor it was, but doctors decided it was benign and we should just watch it for a while. The eight-inch incision on the outer side of Becki's leg healed and she went back to running hurdles in track. The incident was pushed to the back of our minds as life continued and as my (Jim's) mid-life crisis really heated up.

But the leg began to swell again. The bone definitely was enlarging. After another biopsy a year later, the specialists decided the growth was malignant and the best solution was amputation. Becki was now sixteen, and I was just coming out of my mid-life crisis.

I wanted to vomit as I saw Becki being wheeled on a gurney to her hospital room after surgery. At first I saw her head with her pretty blond hair. The sheet was pulled up tightly under her chin. My eyes followed the contour of her body from her neck down her body. I could see her right leg supporting the sheet all the way out to her toes. Then my eyes followed the sheet where her left leg should have been. The sheet was raised for about six inches and then fell off in a sickening, flat manner all the rest of the way down the bed. There was no strong muscular leg. There were no toes pointing up and holding the sheet in line with her other toes. That leg was gone.

What would happen to her now? Would she be able to finish school? What would she do for a life's work? Would any man ever want to marry her?

Suddenly I found myself at the bottom of the mid-life crisis pit again. The last time I was down, I had known God was there. This time I wasn't sure that he existed or, if he did, that he cared.

ONLY OTHER PEOPLE DIE

Every person knows that death is a reality. Remember when you were twenty-three? You knew about death, but it always was to happen to somebody else. Until mid-life we keep living with the illusion that death happens to someone else in some other distant place. When you were a little girl, a whole line of people ahead of you had to die before you did. Those people, in a sense, protected you from dying. By the time you get to mid-life, some of those protective people have been snatched away. You become aware that you are more vulnerable. In fact, you may already have been startled by the death of somebody in your peer group. Gradually you begin to realize that you are no longer young and that you are not immortal.

When you looked in the mirror this morning, did you notice how your face had changed since yesterday? Probably not. You noticed a difference from a year ago, perhaps. More likely, you notice only the change that takes place over several years as you compare old photographs. Aging is like that—gradual, almost unnoticed.

Yesterday you were in college; today you are a mid-life woman with children who are moving toward independence and a husband nearing the peak of his career. Crazy as it seems, you still think of yourself as a young woman. Aging is tricky. It sneaks up on you and catches you when you're not looking. You don't notice you are aging until you go to your high school reunion and wonder why they let all those old people come to the meeting.

"Death and aging are different, though they may be intimately intertwined: One dies alone, one ages in a context; death is solitary, an act in itself, while aging is social, a process within a group; death is absolute—or infinite, aging is forever relative."[4]

Death isn't gradual. An illness may lead gradually to death, but the moment of death is definite. Death is traumatic at mid-life because it's not supposed to happen then.

The death of a significant person at any time in your life can be traumatic for you. The death of an important person, along with the other pressures of mid-life, could trigger or accentuate a mid-life crisis.

THE NIGHTMARE

If a wife loses her husband in mid-life, she will experience many feelings. One of these is anger which may be directed at several different people.

Harry had a history of heart problems. Each time he had an attack, Suzanne was afraid. One night when Harry got up to go to the bathroom, he felt a stabbing pain in his chest. Instead of waking his wife, he went downstairs to get his medicine. Before he could take the medicine, he collapsed and died on the kitchen floor. Suzanne chastised herself. Why hadn't she awakened? Why hadn't she been more thoughtful to have medicine in several places in the house? Why had she been irresponsible? Her anger was mixed with guilt, because she felt she could have kept him from dying.

Strangely, anger may be directed at the person who died. In a sense, the remaining mate says, "Now why did you go and die on me? You've left me at a terrible time." Anger directed at the person who has died is sometimes a way of saying, "I can't get along without you. You're crucial to the support of my life." In some cases the anger directed at the person who has died means, "You lucky duck, you got out of this massive responsibility and I'm left holding the bag." The problem with leftover anger is that you can't sit down and work through it with the one who has died.

TOO BUSY—EXCEPT TO DIE

A mid-life woman who loses her husband also experiences guilt. She feels guilty for overt actions, thoughts, and words that were wrong and unkind. "Why did we have that dumb fight just the day before he died? Why did I insist on my own way?"

She also feels guilty because of omission. Mid-life is a very busy time of life and it's easy to put things on the back shelf. She confesses, "We had always planned to. . . . We talked about. . . . We enjoyed . . . so much, but we never had a chance. All the blanks are left. And I keep getting hit with the feelings that I was responsible for not filling those empty spots, for allowing our lives to be pushed along by the tyranny of the urgent. Why didn't we stop to reevaluate and live life according to our priorities? Why is it now, after he's dead, that I think about reordering my values?"

HIS AFFAIR

The mail this morning brought the usual flow of hurts from mid-life women whose husbands are involved in an affair or who have decided to end the marriage through divorce. One letter, typical of hundreds, read like this:

"I know that you don't know me, but I've read both of your books and they describe my husband very accurately. We've been married for seventeen years. He has been a loving, kind husband who has been thoughtful and gentle. He is a good provider. He loves the kids and is a good father. He's been a strong Christian and has been a highly respected leader in our church.

"One morning he announced to me that he can't stand me. Just my presence in the room disturbs him, even if I only sit and read quietly, even when I don't say a thing. Just my walking through the room drives him crazy. He told me that our marriage has always been bad and probably we never should have married. He's involved with another woman. He wants a divorce.

"My life has been so complete and happy up to this time. Now I'm shattered. I don't know which way to turn. Even the Christians in our church have turned their backs on me. I almost feel like I don't exist, or I wish I didn't. Where do I go from here? Please . . . I need some help."

If your husband has become involved in an affair, certainly you will feel a loss of self-esteem, a sense of inadequacy or failure. "I didn't please him, I somehow didn't meet his needs." You realize your communication broke down. You probably feel wronged and betrayed. You may feel guilty: "I could have changed this, or that, but I just didn't do it." Perhaps you feel shame and that you must carry your burden in secret. You don't just say to your small Bible study group, "Well, Tom isn't here tonight because he's having an affair with his secretary. I'd appreciate your praying about that." Most women tend to carry these feelings inside, too embarrassed to share this problem or ask for help.

A man involved in an affair causes great devastation to his wife, but there is still hope. Many marriages *are* restored after an affair, but your husband's affair may push you over the edge into a mid-life crisis.

THE DIVORCE BOOM

The telephones in our office are busy nearly all day long with people calling from around the United States to receive counseling. Again and again we are startled when the women who are calling say that their local pastors and/or Christian counselors have advised them to get a divorce because of an affair.

According to the U.S. Census Bureau divorce has increased over 900 percent since 1900 for women age forty-five to sixty-four.[5] With the sharp rise in divorce, we would like to hope there would be a sharp rise in commitment among pastors and counselors to keep marriages together and to help couples work through their problems. Unfortunately, pastors and counselors display a growing sense of futility about mid-life marriages that are breaking.

We believe that pastors and counselors give up on troubled mid-life marriages because they do not understand the mid-life crisis. They do not see it as a temporary problem because of difficulties in working through the mid-life transition. They think the situation is a hopeless, forever-after pond of quicksand, sucking people down to permanent destruction.

If you are going through a mid-life marital breakup, it is *not* hopeless. Don't believe all that you hear from pessimistic leaders or friends, and don't believe that life will be rosier if you get out of this marriage.

One woman told us, "I went to my evangelical pastor when my husband asked for a divorce. He said, 'Just give up on the bum.' I went to a well-known Christian counselor in our community, and his observation was that my husband was too old to change and our marriage could not be restored. He said the wisest solution was for me to face reality and prepare for the divorce."

Each time this woman called us, she asked, "Does that sound right? Isn't there any hope at all? Where is God in this whole situation? Can't he make a difference?"

We encouraged her that she ought not to give up, that there was hope, and that God does make a difference. Some marriages do end in divorce, but we have seen many restored when each mate worked on the relationship. In most cases one mate started working on it before the other, and because she or he didn't rush into agreeing to the divorce request, they have their marriage today.

THE CHILDREN

Mid-life women have a difficult time adjusting to marital separation. In a 1982 report by David Chiriboga, women in their thirties showed more social disruption stress and personal disruption stress than women in their twenties or forties. They also had more health problems and visits to the doctor than women of other ages.[6] Perhaps the increased stress reported by women in their thirties is directly linked to the responsibility they bear for their children during a marital breakup.

Children in divorce situations have a difficult time of

recovery and often bear lifelong scars. Wallerstein and Kelly in *Surviving the Breakup: How Children Actually Cope with Divorce,* report, "Five years after the breakup, 34 percent of the kids are happy and thriving, 29 percent are doing reasonably well, but 37 percent are depressed."[7] Other studies confirm these findings by reporting that children of divorce often experience fear, anger, depression, and guilt that carry into adulthood so that they continue to be classified as less happy, more prone to anxiety, and experiencing a lower self-esteem.[8]

To verify the effects of divorce on older children, we carried out a study with University of Illinois students whose parents had been divorced within the previous five years. We found a great number of troubled students who were not able to function at full capacity in school or other activities. They struggled with self-worth, were afraid of close relationships, and were fearful of the future, especially of marriage.

DEATH WOULD BE EASIER

E. O. Fisher in "A Guide to Divorce Counseling" has a graphic and gruesome description of the divorce process: "Divorce is the death of the marriage: The husband and the wife together with the children are the mourners, the lawyers are the undertakers, the court is the cemetery where the coffin is sealed and the dead marriage is buried."[9] Unfortunately, however, divorce does not really bring death to the marriage relationship. It usually only separates the combatants who go on feeling antagonism and anger toward each other for the rest of their lives.

In most death situations, the bad is forgotten and the good is remembered. In most divorce situations, the good in the marriage is forgotten and only the bad is remembered. This is aided by the legal process, in which battles rage around money and child custody, and each mate must be shown to be defective.

Since a woman's identity traditionally has been tied to marriage and family, a part of her is lost when she loses her marriage. As human beings, we are inescapably connected to our roles, and when one or more of these is lost, part of us is gone. The mid-life woman facing divorce is experiencing the loss of one of her roles along with loss of identity. Depression would be a normal consequence, and it may be enough to push a mid-life woman into mid-life crisis.

GOD IS ALWAYS THERE

We need to be reminded that even though we experience many traumatic change events and losses at mid-life, God does not intend for those events to overwhelm us. He doesn't promise to shelter us from problems, but he does promise to be with us: "When you go through deep waters and great trouble, I will be with you" (Isa. 43:2a).

We can use the difficulties to produce growth and beauty in our lives such as Shirley reveals in this letter:

"I wanted to get in touch with you again to bring you up-to-date. . . . Roy finally did file for a divorce and it has been final for a year now. [She then recounts additional things she had done to try to restore her marriage since we had talked.]

"Once I worked through my anger and disappointment, I have been able to move on. I have really changed and grown through all this, and I do like much about the 'new me.' I have taken classes and obtained my realtor's license. I love selling, although the market isn't so great right now. I have had an exciting trip to visit my missionary sister in Kenya and got to stop in several countries in Europe and Asia. I've taken up some exciting new hobbies—things Roy wouldn't believe I would ever do. I go sailing quite often and have become quite an able sailor. I've started scuba diving lessons and want to continue.

"Even though things didn't turn out as I planned and

especially after I worked so hard at it, I'm glad I now have a better sense of who I am. I've learned that there's a lot I can do. I also know God more intimately. I wish growth didn't hurt, but I'm glad that since I had to go through the pain, I can feel that I'm a more complete, more interesting person than before. . . ."

Chapter Ten

THE MARKS OF TIME

There are four ages for women—childhood, adolescence, young adulthood, and "you-look-wonderful." Ever since the beginning of time, people have had a deep desire to prevent death and any of its indications or foreshadows. Fighting the aging process seems to be inborn.

Resisting aging isn't just a social conspiracy pushed by advertisers, but people have a deep-seated dread of losing what they now have. The only way to beat the game, it seems, is to figure out some way to make youth last a lifetime.

"Someone your age should expect such trouble," was one of the lines my gynecologist was saying to me (Sally) as I sat draped in a sheet on the cold, hard table. I vividly remember what happened that day one particular year when I went for my annual gynecological exam. I always accumulated a list of the little medical problems that arose between my yearly visits and would ask for answers during that one appointment. Every year my doctor would politely try to give medical solutions for each of my rather insignificant troubles. Then one year he seemed to give little thought to any of the problems on my list and would answer with remarks such as, "Well, at your age your body doesn't. . . ." or "Now that you're older, you have to expect that. . . ." I laughed and said to him, "You're going to have me walking out of here an old woman!" He didn't say a thing in reply! As I walked out the door, wondering about his changed attitude, I realized he must have taken time to deduce by the birth date on my medical records that I was now forty years old.

Two or three years later I wanted to know more about menopause so that I could be adequately prepared and be able to go through the time as positively as possible. The doctor brusquely said, "When it happens, you'll know!" I asked if he had some materials I could read on the subject. He thought a minute and excused himself from the room. While I waited for him, I noticed that sitting around his office were little display boxes containing booklets on family planning, natural childbirth, breast feeding, and other topics for young women. After about ten minutes he returned with a rather shop-worn little pamphlet on menopause. "Here, take this. We don't seem to have much," he mumbled. This was at a large clinic with six or eight gynecologists on staff!

I felt very much as if I had crossed some line into the land of the undesirables. One of the nurses, who is my personal friend, bluntly told me the answer to the problem, "These doctors are men and men are not interested in older women. They'd rather spend their time looking at younger women's bodies. You should hear them joke about the 'old crocks' over forty and that they'd rather have a new road map than an old, worn out one for a patient."

AN "AGE-OLD" BATTLE

In recent years I have had opportunity to see younger and older women in various stages of undress (this is still Sally writing!) in women's locker rooms and in our daughters' college dorm. The comparison between the old and young bodies is shocking. Even though some young girls may be overweight, most of them have good muscle tone with their breasts in full form, thighs thin, and buttocks and stomachs tight.

Mid-life and older women may be thin, but they have flabby abdominal muscles and thick waists. They may have been skinny in their twenties, but it's hard to say that about most of them after thirty-five. They usually have varicose veins and many have various sorts of scars from surgeries. They look as if they had dozens of marbles tucked away just under the skin of their thighs. (It's strange that when we buy a half of beef for the freezer, we like it well marbled with fat and call it prime beef, but when a woman gets well marbled with fat, we just call her fat and old.)

That frightening battle against "old" is what gives the hucksters an opportunity to push all their magical potions on us. The benefits are mostly for the people who sell them. Women in mid-life wildly go after "fad diets, lotions, sunlamps, wrinkle-removers, vitamins, plastic surgery, beauty preparations made from exotic insect ingredients, facelifts, exercise salons, machines guaranteed to restore youthful tone to age-slackened skin and muscles, and cures for impotence, among them those mail-order books on techniques for 'sex after forty.' . . . it reassures us that everything is not yet lost, and there's still a magical chance that we might, like middle-aged Cinderellas, be restored to our youthful glory in the nick of time. Lots of luck. . . ."[1]

THE PRIME OF LIFE

Unfortunately, our society has a crazy double standard. When we were pastoring, Sally would say to me (Jim), "The way some of the girls fall all over you isn't fair. They want to come to see you in your office. They offer to do things for you and to help with just anything around the church to be near you." Yet, my sideburns were turning gray and my face had lots of wrinkles. You see, a man with gray sideburns seems to be wise, and wrinkles on a man are just laugh lines that show he has a lot of character and quality. Sally is a very pretty woman, but the young guys who sought her out were genuinely wanting her for counsel, motherly advice, and insights as a woman. They were not flirting with her.

We live in a funny world. The two of us say of ourselves that in spite of our age we at least think young, and we're glad when our kids tell us that we look young. At the same time, Barbara, our oldest, at age twenty-seven is saying she'll be glad when she gets into her thirties so she'll get more respect as a counselor.

When *is* the right age? For a woman, it seems to be somewhere between thirty-four-and-a-half when you're still young enough to be admired and thirty-five when you fear you're about to be put out to pasture. It's interesting that "an infant hears a very high pitched sound which his big brother cannot hear. The faculty starts to decline at the age of two and is gone by 20."[2] If our society valued the ability to hear high-pitched sounds, age two would be the prime of life.

THE BITTER FIGHT

Biologically speaking, from the very beginning of life our cells are dying off. They do increase faster than they die until about age twenty-one, but after that we spend the last three-quarters of our lives with cells dying faster than they are being created.

There isn't a lot of physical loss from young adulthood to mid-life, but during mid-life the changes occur more rapidly. After age thirty-three, hand and finger movements are progressively more clumsy. By age fifty, most adults have at least one pair of glasses. There's not much change in taste sensitivity until after about age fifty. Sensitivity to smell decreases slightly after about age forty and sensitivity to touch after about age forty-five. Hearing is about the best at age twenty and then there is a gradual loss of the high tones. Balance, interestingly, is at its best between age forty and fifty. The voice also begins to change and by mid-life many singers have retired, but it isn't until old age that the voice will lose its lower ranges and become more high-pitched.[3]

But these areas are not really where the sting is. Changes in appearance are the most devastating to mid-life women. Susan Sontag, a poet, writes passionately about a woman's loss of beauty in mid-life. "Beauty, women's business in this society, is the theater of their enslavement. Only one standard of female beauty is sanctioned: the girl. . . . The standard of beauty in a woman of any age is how far she retains or how she manages to simulate, the appearance of youth. . . . Most of the women who successfully delay the appearance of age are rich. . . ."[4]

DOES SHE OR DOESN'T SHE?

The Big Three that mid-life women work on for appearance are their hair, skin, and weight. The hair, for example, begins to thin by age forty, and by age fifty most women have gray hair—although only your hairdresser really knows for sure. Before 1938 the *New York Times* would not accept advertisements for hair coloring,[5] but when you look at the women around you now, you realize what an impact Miss Clairol has made. Our sewers are filled with a lot of gray that has been washed away.

Joyce Brothers reminds us that we believe "beautiful people have beautiful personalities. . . . We may not be aware of our bias, but we consistently judge them to be more sensitive, kind, intelligent, interesting, sociable, and exciting than less attractive people."[6] Since gray is judged as not beautiful in our society, that leaves a lot of gray-haired people with a problem.

A NEW WRINKLE

The skin, the second battleground of appearance, begins to show more wrinkles because the fatty tissue just under the skin on the face and arms begins to disappear as one ages. The skin then sags over the bone structures. No face creams can really restore the fatty tissue under the skin to give a youthful, full face look.

One author's description is grim but accurate: "The skin loses elasticity. It becomes coarser and darker on the face, neck, arms, and hands, and wrinkles appear. Some of these skin-associated changes result from muscle flabbiness underlying the skin. For example, bags and dark circles form under the eyes. These are particularly noticeable because the rest of the skin pales."[7]

Perhaps the battle for aging is fought so often at the skin level because a woman's skin shows her real age. A good bra, control top pantyhose, and a lightweight girdle can pull a lot of things into shape, but it's difficult for her to cover up the crows' feet around her eyes and those little wrinkles at the corners of her mouth. If she didn't have to move her eyes or mouth, then maybe makeup would cover the lines. On a man, wrinkles say he's "experienced." On a woman they say "old."

Cosmetic surgery is one solution women try in order to tighten the skin and remove some of the bags under the eyes and chin. It's important to investigate this kind of surgery thoroughly before proceeding, because there are a number of risks involved, including nerve damage and permanent deformity. In spite of the risks, it is estimated that forty-five to fifty-five thousand people a year submit to having their faces lifted.[8]

Perhaps columnist Nancy Stahl sums it up best: "When I was 15 I was given to spending half an hour in front of the bathroom mirror, experimenting with makeup in an effort to look 21. I do the same thing at 39."[9]

THE WAR ON WEIGHT

The third big enemy in the physical war game is weight. Once you decide that "fat is old" and you don't want to look that way, you probably will start on a process of losing weight. However, some forces work against you, apart from how much you eat or exercise. Every mid-life woman has an increased tendency to gain weight, because body fat is redistributed and muscle is gradually converted to fat. Body fat makes up only 10 percent of body weight in adolescence, but it is at least 20 percent by middle age and most of it settles around the waist. The bust becomes smaller and, unfortunately, the abdomen and hips become larger.[10]

Perhaps at this point, you're saying, "That's me! I'm not what I used to be." Your ideal weight is what you weighed after you attained your full stature and you were in your early twenties, assuming that you were not overweight then. Given the normal conditions of life in our society and the change in body metabolism as you grow older, you will have to deliberately work at keeping off excess weight. Not only is fat ugly and old, but it produces stress on the rest of your body systems.

THE PROTECTIVE LAYER

Keeping weight off is more than watching calories and exercising, however; it is also mental attitude. Often the battle is waged at a deeper level than the body tissues. Many mid-life women are also struggling with feelings of personal inadequacy and sometimes a deep-seated hatred of themselves. Frequently an overweight woman has an unhappy past or present, or both.

Doris was an early mid-life woman who had all of the potentials for being a very attractive woman, but she was about seventy pounds overweight. Her hair was not cared for, and she seemed to have no understanding of how makeup could be used to enhance her natural beauty. As she talked to me (Jim), she eventually poured out a history of sexual exploitation. First her father sexually molested her and later an uncle did. When she was a teenager, she had a pretty face and sexy body, and her contacts with boys tended to be very physical. She thought in her mind, "I'm a dirty person already, what difference does one more make?"

While she was a college student, God brought her to himself in a beautiful way and began to change many of her directions in life. But since she was still under the influence of her negative self-image, her weight did not respond immediately.

When she was in her late twenties, God led into her life a caring Christian man who wanted to see her reach her full potential under Christ. She had experienced much growth in her life in her early years of marriage, but she was still wrestling with her self-image and weight problem by the time she entered mid-life. Again and again she had tried diets, only to fail.

After we talked for a few sessions and worked a bit on her self-image, she came to see that her accumulation of weight really had become a protection against the sexual approach of men. Only as she confronted the distorted sexual area of her life was she able finally to make headway in the weight battle. She had to go back in her mind and forgive all the men who had exploited her. She needed to accept God's forgiveness and realize that before him she was a clean and forgiven person. She then came to a new understanding of God's intention for sex and also was able to lose her excess weight.

It may be that the weight you're struggling with has more to do with emotional and spiritual battles than with liking chocolate brownies and hot fudge sundaes. Perhaps a counselor can help you resolve the real issues that cause your weight problem.

NEVER SAY, "DIET"

The body's nutritional malfunctioning may also cause weight problems. In *Feel Like a Million*, Catharyn Elwood says, "Overweight is as much a symptom of malnutrition as underweight. And just as soon as the missing food elements are supplied, the water and fat roll off."[11] Adelle Davis stated, "What causes so many people to be overweight today is that too few nutrients are supplied in their diets to burn fat readily."[12]

Dozens of fad diets and quick weight loss schemes are available. The fad diets may burn off fat, but they tend to put the body under stress and, at the same time, may destroy muscle tissue. Some of the severe low calorie diets that are below 500 calories per day have been demonstrated as being harmful to the body's overall health when used for more than a few days. In fast weight loss your skin has to adjust to cover less territory, and it cannot adjust as rapidly as it could when you were a teenager. So, if you go on a crash diet, you may lose a lot of weight, but at the same time, you may lose some of the smooth appearance you had with extra weight. Bluntly speaking, you may become saggy and crepey looking. Joyce Brothers puts it this way, "No woman really looks sexy no matter how great her figure when her shape is slipcovered in prune skin."[13]

A *Reader's Digest* article, "How to Stay Slender for Life," suggests that there are small changes we can make with our diet that will have impact on our body weight over the long haul for many years. For example, if we eat just one less pat of butter or margarine daily, we will lose three-and-a-half pounds in a year. Cut out one slice of bread daily and we lose six pounds in a year. Give up two doughnuts a week and lose four pounds a year. Omit just one piece of cake a week and lose five pounds a year.[14]

Eating less is only part of losing weight. We also need to eat the right kinds of food in a balanced diet and get good exercise. The two of us try to go for a walk together every day. It does several things for us. It gives us a break from our heavy work load, and we get an opportunity to talk with each other. Exercise also helps to improve our mental attitude as we'll discuss later. On top of that, if we walk twenty minutes at a brisk pace, over a year's time we're each burning off about eighteen pounds.

TOO OLD FOR SEX?

Two outside forces work on an early mid-life woman regarding her sexuality. The one is from our culture which fosters the notion that older people do not have sexual relationships. There is, however, considerable research that shows that sexual interest and activity can exist into the ninth decade and beyond.[15]

Another author points out, "Our society is basically anti-old. . . . Sex in our society is not for older adults. You are supposed to have outgrown sex a long time ago! If you listen long enough to this kind of attitude, you start believing it, and before you know it, you are living it. You are too old for sex, you are too old for your job, and just too old to be around."[16]

The second force against a mid-life woman's sexuality comes from her children's thinking. As they learn about sexuality, they think of it in terms of fun and games and babies and it logically follows that "since my parents are no longer interested in babies and they are not having any fun in life, certainly they must not be having sex."

A study from Illinois State University, Normal, Illinois, showed that college students didn't think there was much sexual activity after forty, and if there was, it wasn't very much fun. Some students reacted very negatively, apparently not wanting even to think about their parents' sex life: "This questionnaire stinks." "Whoever thinks about their parents' sexual relationships except perverts?" "What stupid . . . person made up these questions?"[17]

Some mid-life women begin to believe cultural opinions

or the attitudes of their children. At the same time, because they have been preoccupied with other facets of life, such as a career and raising children, the marriage relationship itself may be very unsatisfying with little sexual expression. If all of these factors are prevailing, our mid-life woman may feel defeated in this area. "Convinced that she is no longer a desirable woman, our unhappy and unwilling heroine begins to express this neuter personality in her body language. Every movement tells us the message that she is no longer woman."[18]

SOME THINGS IMPROVE WITH AGE

Another force is at work in the mid-life woman, that of an increase in sexual drive. Most mid-life women tend to become more assertive, have a greater frequency of orgasm, and can experience repeated orgasms with little time lag. In other words, the mid-life woman is really coming into her sexual prime.

Because most sexual literature has been written by men, studies of the sexual development of adults have tended to follow male thinking and ignore the reality of women's experience. Males often have a shocking experience at mid-life, when they may be slowing down sexually but their wives are just reaching their peak.

TURNED ON AT THIRTY-NINE

Arnie was having a struggle with some of this difference in sexual interest between him and his wife. "I've never talked with anyone about this before, but I'm beginning to pick up from other guys that I'm not the only one with the problem. You see, it wasn't until we'd been married for a long time that Pat seemed to like having sex. Oh, sure, we had sex a lot when we were first married, but I think she didn't enjoy it very much. She usually just put on that she did just to make me feel good. Then she would go for long spells where she would put me off with headaches or being too tired.

"Of course, she was tired with three kids all over the place. I wanted to be considerate, so if she didn't want sex, I'd forget it for a few nights. After awhile, though, it would build up so that I really needed it and she'd give in.

"Eventually this got old. Besides, Pat's figure kind of went to pot and she started letting herself get fat. She wanted me to touch her more before we had sex, but I didn't find myself turned on by her body as much anymore. In fact, I was beginning to find that the whole thing wasn't very great.

"Then, whammy! When she was about thirty-nine she started wanting more sex. She would make moves on me as soon as I'd get home. I'd be tired, but I'd try to go along with her. In fact, I was glad for the change for awhile, but she seemed inexhaustible with an urge I couldn't quench. After awhile I couldn't keep up with her.

"Then one time, it happened. I couldn't get an erection—I'm embarrassed to even say this. I felt crummy. And she felt I didn't love her any more. I felt like I'd just lost my manhood and she was sure I had somebody else. That made me mad, so we had a big fight.

"I can't understand why she's so turned on now when she wasn't earlier. She gets excited before I ever get home. I get tired just thinking about it. Even when we do have sex, she never gets enough."

THE SECRET IS OUT

Sometimes the woman who has an aroused sexual interest at mid-life wonders if she is out of line, because society, her husband, and her kids think she ought to be slowing down. Instead she wants to have more sexual times with her husband and she's interested in variety and experimentation. How do you handle all of that in the context of being a Christian woman and not think of yourself as a dirty old woman?

A mid-life woman needs to understand that the changes are normal and that she is likely to have a high sexual interest through the rest of her mid-years. In fact, the decrease of sexual activity in older women has less to do with their interest or drive than with their opportunity. Most sex is still initiated by the male, and women in the later years of life are quite often widowed, frequently do not remarry, and, in a sense, voluntarily surrender that sexual interest.

MIRROR, MIRROR

Some of the mid-life woman's increased interest in sexual contact is because of the physical changes she sees in the mirror. Ever since she was a young woman and became aware of her sexuality, she realized that her sexuality was correlated with her physical body. Now as she sees her body begin to change shape, sag, show a few wrinkles and gray hairs, she asks, "Am I still sexually interesting to males, to my husband?" This sexual insecurity can cause a mid-life woman to question herself and may even force her into a panic situation to attempt to prove herself. She may become increasingly flirtatious with her body, her eyes, her walk, her conversation. It's almost as if she is saying, "Time is really running out on me. In the past I've always known that I am worthwhile because men have been sexually attracted to me. Now I'm not sure about that anymore and if I lose that, maybe I've lost myself."

Recently I (Jim) was on location where advertisements were being filmed. The group included a number of extras who were hired just for the day. One of them was a mid-life woman, about age forty, who was fairly attractive. She apparently had a need for men to be attracted to her, however, to make her feel good about herself.

She made several passes at me with her eyes. She complimented me on how fit and trim I was. Then she moved in really close. While we were moving along the buffet table during the lunch break, she reached ahead of me several times for some item of food. Her movements were strategically planned so that her breast would rub against my arm. She obviously was looking for a response. Part of me was flattered that this attractive woman was trying to come on to me, yet on the way home I thought to myself, "Isn't it tragic that this woman seems to be able to develop relationships only through her body. She doesn't feel she can make it with just her personality or her being, apart from sex."

Let me put it to you bluntly. There comes a time in all our lives when we have to learn to live on something other than our physical bodies. Most women are taught from childhood to be pretty and attractive. By the time they get into adolescence they're also learning to be sexy. Mid-life is the time when you *must* learn to live by other qualities in you as a person and not only by your sexual being.

Emphasizing your other attributes doesn't mean you can't have good sexual times with your husband. But the physical aging of your body should cause you to redirect your energies so that you are attractive to people because you are a loving, caring person who has intellectual and spiritual contributions to make.

THE MENO MONSTER

Sometimes mid-life women panic sexually because they dread the thought of menopause. (The cessation of menstruation can occur at any age but usually takes place in the late forties.[19]) Changes do take place, but you will hear a lot of old wives' tales about menopause.

Menopause does not mean you're going to become sexless. Instead, you have a new freedom because you don't have to bother with contraception or worry about pregnancy. This freedom may cause a rise in your sexual interest and activity. Perhaps, for the first time in your life, you will be instantly available for sexual relationships with your husband. Maybe the *hunted* will now become the *hunter.* Remember, you don't become a senior citizen merely because your ovaries cease functioning.

Perhaps you've heard that menopause brings on emotional instability with rapid mood shifts, hot flashes, nervousness, irritability, insomnia, and fatigue. You also may have heard that vaginal lubricating fluids diminish and cause intercourse to be painful, and sometimes there is itching, burning, and bleeding. All of these are potentially true, but if a woman is experiencing some of these symptoms, she needs to get help from her doctor.

Many of these physical and emotional changes can be eliminated or minimized by the replacement of the estrogen hormone, which after menopause is no longer produced naturally by the body. However, doctors carry on a running debate about the use of estrogen therapy. Opponents argue that it causes an increase in the incidence of uterine cancer, especially if large doses are used. Smaller doses do not seem to carry the same risk.

The opposite side of the argument is that, in addition to stabilizing emotions, hormone therapy reduces the loss of calcium from the bones preventing a condition called osteoporosis. Estrogen therapy also combats loss of muscle tone and loss of elasticity in the skin. Also, strong evidence shows that estrogen treatment protects women against the incidence of heart attack that rises after menopause.[20] We recommend that you consult a doctor who works with hormone imbalance at mid-life and ask about estrogen therapy. If estrogen cannot be used, a concerned doctor will see that you get help by way of vitamins and other medications. (Ask about B vitamins to lessen depression.) You may have to hunt to find a doctor who cares about women at mid-life, but the effort will be worthwhile.

A CUTTING EXPERIENCE

Mid-life is when many women have a hysterectomy. Some medical professionals have the attitude that "when a woman is finished with child-bearing, her uterus is expendable. Dr. William A. Nolen, Chief of the Department of Surgery at Meeker County Hospital, Litchfield, Minnesota, castigates this as 'male chauvinism at its most flagrant.' 'A patient's ovaries,' he adds, 'are another favorite target of both gynecologists and general surgeons. There's a saying in surgical circles that if ovaries were testicles, there'd be a lot fewer of them removed. I know that's true.' "[21]

Sometimes a woman herself is convinced that her "uterus is expendable" and that monthly periods are a distasteful, painful bother. She should realize, however, that a hysterectomy often results in hormone imbalance that will cause emotional stress. Stress also may be caused if a woman has a hysterectomy and later, through changed circumstances such as a child's death or her remarriage, she wishes she could have another child.

Another common operation for early mid-life women is a mastectomy caused by breast cancer. Breast cancer accounts for 20 percent of all female malignancies and involves 110,000 American women each year. Approximately one woman in fourteen gets breast cancer. However, there is reason for optimism. "Dr. Vincent DeVita, Director of the National Cancer Institute, says, 'In the 1980s we're going to see the common cancers begin to fall. With breast cancer, it's already happening. Indeed, some 87 percent of women with localized breast cancer now survive at least five years, . . . over 70 percent with localized breast cancer live at least ten years after diagnosis.' "[22]

MIND OVER BODY

If you're troubled by what aging, menopause, and mid-life surgeries might do to you, let us suggest that the problems may not be only physical but also psychological, particularly in your view of yourself. Remember that as we move along through life, any unresolved problem from the past is usually carried over into the next era. If you have some old unsettled problems, they may become exaggerated as you face mid-life.

Suppose that as a teenager you were disgusted with your physical body. You may have thought that your arms and legs were too skinny, your hips too big, your breasts not big enough—in other words, you didn't like your proportions. If you didn't settle that problem in adolescence, it was probably carried over into young adulthood. If you still didn't accept it, you probably are going to deal with it again now in mid-life, especially as your torso picks up more weight, your limbs get thinner, and everything, including your breasts, begin to sag a little.

You see, we're dealing with self-image and perfectionism. Raquel Welch is reported not to like the proportions of her body. She says she isn't well balanced. Really! When is enough enough?

Self-acceptance is crucial at mid-life. Self-acceptance is cyclical, also. That is, when you don't like the way you look and you're afraid of getting older, losing your shape and figure, being rejected by your husband, and losing your sex drive, you may act out the fears caused by your negative thoughts. You then begin to lose the sparkle of your life, which is what makes you attractive in the first place. Then when people are not attracted to you, the feeling that you are unattractive is reinforced. Somewhere you have to break the cycle, or the physical aging process will destroy you.

ONLY WOMEN GROW OLD

From a study done by Carol A. Nowak, she concludes: "To be 'old' in this society is certainly not good. But to be an 'old bag' is decidedly worse. Getting old happens to everyone. Becoming shapeless, wrinkled, and unattractive happens to women. Just ask anybody. While middle-aged men with 'touches of gray' look 'distinguished,' women who haven't 'colored away the gray' look drab. While middle-aged men with 'lines' and 'furrows' have 'character,' middle-aged women with 'wrinkles' and 'crow's feet' look ugly. While middle-aged men are generally taken for a handsome lot, middle-aged women are typically judged as 'over the hill.' And middle-aged women themselves are most guilty of perpetuating these expectations. They are their own worst critics."[23]

In this study by Nowak, she wanted to see how different age groups and different sexes would respond to colored slides of people's faces. Would they judge them as attractive, plain, or unattractive? How would they rate them as to youthfulness? She sums up her study of 240 men and women by saying, "As I'd expected, middle-aged women, significantly more than anybody else—all men or younger or older women—judged the most 'attractive' models, regardless of their age, to be most youthful."[24] The tragedy is that these mid-life women were judging themselves as being unattractive because they had agreed that the most attractive women were the young adults.

Joyce Brothers summarizes some studies on the correlation between attractiveness and self-image: "The findings of all these studies add up to the fact that it is really not so much how you look, as how you feel about yourself and your looks that matters. For instance, fifty percent of the women taking part in one study said that they considered themselves attractive. This same group also rated higher in self-esteem than the women who did not consider themselves especially attractive. Another study revealed that women who feel that they are good-looking also consider themselves to be more intelligent, more conscientious, more forthright—and more downright lovable than other women."[25]

Another author comments, "It is perfectly true that the cosmetic industry has terrorized us about what it means to be sexy and attractive to men, and that if they have their way we would all be Barbie Dolls. It surely *is* high time that we insisted on what we know, somewhere deep-down, below the TV-level of consciousness, that beautiful, sensuous, feminine women come in all shapes, sizes, ages, hair color and skintones, and that what makes them that way is not false eyelashes, dyed hair, corsets, lanolized skin, but something deep inside which exults in being female."[26]

WHAT ARE YOU WORTH?

The woman who comes to mid-life and has nothing going on inside of her regarding her own value structure, her own sense of self-worth, and a purpose for living is like a sailboat in a storm with a rudder broken off and the sails in shreds. The sailboat is at the mercy of the wind and the waves. It probably will be smashed onto some shore and finally battered apart. If you're a woman at mid-life without internal spiritual direction and purpose, and you're listening only to voices on the outside, you probably will then experience your mid-life physical aging as very negative. Growing older may be in itself the force that causes you to enter into a deep and prolonged mid-life crisis.

PART **IV**
DIS-
COURAGED
ON THE
INSIDE

Chapter Eleven

DEFEATED BY A SAGGING SELF-ESTEEM

MaryAnn is a deeply committed Christian woman with strong leadership abilities and a deep love for her three children and her husband. She recently wrote cryptically, "The past two years have not been nice." She went on to explain how her self-image was smashed through a series of experiences related to the loss of her job, friends, physical appearance, and her husband when he moved out.

"I had been an administrative supervisor for a health department for several years. I supervised from three to five women, depending on funding. I also ran a clinic for pregnant teens. Generally, I had a lot of responsibility and respect from fellow workers and patients. I enjoyed my job.

"Then, cuts in funding caused my department to close down all clinic activities except immunizations. I was kept on as secretary at my normal salary. I enjoyed the quiet for a time but gradually began missing the previous responsibilities and challenges. I felt I had been demoted and my self-esteem began to plummet. My secretarial skills deteriorated and generally I began to feel worthless.

"In January I learned that a girlhood friend had died of

cancer. I think that more than anything else threw me off center. She was a year younger than I, and while we were not close at the time of her death, we had maintained our friendship over the years through letters.

"In February I turned 40, in March I got bifocals (a silly thing to cause so much trauma) and in April I wondered who I was . . . what was my reason for living . . . had I ever been happy in my whole life . . . and if I died tomorrow what would I leave behind of myself that was worthwhile? I wasn't sure that I loved anyone—actually, I wasn't sure I was capable of loving anyone. I felt cold, uncaring, and dull. I didn't think my children cared for me a great deal because they never listened to my 'wise counsel.' I was sure my husband didn't love me."

THE CONFORMERS

Mid-life women may experience sagging self-esteem because of the many losses at mid-life and because of early life training. Girls are socialized in self-image quite differently from boys. Boys are encouraged to give up childish ways, to be tough and hard, to be independent, and to prove themselves. Girls, however, are encouraged to be conformists, to be compliant, to be "good girls."

In Her Time gives the results of a study in which "mothers of four-year-olds were asked such things as at what age they thought parents should expect or permit their children to cross the street alone, use a sharp knife without supervision, or be permitted to play away from home for long periods without first telling their parents where they would be. Consistently, the mothers of boys gave younger ages than the mothers of girls—despite the fact that girls mature earlier and are less impulsive."[1]

The ways in which girls are socialized causes a delay in their search for identity and in the development of their autonomy and internal standards for self-esteem. The socialization for low self-esteem in women also continues in adulthood. College men and women were asked to read and evaluate a number of articles. One group was told that the articles were written by women. The second group was told that the same articles were written by men. Both sexes rated the articles that were said to be written by men as more worthwhile.[2]

WHAT IS SELF-ESTEEM?

Many times the words *self-esteem, self-love, self-image, self-worth,* and *self-acceptance* are used interchangeably. There are some distinctions in the words that will help you to understand yourself better, especially in the meanings of self-image and self-esteem.

Self-image is how we *see* ourselves. Self-esteem is how we *value* ourselves. Quite often these two concepts are linked together. If a person has a low self-image, she also will not value herself very much. The reverse is true. A person who does not value herself much tends to have a limited view of who she is as a person.

In discussions of self-image and self-esteem, Christians often raise questions about pride and humility. Pride is claiming that all we are is the result of our own effort and strength. Pride implies that God and other people have not contributed to our lives. We claim to be self-made people. Humility means that we accurately assess who we are, with both strengths and weaknesses. "Be honest in your estimate of yourselves, measuring your value by how much faith God has given you" (Romans 12:3b).

HOW THE SELF DEVELOPS

Before we are born and continually throughout our lives, we are receiving impressions about ourselves from other people and the environment around us. We interact with those impressions and decide how much we will absorb or allow those impressions to affect us. The sum total of those impressions and how we accept them becomes our self-image.

When people grow up, they will, as James Dobson says, either hide from life or seek life. Archibald Hart in *Feeling Free* shows that they will think of themselves either as giants or midgets.

We have found it helpful to think of the development of the self-image in terms of "love dollars" and "love debits." When you were a child, your mother and father, brothers, sisters, grandparents, other relatives, friends, school teachers, and even the dog, had input into your life. Each interaction helped to form your self-image. You accumulated either a lot of self-image love dollars (plusses) or self-image love debits (negatives). (See the chart below.)

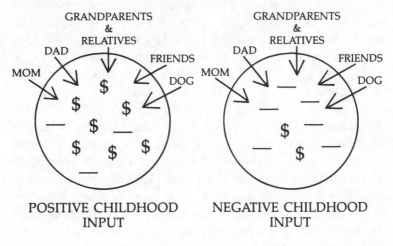

POSITIVE CHILDHOOD   NEGATIVE CHILDHOOD
        INPUT   INPUT

Figure 1

If you grow up receiving a lot of love dollars into your personality, you'll be a person who is outgoing, trusting, eager for life, willing to take risks, and willing to give love to other people. If, on the other hand, you accumulate a lot of self-image debits, you will be afraid of people, unwilling to give love, afraid to try new things, and will tend to be critical, intolerant, angry, and easily defeated by life.

The tragedy is that the person who needs love the most is the one with the debits. This woman then builds a strong wall of protection around herself so no one can come in and take any of her few remaining love dollars from her. The woman with many love dollars needs extra love the least and yet is the one most open to being loved. Later we'll show how you can break the vicious circle of low self-image and love debits.

CULTURE'S FIVE B'S

Our culture has defined several ingredients that are supposed to make you a worthwhile and acceptable person. One is *beauty*. Culture says that from birth on, girls must be beautiful. All through life, much of a woman's value and self-esteem are linked to her "looking good." Brawn and bulging muscles give definition to males, and in the last few years physical fitness has also become a goal for women. They are running and doing other exercises so they can present to the world a well-fit body.

Brains are the second commodity our culture seeks after. Intelligence is important for a girl during the school years, but she is taught not to compete in "boys' subjects," such as math and business. She is to stay in "girls' subjects," like English and poetry. As an adult she is to be bright but not aggressive.

Bank accounts also define a person. What kind of clothes do you wear? Where do you live? What kind of car do you drive? Are those real diamond earrings? Is that heavy gold necklace you're wearing 14 karat or only gold-filled? Culture evaluates you by your net worth, implying that a high dollar worth means a high personal worth.

The fourth cultural demand is *busyness*. You are to produce. If you're not beautiful, don't have brains, or aren't wealthy, you should at least produce something in your life. How high is your productivity? What are you accomplishing in the world?

The fifth "B" is *belonging.* Do you conform? Do you belong? Are you an insider? The conformity yardstick is used frequently by Christians who say you've got to act and think as we do, or you cannot belong to our group. Conformity sticks out when certain issues come up: whether or not to have a career, divorce and remarriage, abortion, women's roles in the church. If you don't believe what "the group" believes, they communicate to you that you're less of a person, and your self-image may take a nose dive.

With all the changes that are taking place at mid-life, a woman may be devalued in several areas. She may be experiencing a loss of beauty and a loss in intellectual areas because she has been out of school and out of her career for a long time. She also may feel she has no access to financial resources because she doesn't work. Her productivity is likely to be despised by the culture if she is "just a housewife." At the same time, she may be experiencing some shifting values as she rethinks life's major issues and may find herself out of step with her religious subculture. In short, she may find herself with a sagging self-esteem.

RESULTS OF A LOW SELF-IMAGE

A person with a low self-image tends to have several of the following traits: One, she becomes a *person-pleaser.* Her self-image has been so severely damaged that she doesn't want to cross anybody. She's afraid to risk, afraid to speak up because she might experience more hurt.

Strangely, a person with a low self-image also tends to become a *leg-chopper.* If it's safe, a person with a low self-image cuts other people down. She feels that if she can make other people look smaller, she will look bigger.

A woman with a low self-image is very *protective.* She hoards, keeps things to herself, generally is not out-going or generous unless she is people-pleasing. She will be generous in order to win someone's approval but not generous just because of someone's need.

Low self-image causes one to be *external*. She looks outside herself for value and worth. She is vulnerable to every situation that happens around her. She is continually being inflated and deflated by the experiences surrounding her. She rejects positive input because she is convinced she's not worth it. She accepts the negative because that's how she has come to see herself.

Another common characteristic is *perfectionism*. A person with a low self-image is constantly trying to be better. Part of her low self-image has resulted from perfectionism and it is her low self-image that keeps her striving toward perfection. Dr. David Seamands says the three favorite phrases of the perfectionist are "could have, should have, and would have." He says that the perfectionist is "always standing on tiptoe."[3]

The woman with a low self-image never really knows who she is, and people around her never really know her as a person. The following poem depicts such a person.

THE MASK

Always a mask
Held in the slim hand,
whitely;

Always she had a mask
before her face—
Smiling and sprightly,
The Mask.

Truly the wrist
Holding it lightly
Fitted the task:
Sometimes however
Was there a shiver,
Fingertip quiver,

Ever so slightly—
Holding the mask?

For years and years and
years I wondered
But dared not ask.

And then—
I blundered,
I looked behind,
Behind the mask,
To find
Nothing—She had no face.

She had become
Merely a hand
Holding a mask
With grace.

—Helen Haiman Joseph[4]

The mid-life stresses that may cause a woman to devalue herself can be, instead, the essential ingredients to help her think through her values, develop a better self-image, and start on a new road to blooming.

HOW TO BUILD A POSITIVE SELF-IMAGE

A woman's self-image can be improved as she works on simple but *specific projects* such as diet, exercise, and proper rest. In *Better Than Ever* Dr. Joyce Brothers tells of her own experience of facing herself at mid-life and how working on these appearance factors helped improve her self-image.[5]

Building a strong self-image also means that you must "be willing to devote time to *unstructured solitude* . . . be willing to daydream and speculate . . . be willing to be reflective, to consider strengths and weaknesses, along with problems, . . . opportunity, . . . a sense of direction . . . be willing to express . . . feelings. Allow the mind to freely associate with such phrases as 'I'd like to,' 'I choose to,' 'I have to,' 'I'm afraid to,' or 'I can't.' "6

You can practice other internal activities to improve your self-image. *Give up self-condemnation* and begin honestly to accept the positive strengths God has placed in your personality. A practical way to stop self-condemnation is to start paying compliments to other people and appreciating their strengths and values. That will help orient you to think positively of human beings in general, then it will be an easy step to think more positively of yourself. As you begin to think and speak positively of others, you in turn will respond positively to people who will help build your self-image.

As a mid-life woman, you also need to *forgive yourself.* Some things *might* have been different; mistakes *were* made, but those are in the past. After asking God, and perhaps others, to forgive you, it is time to forgive yourself. (See Philippians 3:12-15.)

You also need to learn to *listen to yourself.* Imagine that your body is hooked to a polygraph machine and then be sensitive to times when the stress level is increased or reduced. Listening to yourself will enable you to modify and restructure your life toward directions that are less stress-producing.

Cecil Osborne in *The Art of Learning to Love Yourself* suggests these practical ways of building a self-image: give love and understanding, learn to receive love as well as to give it, join a sharing group, share your guilt with other people, distinguish between neurotic fantasies and realistic goals, choose goals well within your reach, and do the things that make you like yourself better.7

Developing a positive self-image means you are willing to *become your unique person.* "When Albert Schweitzer, the great missionary doctor, was a boy, a friend proposed that they go up in the hills and kill birds. Albert was reluctant, but, afraid of being laughed at, he went along.

They arrived at a tree in which a flock of birds was singing; the boys put stones in their catapults. Then the church bells began to ring, mingling music with the birdsong. For Albert, it was a voice from heaven. He shooed the birds away and went home. From that day on, reverence for life was more important to him than the fear of being laughed at. His priorities were clear."[8]

Building a positive self-image includes taking a look at what you do, what you think, the people with whom you relate, and the process by which you internalize all the information that comes to your life. We are also convinced, after working with people for many years, that a vital, personal *relationship with God* will assist this internal integration that produces a stronger self-image.

A certain level of self-esteem in every woman's personality cannot be touched by what other human beings think. Other people need to encourage you to utilize your gifts and abilities and to grow in new dimensions, but you can still feel empty. Even others' affirmation does not touch the very deepest level of self-worth. A vital, personal relationship with God can provide nourishment for the depths of your personality and build your self-image so you can move through the stress periods with confidence.

The Apostle Paul shares about the confidence God can give within the depths of the personality: "If God is on our side, who can be against us? . . . Who dares accuse us whom God has chosen for his own? Will God? No! He is the one who has forgiven us and given us right standing with himself. Who then will condemn us? Will Christ? *No!* For he is the one who died for us and came back to life again for us and is sitting at the place of highest honor next to God, pleading for us there in heaven. . . . When we have trouble or calamity, when we are hunted down or destroyed, is it because he doesn't love us anymore? . . . has God deserted us? . . . For I am convinced that nothing can ever separate us from his love. . . . Our fears for today, our worries about tomorrow . . . nothing will ever be able to separate us from the love of God demonstrated by our Lord Jesus Christ when he died for us" (Romans 8:31-39).

SOURCE OF CONFIDENCE

A solid confidence in God comes first from a personal relationship with him. Invite Jesus Christ to come into your life to forgive your sins. Mentally exchange your weaknesses for Christ's life and his strength. Receive his righteousness as he takes your guilt upon himself (2 Corinthians 5:21).

Second, this confidence comes from a knowledge that God genuinely cares for you and is working the best for you in all events of your life. Romans 8:28 says, "And we know that all that happens to us is working for our good if we love God and are fitting into his plans."

Picture yourself now as a woman who has given her life to God. You have exchanged your unrighteousness, weakness, sin, and the failures of the past for Jesus' righteousness and sufficiency. You are deeply conscious that God loves you and is working all the events of your life together for good. You look forward with anticipation to the future and to becoming all that God has in mind for you to be.

The third concept that will help produce a positive self-esteem is that God is moving you toward growth. You have a future. God is not finished with you; you are still under construction. Amazing things are yet to be accomplished in your life. Romans 5:1, 2 assures you that you are in a place of high privilege now, but more than that, something good is going to happen in the future because of the supernatural activity of God working in your life and in the events around your life.

Spiritual commitment to God comes as you spend more time meditating on what God has said in the Bible and reflecting on these ideas in prayer with him. You *will become* like the ideas you take into your personality. That is why the Scripture encourages us to "fix your thoughts on what is true and good and right. . . . and the God of peace will be with you" (Philippians 4:8, 9).

ALWAYS PERFECT

To develop a positive self-image, you may have to deal with your perfectionism. Perfectionism is the all-or-nothing, feast-or-famine type of thinking. "One dieting physician ate a tablespoon of ice cream and scolded herself by saying, 'I shouldn't have done that! I'm a pig.' These ideas so upset her that she went on to eat an entire quart of ice cream."[9] Dr. David Burns from the University of Pennsylvania School of Medicine suggests several work projects to help perfectionists correct their distortions:

"We urge them to make a list of the advantages and disadvantages of attempting to be perfect."[10] (Take a specific situation in your life and list all of the advantages of doing it perfectly.)

Dr. Burns tells us about one of his clients: "Jennifer was able to list only one advantage of perfectionism: 'It can produce fine work. I'll try hard to come up with an excellent result.' She listed six disadvantages: 'One, it makes me so tight and nervous I can't produce fine work or even adequate work at times. Two, I am often unwilling to risk the mistakes necessary to come up with a creative piece of work. Three, my perfectionism inhibits me from trying new things and making discoveries because I am so preoccupied with being 'safe.' Thus, my world becomes narrow and somewhat boring, and I lose out on the opportunity for new challenges. Four, it makes me self-critical and takes the joy out of life. Five, I can't ever relax because I'll always find something that isn't perfect. Six, it makes me intolerant of others because I am constantly aware of the errors people make, and I end up being perceived as a fault-finder.' "[11]

Obviously the disadvantages of being a perfectionist were very strong in Jennifer's mind but had never been put out on paper where she could look at them.

TOTALLY, COMPLETELY PERFECT?

A second suggestion from Dr. Burns is to "ask perfectionists to spend a day investigating whether or not the world can be evaluated in a meaningful way using all-or-nothing categories. As they notice people and things, they are to ask themselves, 'Are the walls in this room totally clean, or do they have at least some dirt?' They might also ask, 'Is that person totally handsome? Or totally ugly? Or somewhere in between?' The exercise usually demonstrates the irrationality of dichotomous thinking. As one client reported, 'I found out that the universe simply does not divide itself into two categories, all-good versus all-bad.' "[12]

Another technique that Burns uses is to confront the perfectionist's thoughts with reality: "If I don't do a good job and have the house absolutely clean, what will happen? Well, then my husband will think less of me or my neighbors will think less of me." The confrontation then involves asking those people, "Do you think less of me because my house is not absolutely clean?" And the reality comes back, "No, we don't."[13]

Another suggestion is to think of setting different goals in your life. The perfectionist always takes the ultimate goal as the standard. Perfectionists set standards so high they find it difficult ever to produce anything. They find it hard to get started because they hate to do something that is inferior to their high standard. Consequently, they never produce a thing. One writer shared with Dr. Burns that he would say to himself, " 'This has to be outstanding,' every time he sat down to prepare a draft. Then he would daydream or obsess over the first sentence and eventually give up in disgust. When, instead, he told himself, 'I'll just crank out a below-average draft and have it typed up,' he found that his resistance to writing diminished, and he was able to improve his output substantially. It struck him as odd that as he began to aim to make his writing increasingly 'average,' other people seemed increasingly impressed. Eventually, he gave up his perfectionism entirely and became addicted, he said, to the idea of being average."[14]

LOVED BUT VULNERABLE

Perfectionism ultimately is an attempt to win approval because of personal insecurity. This insecurity can be changed by realizing how deeply God loves you. The Scripture teaches that before the world ever began, God the Father loved you. His Son, Jesus Christ, came into the world in order to die for you, to exchange places with you, and—if you have accepted his work for you—the Holy Spirit lives in you to shepherd, guide, and enable you. When you wonder whether you're worth anything—when you think about having to earn people's love—remember that God loves you with an unconditional love demonstrated by all three members of the Godhead.

Mid-life is a dangerous time for the self-image, because it can be smashed by many different negative events. This can also be a positive time for the self-image, because it gives the person an opportunity to grow. Mid-life is something like the time when the lobster must shed its shell in order to grow larger. For a time after it has shed its shell it is naked and vulnerable. It is in danger from a number of predators of the sea. But without the shedding of the shell, it cannot grow any larger.

So it is at mid-life. You are shedding the old shell, the old constraints, the old limited self-image. You are now becoming a different person. Yes, you are vulnerable now. You may experience damage to your self-image. But God is there and says, "I will not abandon you or fail to help you" (Joshua 1:5b).

Dietrich Bonhoeffer, in his poem entitled "Who Am I?" says,

. . . Who am I? This or the other?
Am I one person today and tomorrow another?
Am I both at once? A hypocrite before others, and
before myself a contemptibly woebegone weakling?
Or is something within me still like a beaten army,
fleeing in disorder from victory already achieved?
Who am I? They mock me, these lonely questions of mine.
Whoever I am, thou knowest, O God, I am thine.[15]

"So now, since we have been made right in God's sight by faith in his promises, we can have real peace with him because of what Jesus Christ our Lord has done for us. For because of our faith, he has brought us into this place of highest privilege where we now stand, and we confidently and joyfully look forward to actually becoming all that God has had in mind for us to be" (Romans 5:1, 2).

Chapter Twelve

TRAPPED BY DEPRESSION

As a young pastor and wife, we had very little experience with helping depressed people. We had been through normal seminary training, but that didn't include much practical help for working with people who were depressed, and we certainly had no actual experience.

So it was a rather startling moment for us when Anna appeared at the church study door. She was a mid-life friend of ours whom we had been visiting while she was hospitalized. We did not know she had been released. She obviously was in deep distress. She walked slightly hunched over, shuffled to one of the study chairs, and dropped into the chair with her head down, her hands just lying loosely in her lap. Her puffy cheeks, disheveled hair, and red eyes added to the total picture of dejection and hopelessness.

After some minutes of silence, broken only by quiet crying, she said simply, "My psychiatrist says he has done all that he can for me and he sent me to see you."

Her problem was depression which had started months before and had kept building. She became so depressed that she thought the only way to solve the problem was to take her life. Repeatedly, in fits of anguish and torment, she attempted suicide.

Sometimes in despair she would run out of the house, down the street, and into an open field—running, running, without any purpose or direction, trying to escape from herself and the terrible depression.

Her husband loved her very much and was continually frightened by what she might do next. Would he come home sometime and find her dead because she had sliced her wrists with a butcher knife? Would she just disappear, driven by her depression?

He finally had decided to take her to a psychiatrist, even though his religious convictions and cultural background caused a deep-seated suspicion and fear of psychiatrists or psychologists. Somehow, he thought, God ought to be able to help without these men, who might even be ambassadors of Satan.

He was desperate, so in spite of his strong negative feelings, he sought out professional help. Anna was admitted into a local psychiatric hospital and was involved in prolonged psychotherapy.

She got no better, and the medical staff displayed a growing sense of desperation. She was shifted from doctor to doctor and finally was moved to another medical facility where she underwent approximately fifteen shock treatments.

This was a whole new world to the two of us. When we walked into these hospitals and onto the locked wards, we felt very alien and inadequate. We visited Anna often and were stunned to see only the shell of a human being. She gave no response to us at all. The medication and shock treatments intended for blocking out her depression seemed instead to be creating a nonperson.

Anna went through endless months of individual and group therapy, physical therapy, and occupational therapy. Finally she was released, with little change in her feelings or behavior. Her psychiatrist gave her the news, "We've done all that we can for you. The best thing I can suggest is that you visit a clergyman."

As I (Jim) sat in my office and listened to her recount her psychiatrist's suggestion, I wanted to punch him in the nose. There he was with those millions of dollars of equipment, and scores of trained professionals with a vast accumulation of expertise, yet he had the audacity to dump this poor, depressed soul into my study chair with my skimpy resources and experience at age twenty-seven.

While I looked at Anna, I spoke to God silently in prayer and said something like, "Lord, I'd like to punch that psychiatrist. You know I don't know what to do with Anna. I don't know how to help depressed people, but for some reason you've dropped her in my lap and I can only trust you to work this thing through."

DESCRIPTION OF DEPRESSION

"The woman who is depressed is weighed down with a pervading sadness, a sense of hopelessness and despair. She loses interest in her family and friends and even doubts that she still loves them. Along with a loss of self-esteem, she also loses interest in herself and can become ridden with self-hate, guilt and a feeling of worthlessness. With a loss of zest for life there is a loss of the will to live. She may want to run away, to hide, to curl up and die. To help deaden the pain, the body seems to deaden itself; there can be a slowing down of body functions—lack of energy, inability to sleep, loss of appetite and of interest in sex.

"Sometimes she finds that her activities become agitated, but most often she finds it difficult and well nigh impossible to get through the ordinary daily tasks which she used to perform with ease. Perhaps the worst part of this bleak condition is that she feels there is no hope for the future and that these unhappy circumstances will continue indefinitely. Depression has been called a woman's disease with symptoms that express harsh, self-critical, self-depriving, and often self-destructive attitudes."[1]

A WOMAN'S CROSS

Depression is a significant problem in our country; in fact, about half the adult population experiences depression at one time or another.[2] In addition, more women than men seem to be affected. When Maggie Scarf was doing some work for another subject, she encountered the statistics on women and depression: "The figures seemed strange—strange almost to the point of absurdity. If they *were* accurate, though, the evidence was clear and overwhelming: women, from adolescence onward—and throughout every subsequent phase of the life cycle—are far more vulnerable to depression than are men. . . .

"The same results or findings—more depressed females than males—turned up, . . . in *every* study, carried out anywhere and everywhere. More women were in treatment for depression. It was so, in every institution—inpatient and outpatient—across the country. It was true in state and county facilities. It was the case in community mental health centers. It was simply true, across the board. And, when the figures were adjusted for age, or phase of life, or social class and economic circumstances . . . the outcome was still the same.

"It cut across all other variables and was a constant factor. For every male diagnosed as suffering from depression, the head count was anywhere from *two to six times as many females.*"[3]

Margaret Crockett, speaking of her work with depressed women in a state mental hospital, says that at the nurses' station a poster hung on the wall to remind them of the stress these patients were experiencing. "It pictured the barely visible face of an unhappy woman floating in space and darkness and surrounded by the printed categories of torments that described her condition: LACK OF ESTEEM, NEG-

ATIVISM, INSOMNIA, ANXIETY, CRYING, GASTROINTESTINAL DISTRESS, GUILT FEELINGS, HOPELESSNESS, FATIGUE, LACK OF INTEREST, INDECISIVENESS."4

DEPRESSED SAINTS

Depression is not a modern phenomenon, nor does depression happen only to bad people or to people who normally are not well adjusted anyway. The Bible shares the accounts of several of God's chosen being depressed.

The prophet Jonah in the Old Testament said, "Please kill me, Lord; I'd rather be dead than alive" (Jonah 4:3). Elijah, following a great victory over paganism in his country, ran away in fear for his life and experienced what we classify as an emotional breakdown. In his depressed state, he said, "I have had enough. . . . take away my life. I've got to die sometime, and it might as well be now" (1 Kings 19:4).

Jeremiah, one of the major prophets of the Old Testament, is sometimes called the weeping prophet. He experienced a number of bad times that we would identify as depression. He said, "What sadness is mine . . . O, that I had died at birth. . . . Lord, you know it is for your sake that I am suffering . . ." (Jeremiah 15:10, 15).

When Moses was leading the nation of Israel away from Egypt and into the Promised Land, at times he felt extreme discouragement and depression. He complained, "Why pick on me, to give me the burden of a people like this? . . . I can't carry this nation by myself! The load is far too heavy! If you are going to treat me like this, please kill me right now; it will be a kindness! Let me out of this impossible situation!" (Numbers 11:11-15).

Here are the words of discouragement and depression of a spiritual woman in the Old Testament who had lost her husband and her two sons: "Almighty God has dealt me bitter blows. I went out full and the Lord has brought me home empty; why should you call me Naomi [pleasant] when the Lord has turned his back on me and sent such calamity" (Ruth 1:20, 21)! She wanted the people to call her Mara, which means bitter.

Perhaps the most classic example in the Old Testament is that of Job. He was the richest man in the world, but almost overnight his entire wealth was taken away. He received word that all of his children were killed in a freak accident. On top of that he was afflicted with boils from his head to his foot, his wife despised him, and her advice to Job was to curse God and die.

Job's response was one of deep depression: "Why didn't I die at birth? Why did the midwife let me live? . . . Oh, to have been still-born!—to have never breathed or seen the light" (Job 3:11-16).

YOU'RE IN GOOD COMPANY

Depression is not just an Old Testament experience; it is also seen in New Testament people, such as Peter, who was disillusioned and depressed after his denial of Christ before Christ's crucifixion. Scripture records that after denouncing Christ, "he went away, crying bitterly" (Matthew 26:75).

We detect a note of depression in Paul as he speaks of the physical problem that he had and his report was "three different times I begged God to make me well again" (2 Corinthians 12:8).

Sometimes we have missed the signs of depression and anguish that Jesus experienced in the Garden of Gethsemane. The Bible records that "he took Peter, James, and John with him and began to be filled with horror and deepest distress. And he said to them, 'My soul is crushed by sorrow to the point of death; stay here and watch with me' " (Mark 14:33, 34).

You probably have, in your lifetime, wrestled with some degree of depression. If you are currently experiencing depression because of all your mid-life stress, we want to remind you that it is not because you are unspiritual or a bad person. Nor does depression indicate that you are an emotional basket case and ready for the "funny farm."

The fact that you are depressed does not mean that you're at the end of the road. Many people experience depression, including exceptionally spiritual people, even the Lord himself. Most of the depressed people in the Bible recovered, and they also found that God loved them during the entire process of their depression.

CAUSES FOR DEPRESSION

A VARIETY OF LOSSES

As you can tell from the examples cited, depression is directly related to loss. Some of the losses were lost relationships through death or, in David's case, through conflict with his son. Others were losses of physical and emotional strength, as with Elijah, or of lost opportunities, as with King Saul.

All depression has some kind of loss associated with it. If you are experiencing depression, it is extremely important for you to identify the loss that is triggering the depression.

Relational Loss. "Middle-class housewives have a higher rate of depression than working-class housewives, and those housewives who have overprotective relationships with their children suffer the highest rate of depression of all when the children leave home," was the conclusion of a study on depressed mid-life women.[5]

This research discovered that 82 percent of housewives who were overprotective and overinvolved in their relationships with their children experienced depression as the children began to disassociate themselves from their mothers. If a woman is getting her satisfaction through the accomplishments of her husband or her children, instead of through her own achievements, she will be very vulnerable to depression.

Depression can occur whenever there is a breakdown in or a termination of any interpersonal relationship. Depression should be expected because of these kinds of losses, and we need to know that it's all right for us to feel depressed. The fact that depression is normal doesn't mean that we should stay depressed, but we do need time to recover.

Sometimes when a woman loses her husband through death or divorce, friends will encourage her to "cheer up." There is almost an unwritten principle that she's allowed to feel bad for about two weeks, but after that she should get hold of herself and get going with life.

We are more realistic if we expect a woman to experience depression of various degrees for at least a year following divorce or her husband's death. Part of the process of recovery is that the person must live through all the events of an entire year and readjust in each of those situations. Each new occasion brings a reminder of the loss and thus some degree of depression.

Loss of Material Things. Sally and I were visiting the Tahitian Islands during our second honeymoon, in celebration of our twenty-fifth wedding anniversary. We had loaded a few things into a small dugout outrigger canoe and were paddling from our hotel to an island about a half a mile offshore. We had gone only about 150 yards when we made a slight readjustment of our weight in the canoe. To our absolute amazement, the canoe started to tip over. The outrigger pontoon which was to keep the canoe balanced was water-logged and absolutely worthless. We seemed to be acting out a slow motion movie as the outrigger pontoon slowly settled deeper and deeper into the water until finally we and the contents of our canoe had slipped into the Pacific.

I had a brand new Olympus OM 1 camera with a 1:2 lens which went straight to the bottom of seventy-five feet of salt water. Soon a ski boat came by, pulled Sally into the boat, and towed me and the disabled canoe back to shore.

We later paid a diver to retrieve our shirts, tennis shoes, and other assorted items, along with my magnificent new camera.

I took the camera to our hotel room and thoroughly washed out the salt water, but it just didn't work. Corrosion had already started to eat at the mechanism so that none of the metering systems functioned. I found I could easily say to myself on an intellectual level, "All things work together for good." But it was difficult for me to shake that gnawing depression, that terrible down feeling.

If you lose something tangible that you value, you likely will feel depressed for a period of time. It's normal. It's all right for you to have those feelings. God has given us a full range of feelings. Feeling depressed is not wrong.

Time Loss. Repeatedly we hear from women who are feeling a degree of depression as they near a milestone birthday, such as thirty-five, forty, or forty-five. These women are experiencing the loss of life and time. You can't go back and relive the years. "And who would want to?" some women ask. Nevertheless, because of our youth-oriented culture, we often are gripped by loss when we recognize that we have moved out of the young adult classification into the mid-life category. It can be depressing to feel that we are losing "the best years of our lives."

Lost Opportunities. A young mid-life woman asked if she could talk to me (Jim) for a few minutes. She had barely gotten seated in my study when rivulets of tears started down her cheeks. Almost involuntarily the story spilled out from her inner person. She was a talented woman in her mid-thirties who felt a deep sense of remorse for a missed opportunity. She'd given up a career in business which by now would have placed her in a vice-presidency, in order to pursue studies for a totally different career. Now she was finding disillusionment and even opposition in the new career, and she could see that her former career would have been more satisfying than she thought when she left it. She asked pathetically, "Why do I feel so depressed? I feel like I'm going crazy." Her depression was normal because she felt she had given up a special opportunity she would never have again.

Loss of Control or Choice. If we go for prolonged periods of time with too many demands on our time and energy without a break for restoration, we can become depressed. When every hour of every day, day after day, is cut out for us, we may feel dejected and weighed down without realizing why. If we feel we have neither voice nor choice in decisions that affect us, we may feel depressed. We were created with intellect and the ability to make choices, so a part of us is stymied when we are constantly shut off in those areas.

Loss, then, in any area of life that we value, may cause us to respond with feelings of depression. We must identify the sources of loss and make necessary adjustments so that the depression will lift and we can move on with living.

PROHIBITION AGAINST EXPRESSED EMOTIONS

Along with any loss we experience, we commonly have other feelings such as anger, fear, guilt, or self-pity. Whenever we refuse to allow ourselves to have these feelings, we only intensify our depression. Sometimes women are not allowed by others or themselves to grieve or to feel loss or the resultant emotions of anger, fear, guilt, or self-pity in common life experiences.

For example, a woman who surrendered her personal career dream to get married when she was a young adult and invested all her life in her husband and children may feel uncomfortable grieving over her children's growing up or her husband's success compared to her lack of success. Sometimes unthinking people make inappropriate remarks: "Why are you depressed over your husband's success?" "You should be glad that your children are growing up and don't need you so much anymore." "Now you have time to play more golf, read, and do the things you want."

If your husband's success has driven a wedge into your

marriage so that you feel left out and unneeded, and if your children are growing independent and sometimes obnoxious so that you feel like a fifth wheel with them, you *have* lost something. It *is* appropriate for you to grieve over it, to be upset about it, and perhaps experience a strong anger, self-pity, and even fear about what the future holds. But sometimes people won't let you feel those feelings.

Trying to restrain your feelings will often deepen your depression. Not only have you lost something, but now you have lost the opportunity for a normal emotional response. You are trapped and that sense of being trapped will increase your depression.

EMOTIONAL FATIGUE

Think of your emotional capacity as a muscle—for example, a leg muscle. Now suppose that you strain your muscle while you are riding a bike with your kids. It's sore, and you limp around for a few days until your leg finally recovers and you are able to carry on normal life.

But imagine that you don't give the strained muscle those few days to rest and recover. While your muscle is still hurting, you go on a family picnic and play softball. One of the kids hits the ball and throws the bat, which hits you right on your sore leg. Now you have tremendous pain. You fall to the ground, rubbing your muscle. But, at the same time, one of your other kids, who's playing on a park swing, is swinging abnormally high. There's a scream; you turn and see that your child has fallen and is holding his arm. Without thinking of your leg, you jump up and run over to discover that your child has broken his arm. It's only after you attend to your child that you realize your leg muscle has gone into a spasm. You can't put your weight down; in fact, you're immobilized.

Emotions are like that. When you're called upon to do something that drains you emotionally, you must have time for emotional recovery or the next panic call will further deplete and damage your emotions. Each crisis that comes along calls for expenditure of emotional energy. Dozens and dozens of such crises arise for the mid-life woman. If your emotions are not allowed to recover, they will gradually become so damaged that you will go into depression. In some ways the depression becomes a way of insulating you from further emotional damage. It is not wrong to do what is necessary to recharge your emotional batteries. Prolonged emotional fatigue eventually will demand that you slow down, by bringing about depression.

PHYSICAL FATIGUE

If you go without sleep for a few nights in a row, your body pays a toll. Your emotions are also affected and may cause you to respond in ways that are not normal for you, including feeling depressed.

Joyce, an overstressed career woman, went to her medical doctor in desperation because there seemed to be something wrong with her. She just didn't have any drive or energy. She was always irritable, and, to top it off, she was experiencing pains in her chest and abdomen.

The physician said, "I'm going to schedule you for a battery of tests a week from now, but in order for the tests to be effective I want you to follow my instructions completely. You are to get ten hours of sleep each night. You're not to attend any committee or board meetings or be involved in any outside obligations."

Joyce objected strenuously, but the doctor assured her that this was necessary in order for the tests to be completely effective. She came back a week later and announced to him that she felt entirely different and didn't think she would need the tests. The doctor gently explained to her that all he had done was to ensure a forced rest.

If you are continuing to overtax yourself physically, thinking that you'll catch up later, you probably *will* catch up. But you also may pay the price with depression.

INCOMPLETE EMOTIONAL DEVELOPMENT

By the time you get to mid-life, you should be emotionally developed enough so you can handle normal life stresses. If, however, you have never learned how to give and receive love, you may have a growing feeling that people don't love you.

Norma had this problem. She had been told repeatedly by her parents that they didn't love her, that she was an accident, and that they wished she had never been born. She married Rob more for an escape than for love.

Rob loved her very much, but his loving words and actions were like rain running off a duck's back. His love, even though profusely poured on her, was never absorbed into her personality. She treated it with suspicion because of her incomplete emotional development.

She repeatedly complained to her husband and to others that nobody loved her, even though this was not the case. As she continued to say that no one loved her and refused to accept people's love as being valid, she gradually pushed them, including her husband, away from her. As people emotionally moved away from her, she then could justly claim that nobody loved her. The growing realization that she really was no longer loved was devastating to her and sent her into deep depression.

The problem started with her incomplete emotional development rather than from an unwillingness of her husband to love her. Women who keep growing and working on areas of emotional limitation will less likely be candidates for depression caused by being emotionally underdeveloped.

PRESSURE FROM ORGANIZATIONS OR INDIVIDUALS

Since the Second World War the church (especially conservative groups) has become increasingly vocal in pushing women toward a marriage-and-mothering-only role. As we've noted earlier, these women are more likely to be depressed and to experience greater mid-life trauma. Secular liberation influences have also created stress and pressure for women by urging them to choose a career-only direction and avoid being "enslaved" as homemakers and mothers.

When a woman accepts a religious or secular movement's directions for her life, and when those ideas violate that internal sense of rightness that God has given her, she is being set up for depression. If God has given you the ability, the interest, and the desire to be a mother and wife only and if you are forced by outside pressures to engage in a career as well, you eventually may fall into depression. If, on the other hand, you follow the rigid religious teachings (which actually are based on questionable biblical interpretation) that insist a woman must be a wife and mother only, in spite of God-given desires and abilities for a career, you also are being set up for depression.

The causes for depression are many, but the key word invariably is *loss.* Therefore, in order to move out of depression, an early priority is to discover the source of loss and decide how that loss will be handled.

THE PROCESS OF DEPRESSION

Depression usually begins gradually. As we've said, the first step, although not always immediately recognized, is the loss of something of value. We may then move into the first level of depression with its normal feelings as a response to the loss. If we continue too long in a depressed state, we may slip into a condition known as clinical depression. This can lead into a serious state of complete withdrawal from life.

YOUR PERSONAL LOSSES

To understand the process of depression and the part that loss plays, let's use an imaginary illustration. Suppose that you value yourself as a woman on the basis of your appearance and your relationship with your husband.

Now imagine that in the past few weeks, as you approach your thirty-ninth birthday, you have been startled with the discovery of gray hair, age lines on your face, your changing figure as your weight shifts to your torso, and that despicable marbleized flesh that shows on your legs when you wear your bathing suit. You have experienced physical loss, and because you so highly valued youth and beauty, you may not feel comfortable with yourself anymore.

A second loss might be in the area of marriage intimacy. When you and your husband got married, you promised each other that you would never allow your marriage to become dull and boring like the marriages of your parents. In spite of good intentions, your marriage has followed the same unsatisfying pattern. You both have become preoccupied with living and with meeting life's endless emergencies, so you have gradually grown apart. Your husband may have become so highly committed to his career success that in reality there is no time for you or for building a relationship.

EMOTIONAL RESPONSES TO LOSS

As we said earlier, some women are unable, or will not allow themselves, to experience the emotions associated with loss. Therefore their depression tends to intensify. Let's go on with some of the possible responses to the loss in our hypothetical illustration.

When you look in the mirror and see how your body has aged, you justifiably may feel some degree of anger. It would be better to face and acknowledge your anger than to bury it and pretend it's not there. You may also feel self-pity: "I feel sorry for me because this is happening. I don't like it." In addition to self-pity, there may be fear: "What if this causes my husband to leave me? He used to comment on how he liked my figure when I was a young woman. What if he leaves me for another shapely young woman?" You may also experience guilt: "If only I had exercised, or if I hadn't always eaten so much chocolate cake, I wouldn't be in this bad shape."

It's OK for you to have these feelings and it's better that you face them. Knowing your real feelings will help you deal with the loss. Sometimes unwillingness to allow your feelings to be expressed is part of a denial system that says, "I am not losing anything. I don't feel any loss."

NORMAL DEPRESSION
The next part of the depression process is the actual stage of depression itself. Normal depression is a grief process because of loss or disappointment. Some of the common experiences you may have:

- A lowered self-image
- A sense of loneliness
- A degree of helplessness
- A feeling of not being loved
- A breakdown in healthy living processes of proper eating, sleeping, and exercise
- An unaccountable physical and emotional fatigue

Let's continue our example of the losses of beauty and marriage intimacy. You normally can expect to think less of yourself if these losses occur. It will be normal for you to feel lonely. You probably will sense some degree of helplessness as you realize that you cannot reverse the cycles, especially those related to your physical aging. With your husband preoccupied in his business and career, you may feel unloved. This normal process of depression will probably have some effect on the way you eat—you may overeat or undereat, gain or lose weight. You also may find that you're sleeping less or that the sleep you get is not sound and deep. You may experience an overall feeling of fatigue—something you can't put your finger on is wearing you out. That something is depression, which has been triggered by these two losses in your life.

FACING THE PROBLEM

At this point most people confront their loss and decide they're going to do something about it. Other people decide to do nothing and allow themselves to slip deeper and deeper into depression.

Some people ask, "Why not stop the process of depression earlier? As soon as the event takes place, deal with it and get it out of the way?" If getting it out of the way means to deny that you've experienced loss and you have the resultant feelings, then you are, in fact, not dealing with it. You are only storing up problems which will explode at a later date.

You can, however, deal with your situation early in the process by saying, "Yes, I did lose my camera and I do really feel crummy about it. I know that I may feel rather uncomfortable about this for some period of days or weeks and I'm going to allow myself to feel that way. No, it isn't the end of the world, but yes, it was a valuable camera and yes, there were pictures that went down with it that we'll never see."

Or, to use the imaginary illustration: Yes, you are aging. True, you don't have the physical beauty of a twenty-five-year-old. But no, it doesn't mean that you are sexless. It does mean you can offer other strengths in the place of the twenty-five-year-old beauty that you've lost.

If you've had losses in your marriage, they too can be confronted. Talk with your husband about some of the good things that you remember from the early days of marriage and consider how to get some of those back. Talk with him freely about some of the feelings you've had— your fear, self-pity, sometimes even anger. Confront it early and you can reduce the depths of depression.

Many of the things that ultimately result in depression have been developing over many years in a gradual, almost imperceptible way. It's difficult to identify exactly at what point you started aging or when your marriage started to be less than satisfying. But at whatever point you do discover loss, confront it. As soon as reasonably possible and without denying any of the attendant emotions, decide what you're going to do for appropriate solutions.

CLINICAL DEPRESSION

If the emotions in the earlier stages of the depression process are not dealt with early, they will combine and intensify to become a cyclical process. The more anger you feel, the more helpless, lonely, and unloved you feel. The more these feelings and responses rage within your personality, the more they break down the healthy living process and begin to change the chemical balance in your body. Chemical imbalance in turn will cause depression and emotional stress. When the body chemistry is disturbed, you cannot handle depression and emotional stress as well.

The situation is something like a time when you were totally physically worn out and then you were forced to solve a number of problems. You probably were short-tempered and angry: "Why does all of this have to happen now?" Unchecked depression wears us down and changes us chemically so that we're less able to handle the next pressures of life when they come.

The cycle of clinical depression—that is, depression which keeps on feeding depression which causes more depression—is almost impossible to break without medication and counseling therapy from a psychiatrist. A psychiatrist is a medical doctor who has a psychology degree in addition to his medical degree. He will look at the physical and emotional conditions and the interplay between the two. Clinically depressed people need the help of a trained person such as a psychiatrist and may need hospitalization.

WITHDRAWAL

The next level in the process of depression is withdrawal into a private world. If the clinically depressed person is not helped, he or she tends to retreat from reality, moves farther from confronting the loss, and withdraws into a secluded little shell. This is called an emotional breakdown. The person now becomes nonfunctioning, many times unable to carry on the normal activities of life such as eating, grooming, dressing, or working.

The woman who has been affected so greatly by depression that she is now in a deep state of withdrawal will need a great deal of care. She probably should be hospitalized to protect her from herself, to help her get physical rest and nourishment, and to receive the emotional counseling and support she needs to work through the loss that has occurred in her life.

IDENTIFYING SIGNS OF DEPRESSION

The following questions may help you identify depression symptoms, evaluate your own feelings, and seek help if you need it:

1. Have you been feeling sad, blue, hopeless, down in the dumps for more than two weeks?
2. Have your eating habits recently changed drastically?
3. Do you have trouble falling asleep or staying asleep?
4. Do you feel fatigued, run down, without your usual energy, and there are no clear reasons for this fatigue?
5. Have you experienced an unusual loss of sexual interest and/or pleasure?
6. Do you have difficulty concentrating or making decisions?
7. Are you feeling jumpy, unable to sit still?
8. Do you have frequent thoughts of taking your own life or wishing you were dead?
9. Are you more irritable, easily annoyed, and do you experience a great deal more anger?
10. Do you feel extremely discouraged and pessimistic about most things?
11. Do you feel guilty and worthless?
12. Are you unable to forget bad things that happened in the past?

13. Do you cry more than usual?
14. Are you constantly in need of reassurance from people?
15. Do you have new stomach and abdominal pains or severe headache or backache with no medical explanation?

As you read through this list, you probably easily identified one or several symptoms that are current in your life. This does not necessarily mean that you are depressed or that you seriously need help. The key concept is in item number one—have you felt this way for more than two weeks? If item number one is true of you and several of the other items also apply, then it would be important to seek help. We'll suggest where to seek help under the Recovery category later in this chapter.

ALCOHOL AND DRUGS

Alcohol or chemical dependency may become a factor in a woman's depression. One writer notes, "Alcoholism climbs a steep 50 percent in the 40-to-60 age group over those in their 30's. In this period of stress and tension when the individual is restless, sleepless, and irritable, alcohol may be resorted to for support and relaxation."[6] About half of the women admitted to institutions for alcohol problems are in the age group forty-five to sixty-four. Over half of the drug-related deaths among white women occur after age forty. Of women age forty-five to forty-nine, 28 percent use prescription psychotherapeutic drugs, and more than one out of every three women in this age category use either prescription or over-the-counter drugs to help them deal with emotional stress.[7]

Drinking by mid-life women many times is not simply a social experience but is used for escape. The mid-life woman with a drinking problem has an emotional make-up that is quite often marked by low self-esteem, self-pity, a tendency toward self-punishment, resentment, and an inclination to project blame. She is impatient, irritable, and marked by depression and anxiety. She looks at alcohol or drugs as a means of helping her cope with life or just plain survival.

Allow us to be very direct and blunt. If you need a drink in order to keep your world in order, or if you find that you continually need some drug like valium or librium just to take the edge off your tension and enable you to handle stress, then you really ought to seek help. You need to work through the issues that are causing stress and depression. Identify your losses and take positive action to reconstruct your life so that those losses don't continue to eat you up.

RECOVERY

Someone who is clinically depressed probably will not be able to help herself nor will she be likely to seek help. Someone who loves and cares for her must be willing to take responsibility and refer her to competent psychiatric help. A psychiatrist may use many resources, including antidepressant drugs which are reported to bring about recovery in 70 to 95 percent of clinically depressed people.[8]

Let's assume, however, that you are not clinically depressed but you are concerned about working out of the lesser depression you are experiencing. Following is the logical progression for recovery:

1. Identify the loss that has caused the depression. It's extremely helpful to talk to a friend you trust or a pastoral or community counselor. Share with that person what you've discovered and let him or her be a mirror to reflect to you what he or she sees and hears you saying, helping you to pinpoint your loss.

2. Gather all the information and truth that you can about the loss. Again, a friend can be very helpful. Remember this is not a whitewash or a coverup; you really are going to confront truth.

For example, if the loss that you're experiencing is related to your youth, then confront all that involves. What does it mean to lose youth? Talk frankly and explicitly about all of the other losses related to the major loss of losing youth. You can't stay up as late at night, you have some gray hair, your body weight is shifting, you've got wrinkles, you're not as athletic as you used to be. You are trying to learn the truth about the loss that you've experienced to understand the full scope of it. If you look at only a little bit, you may be leaving some important sections unexplored, and this will produce depression. So, get all of the information out so that you can deal with it.

Remember that some of the truth about your loss has a very positive side as well as negative. You might ask, "How can there be any positive side to the fact that our marriage is not what it should be and I've lost intimacy with my husband?"

The positive side is that instead of allowing yourself to continue to slide into increased depression, you are now confronting the loss. Confronting this loss in marital intimacy now will help your husband reorder his priorities so that he will be less likely to experience a marriage-related crisis at mid-life. Another positive truth is that you will see that your unsatisfying marriage can be corrected now before it gets so bad that nobody wants to work on it at all.

3. Allow your feelings to be expressed. Obviously, some of your feelings are going to be coming out as you identify the loss and explore the truth about it. But at this stage deliberately ask yourself what you *feel* about this loss—not what you *think*, but what you *feel*.

Sometimes writing out your feelings will help you understand them more accurately. Verbalize to another person exactly what you feel and the intensity of those feelings.

You may find yourself expressing feelings we mentioned earlier—anger, fear, self-pity, guilt. Let them all spill out. In the process you'll have a good cry or several good cries. Don't sweep crying under the rug saying, "Well, that's just another expression of the weakness of women." An article entitled "Go ahead, cry your eyes out!" reports from several clinics around the country that women are joining the male population in repressing their emotions. We are becoming a nation of people who do not cry. The price for these repressed emotions, according to these studies, is an early death.

The experts report that a good cry can:

> "Help you rid your body of harmful chemical by-products of stress.
> Give your vascular circulatory, respiratory and nervous system a work out.
> Provide psychological relief.
> Relieve tensions."[9]

Let your tears spill out. Don't believe those false comforters who try to hush you up. Express your feelings. You're going through a grief process that is necessary to carry out before you can go on to step four.

4. Decision-making is the next step. Now that you have identified the loss, understand all the truth about it, and have expressed your feelings, what are you going to do about it? Remind yourself that you're a survivor and that you're going to make decisions that will move you toward health, growth, productivity, and effectiveness. What decisions will help to move you in that positive direction?

Again, let's imagine the loss to be that of losing youth. Your decision might be to deliberately emphasize the strengths that you have now as a mid-life woman with a great deal more insight and knowledge about life. You deliberately are not going to compete with young bodies. Don't make the bikini your point of competition, but use your brains and your experience.

If you've experienced marital loss, make decisions for reconstructing that marriage. Do whatever you can to develop true communication, meet your husband's needs, make changes in yourself, or whatever must be done to restore and enrich your relationship.

5. Develop a climate of support and love. Put yourself in situations where you are with groups of people who are very supportive, loving, and optimistic, and who will extend themselves to you. Carefully cultivate any people who have opened themselves to you so that you have the emotional support you need to help you recover.

Encourage this person or group of persons not only to hear you out as you work through this process but also to call you to be accountable for any decisions you make. Groups of caring people are frequently found in churches, but look especially for people who have been touched deeply by God's love. These are the people who look at life as a great privilege and are awed by God's graciousness.

6. Get inoculations of hope. You need a steady diet of positive, hopeful messages being introduced into your life. You need to deliberately turn away from the loss now that you have fully experienced it and completely grieved over it. Turn your face toward the future and toward God.

A helpful procedure that we have often recommended is to read through the Psalms thoughtfully, with personal application. The Psalms were written by people who struggled deeply with life but who also had learned about hope.

Yes, life has many experiences of depression and trial, but God is there to walk with you through those low valleys. "But now, thus says the Lord, your Creator, . . . He who formed you, . . . 'Do not fear, for I have redeemed you; I have called you by name; you are Mine! When you pass through the water, I will be with you; And through the rivers, they will not overflow you. When you walk through the fire, you will not be scorched, Nor will the flame burn you. For I am the Lord your God, The Holy One of Israel, your Savior . . . ' " (Isaiah 43:1-3, NASB).

Chapter Thirteen

TEMPTED TO ESCAPE

THE RUNAWAY

The crowd was leaving after the conference, and a woman stood off to the side, obviously wanting to be the last one to speak to us. When everyone had left, she asked for a few minutes to talk and, in a rather deliberate, detached way, Elaine explained that her marriage was in bad shape.

She said they had had trouble for the last four years, but Tom was not willing to go to a counselor. He said their problems were all her fault. If she would just quit worrying about her needs and do her job with the family business, everything would be OK.

She finally did persuade Tom to go for marriage counseling, but he clearly resisted the whole process. Each time after they left the counselor, Tom made fun of what had taken place during the session, and seemed to be even more determined not to change and to be disinterested in her needs. He would promise the counselor he would carry out certain changed behaviors, but afterward he would only laugh about that.

After the counseling experience collapsed and things were no different, Elaine decided she was going to have to do something for her own sanity. She told us that day after day she would have long crying spells. She felt she was alone, unloved, and unneeded; yet, she couldn't share this with her husband. He kept saying, "It's all in your head. Just forget it and you'll be better," so she would never allow him to see her crying.

During these years, he had an increased need for sexual intercourse, and each time, she reported, she just felt used. She would lie awake hours after having had sex, crying quietly into her pillow.

As the months and years went by, she seemed to experience a hardening in her emotions, almost as if she were dying inside. She felt something had to be done or she really would die.

She was the business manager and bookkeeper for their small business. Much of the business was done in cash, so she began secretly to skim some off the top to put into a private savings account. At the time she talked to us, she had put away a little more than $12,000 over a period of eighteen months.

Now her question to us was, "Is it wrong for me to run away? I'm secretly planning to leave as soon as the kids are out of school. I won't tell Tom or the kids that we're going. I'll just take the kids with me and go to a cottage that I've located and spend the summer. We'll have a vacation, and I hope it'll drive him crazy wondering what's happened to us."

THE RUNAWAY WOMAN

In our culture we still believe the husband is the one who leaves the home. But ". . . the runaway wife is one of today's fastest growing phenomena. In the last twelve years, the ratio of bolted wives to runaway husbands has gone from one in 300 to one in two."[1]

The runaway wife is a more common phenomenon to-day because she is more willing to admit her needs and also is better able than she once was to make it on her own in the world. Fifty years ago women stayed in difficult marriage situations because there were no options. But the innumerable options for a woman today provide an easier opportunity for an unhappy woman to run.

In one sample of women we studied, approximately 78 percent of the women physically ran away from their marriage relationships for some period of time. The women in our survey were ages twenty-eight to fifty-five. Those who reported they had physically run away at some time averaged 2.5 experiences of running away. The average age of the runaway woman was thirty-four, however, the runaway eras grouped around two distinct times—one in the late twenties, the second in the late thirties.

A noted anthropologist has said, "I think the principal rebellion today, following the rebellion of men in their forties, is the tremendous number of women who are leaving their husbands *before* they're deserted. These are women . . . of 35 who feel, 'This is my last chance.' "[2]

The runaway woman is a topic infrequently discussed and yet, if our findings are a reliable indication of the situation, running away some time during life is a very common experience in America. If it is this widespread, then we need to begin asking ourselves who these runaways are, why they run away, and how they can be helped.

TYPES OF RUNAWAYS

Human beings are unique and don't easily fit into categories, but sometimes we can understand other people and ourselves better if we look at some obvious groupings. There are two kinds of runaways: the ones who physically leave home and the others who run only in their emotions. Some of the women who run physically go for just brief periods of time; others plan for extended times away, as did Elaine. The emotional runaways are the explosive ones who obviously and verbally detach themselves from their marriages and the silent ones who say nothing but simply die inside.

SHORT-TERM PHYSICAL RUNAWAYS

As I (Sally) was interviewing a woman for the research on this book, I asked her if she had ever run away. "Yes, I have, but it's been for only short periods of time."

I asked her, "What do you mean?"

"Oh, like once when we were driving across town to visit some friends, and my husband and I were having a fight, which is very common for us. He doesn't seem to understand me, doesn't try. He's always putting me down and treats me like dirt. The same process started again. I was feeling humiliated. The more I verbally fought back, the more he smashed me with his words. We pulled up to a traffic light, and I just jumped out and started running. I cut through some yards so he couldn't find me and went and sat in a park for a few hours, feeling sorry for myself and, at the same time, hating him because I knew that I'd go back."

Another woman reported that after a very tense dinner time, her husband simply walked away from the table, sat down, and turned on the TV while she was left to care for the children and clean up the kitchen. She grabbed the youngest child by the hand, walked out the door, got in the car, and drove off. She parked the car a few blocks away and sat there. Then she said pitifully, "I had no place to go."

LONG-TERM PHYSICAL RUNAWAYS

A woman who runs away for a short period of time tends to have some experience like the straw that breaks the camel's back. She is likely to be a woman with a short fuse, and running away even for a short time or a short distance will help her to get perspective. The woman who runs away for the long term has a different need. Generally, she has been hurt over an extended period of time. Her emotional batteries are so run down and she feels so emotionally battered that she needs a longer period of time to recover.

Sometimes the long-term runaway woman, like Elaine, makes elaborate plans to enable her to get away. Occasionally the long-term runaway makes her leaving appear socially acceptable by going to live at her mother's or with some other relative for the summer.

THE EMOTIONALLY EXPLOSIVE RUNAWAY

Runaway is perhaps not the correct term for this woman, but in a sense she is escaping from her home. She doesn't leave physically, but in very clear terms she lets her husband, and perhaps the children, know that even though she is there physically she is not emotionally involved with the home.

Joanne had talked to Bill repeatedly about her emotional starvation in their marriage, but he was a busy contractor trying to manage a multimillion dollar business. He kept saying to her that things would get better, but they never did.

He came home one night to find that their two younger sons had been fed and were watching TV. Joanne was in the living room reading a book. He came and asked her, "Where's supper?"

She said simply and directly, "You make your own supper."

"What do you mean?" he demanded.

"I mean, from now on, I don't care for you or do anything for you—in the same way that you don't care for me."

"What are you talking about?" Bill asked.

Joanne replied, "I mean I'm not going to ruin your reputation in front of all of your business associates and Christian friends, but I want you to know that I'm not having anything to do with you anymore. I've put all of your clothes and things in the guest room. From now on, you sleep in there."

Bill went storming out of the room into the guest room to see if this was true. He came back into the living room and insisted that Joanne get up and make supper for him. She told him in no uncertain terms that he was on his own and that if he pressed her too far, she was going to pack her bags and leave him to take care of the kids. Then he could try to explain the situation to the other men who served with him on the Board of Elders at the church.

Bill continued to fume, but he backed off. During the next several months Bill and Joanne lived in the same house while Joanne lived out the role of an emotional runaway.

THE SILENT RUNAWAY

The woman who escapes by withdrawing is the most pathetic. She has chosen to coexist with the problem instead of trying to change it.

Margaret's husband was a full time Christian worker. He held a state office in his denomination and was on several national committees for evangelism projects. He was extremely competent in evangelism, but a total misfit as a husband and father. He knew how to manipulate people politically, but he did not know how to relate to people as persons. They were always just things.

Margaret had decided as a young wife that she was not going to leave the unhappy marriage; instead, she would do her very best to help Ed be successful. Deep down inside, Margaret felt that she was the cause of their marital friction. If only she could be a more submissive wife, just as Ed kept telling her, certainly their marriage would get better.

Margaret continued running away deeper inside herself until finally she was almost in another world. She would stand at the kitchen sink, peeling the same potato for fifteen minutes, carefully taking off each strip of peeling and laying it neatly beside the other strips in a row on the counter. She was consistently late with serving meals and with every household task.

Later, Ed got involved in an affair and felt quite justified within himself. After all, he rationalized, he didn't have a complete woman for a wife; she was emotionally disturbed. Their problems had always been her fault.

WHY DO WOMEN RUN AWAY?

Women gave us many different kinds of responses to the question of why they ran away. Many were so dissatisfied in their marriages that they wanted to escape. Sometimes they ran when their husbands got involved in affairs or when there was incest in the family.

Many responded that there was just too much work and not enough appreciation from their husbands and families. Some felt a sense of hopelessness—"Nobody caring about all that I did." They felt constant fatigue and unceasing demands from husbands, children, and sometimes the church. Some women were very angry because they felt their husbands had left the raising of the children to them.

Other women reported that they ran away because of physical abuse. Others left because they felt they were trapped in their roles and were not significant in life. Some ran as a protection from going crazy from the things their husbands said to put them down or otherwise verbally abuse them.

The most common reason for running was that a marriage was in trouble. Sometimes the running was to punish the husband for his lack of concern. Sometimes it was a means of getting his attention, saying, in essence, "Hey, I'm serious about this. Listen to me." Other times the bad marriage relationship and running away became the beginning of a bridge to an affair. Most of these women did not have affairs first and then run away to their lovers, but they were running away out of desperation and then affairs developed.

Running, for most of the women that we have surveyed, was an escape response. And if she didn't get help, the woman on the run was likely to be the woman who would then seek the closeness and companionship of an affair.

THE AFFAIR

Webster, in a brief few words, describes the affair as "a romantic or passionate attachment, typically of limited duration." But the dictionary in no way describes the intensity and elation, or the pain, agony, and tragedy that we have seen in the lives of people who are involved in affairs.

WHAT IS AN AFFAIR?

We will enlarge Webster's definition to include the word, *extramarital*, meaning that one or both of the people involved in the affair is married to someone else. An affair need not have a sexual dimension, but it certainly has a dimension of emotional preoccupation, with thoughts continually drifting to the other person and commitment shifting away from the marriage to the other person.

One woman in her early thirties tells about getting involved in an affair. She said that at first her times with the other man were very innocent, then "his joking around with me became flirty, and eventually, he made several passes at me . . . I also was strongly attracted to him." She decided to break if off and did not see the man for several months. But whenever she would think about him, she would realize she was still in love with him.

Then she said, "One day we saw each other again at a meeting. As I was leaving, he came to me and said that he missed me. Then he said it really was more than loneliness; he was in love with me. I left the room, feeling confused. I was excited that someone loved me, but then I came to my senses. We could never be together."

An affair, then, may be something that is very casual. It

may be, as in the movie *Same Time Next Year,* only a yearly contact. It may be only a deep caring and sharing relationship, including touching, and it may include sexual intercourse. It isn't so important to describe what happens in an affair as it is to realize that you are actually involved in an affair if another man is drawing your emotions away from your husband. If you are spending energy, time, and money on a relationship with another man instead of your husband, no matter how innocent that relationship may appear, you are in an affair.

A SHORT-TERM HIGH

As we describe an affair, two other words are key: *infatuation* and *temporary.* Infatuation means a foolish or extravagant and intense relationship. There is a sense of losing your head, losing perspective and direction, or selling your soul for something that seems worthwhile but in the long run really is not.

Affairs are temporary. Most affairs follow a six-month pattern. Great intensity, enthusiasm, and exhilaration abound at the beginning, but then the pain begins to rise. Reality starts to creep in and a woman comes down from the clouds. She realizes that if she were to live a normal life with this man, she would find he had human limitations and problems like every other man. She would just be trading one set of problems for another.

Affairs are like amphetamines. They promote a short-time high but they do not cure the problems of your life, and when the drug wears off you find yourself crashing again.

WHY DOES POPCORN POP?

Why do people get involved in affairs? What are the causes?

Our world is saturated with sexual stimuli. An ad for jeans shows a young woman lying on a young man with his shirt off. Of course, they are both wearing the jeans that are being advertised, but the jeans aren't what make your juices flow. Invitations to sexual arousal are everywhere—magazine ads, television programs, commercials, plays, films, books, magazines, music, bumper stickers, jokes, clothing styles. It's as if our culture were programmed for sexual turn-on.

Besides all the visual turn-ons, we are continually bombarded with "easy sex, irresponsible sex, sex without commitment, sex to escape the pressure. At the heart of this sexual overload is the popular lie that sex is an answer for our larger human needs and pressures."[3]

Even though we are surrounded by sexual stimuli, we respond to it because of another reason. That reason, basically, is depravity. We are people who by nature are attracted to sin; we are interested in things that are un-Godlike and we are self-centered and self-serving.

On July 21, 1976, Jimmy Carter made a statement that shocked the world. It was later published in *Playboy* magazine: "I've looked on a lot of women with lust. I've committed adultery in my heart many times. This is something that God recognizes I will do—and I have done it—and God forgives me for it."[4]

The problem then is not only the bombardment of sexual stimuli around us, but also that we have a nature that is attracted to it. Jimmy Carter was simply saying that even though he was President of the United States, he still had a sin nature that could be appealed to and that would respond with lust.

WHO WILL FALL?

Our personal depravity and the sexual stimuli all around us certainly are strong factors in causing affairs, but still there are people who are never involved in affairs at any time. What makes the difference?

We have found that the key word is "vulnerability." A woman becomes vulnerable through some loss in her life, physical fatigue, sickness, depression, years of singleness, divorce, or a sagging marriage. Whatever the aggravation, she becomes susceptible to an affair. She reaches out for some way to solve the desperate loneliness she feels, that lack of relatedness with another human being.

In an article entitled "The Promiscuous Woman," Maggie Scarf says, "I have noticed in my interviews that . . . a high degree of sexual wheeling and dealing appears to exist in tandem with . . . very powerfully depressive feelings. The woman's suddenly increased sexiness seems to be, in this sort of instance, a kind of antidepressant maneuvering."[5]

As we noted earlier, whenever loss occurs in life, we experience a degree of depression. If a woman has sustained a loss in her life, she very well may feel depressed and may respond by acting sexier, as if making a desperate grab to relieve the depression and loneliness she feels. The irony is that most affairs are temporary, and even though there is the initial exhilaration, the woman ends with another loss. She quite often feels a deepening sense of worthlessness and thus more depression. At first she may think the affair is an invigorating lift, but for most people it becomes a massive letdown. Then she must also struggle with guilt.

MEANINGLESS MARRIAGE

A major cause for married people getting involved in affairs is that the marriage relationship is no longer nourishing. One or both partners don't put enough into the relationship to make it a true marriage. They are still legally married, but nothing exists in the relationship between them.

Lewis Smedes calls this "negative fidelity." He says "a man or woman can be just too busy, too tired, too timid, too prudent, too hemmed-in with fear to be seriously tempted by an adulterous affair. But this same person can be a bore at home. . . . "[6]

The hundreds of unfaithful married people with whom we have worked almost always have had a neglected marriage which created vulnerability for an affair. Remember that affairs seldom start with a deep commitment to the third person or because of a search for sexual involvement. They start with two people who are vulnerable because of needs in their lives.

Some people—even some intelligent marriage counselors—suggest that an extramarital involvement should not be criticized because it quite often will stimulate the marriage and restore some of its lost luster. While it may be true that there is much good food to be found in the garbage dump, that isn't where we choose to have our wedding anniversary dinner! A few marriages may be helped by an affair, but for every one that is helped, we see dozens, scores, perhaps hundreds, that are broken or at least severely damaged, with great loss to the people involved.

THE DANGER SIGNS OF AN AFFAIR

"I'm a thirty-six-year-old woman and a director of Christian education. I never dreamed of being involved in an affair, but it all began when I went to a four-week course of training without my family. During those four weeks I often chatted with one of my classmates named Bruce. He was so easy to talk to, understanding, highly intelligent, and a very sensitive person. Sometimes, just to get away from the pressure of studies, we would take a walk together and talk about philosophies and interests, but he never made a pass at me. It was beautiful, it was innocent, and it was refreshingly honest.

"At the end of four weeks we were invited by an engaged couple to go to a movie to celebrate the completion of our course. After the movie, the four of us drove around and laughed and talked together. We stopped near a lake and the engaged couple drifted into their own world of hugging and kissing.

"I don't even remember what I was talking about at the time, but I do remember being stopped in midsentence by Bruce kissing me. He later remarked that 'I didn't know I was going to do that until I was doing it.' I was surprised and thrilled. I told Bruce that was awfully nice. So we did it again, several times, to the chimes of encouragement from the back seat.

"But all good things must come to an end, and the time came when we had to return to campus. Bruce let the three of us out near the dormitory, and I waited for him while he parked the car. Since there were few students, we were all housed in the same building, with men on the first two floors and women on the third. When we reached the second floor landing, we gave each other a good night kiss. Then another and another with increasingly more body pressure.

" 'Chris, let's go to my room,' he proposed.

" 'We can't do that; I've got to go upstairs,' I said. Another kiss.

"Bruce insisted, 'We can't say good night now.'

" 'I know we can't, but we're going to have to anyway.' Another kiss, and he led me through the door to the hall, then into his room.

"I said, 'Let's just sit and talk awhile.' He moved in closer. 'What about Marie (his wife)?' I asked.

" 'Marie's not here.'

"I raised a couple of other objections. . . .

"I have never been loved so sweetly, tenderly, or have I ever felt such a desire to respond . . . I know that I didn't want to leave. . . .

"But the next morning, after a hug and a hand shake, we and all the other students, went our separate directions. . . ."

There were obvious signs of vulnerability that each of these people were aware of but chose to ignore. There were needs in both of their lives. Both of their marriages were unfulfilling, and each of them was using Christian ministry as a way to provide meaning in their lives and to ignore the stress in their marriages.

LONELINESS BREEDS RATIONALIZATION

They were both lonely. Back home they had a network of friends and associates who filled the gap that was being left by their poor marriage relationships. These friends and associates also provided stability so that their marriages were not threatened. In this conference situation, away from home, they didn't have that network of friends, and they could easily be victimized by Satan. In fact, they were so deceived by Satan that they believed wrong was right. "Woe to those who . . . say that what is right is wrong, and what is wrong is right; that black is white and white is black; bitter is sweet and sweet is bitter" (Isaiah 5:20).

Chris speaks of a later time when she and Bruce once more got together. Again, the meeting was related to church duties. This time Bruce was serving Communion. She says, "There was such love in his eyes as he offered me our Lord's body and blood that I knew beyond all else that the Lord was with us and would continue to be. Never have I been so close to seeing Jesus face to face as I was on that evening."

These two vulnerable people experienced what many others have—that Satan will attack us at the weakest point of our lives and he comes, as the Scripture says, as an angel of light, convincing us that what he has for us is good and intended only for our growth and pleasure.

Another danger sign was their common interests. They could rationalize that they belonged together because they thought so much alike. They had so much in common. It was also easy for them to have opportunities to be together that appeared quite legitimate because of their common interests.

COMPULSIVE IMPULSES

Another danger sign was their compulsive thought life. After they returned to their separate ministries, they couldn't quit thinking about each other. Chris continues, "One day early in September, I impulsively called him at his church office. It was then that he suggested we write to each other, and soon after that, a letter came: 'You have no idea the explosion that took place in my solar plexus when I heard your voice on the phone . . . I feel like an adolescent boy must feel, and I like the feeling, even though it scares me, for all the obvious reasons as well as some I haven't even admitted to myself yet.'

"Soon we were writing at least once a day and conversing on the phone twice a week. We talked of our trip around the world, fantasizing that we'd set up housekeeping on a South Sea island. Through our letters we grew to know and love each other more. We tried to limit our telephone conversations to an hour, but weren't always successful!"

The compulsive thought life and actions that focus on the partner in the affair are very obvious danger signs that should throw up red flags as signals to stop and change directions.

If you wonder if you're having an affair, ask yourself some hard questions. Can I stop thinking of this person? Is there a compulsion to contact him, to be with him? Do I plan my day's activities so that our paths will cross? If you're responding "yes" to any of these questions, you're in trouble. You're already deeply committed. You are already in an affair, whether it has become physical or not.

SMALL STEPS—BIG CHANGES

Another danger sign is the small steps that soon become giant shifts in values. This couple started with very casual talking and walking, then they moved to deeper conversational sharing of their lives. They crossed over an emotional bridge when they responded to the invitation to go to the movie. Now they were thinking of themselves as a couple. They crossed another bridge when, with the emotional excitement of the couple necking in the back seat, he reached over and impulsively kissed her. It wasn't a big step from where they were, but it was a huge step from where they started.

The good night kiss was another emotional bridge and another danger sign. That kiss wasn't very far from the kiss in the car, but neither was it very far from sex in his bed a few minutes later.

Listen to the danger signals. Look carefully at the signs. You start out thinking you're going to just innocently meet a few of your needs and you end up forgetting who you are—a child of God.

We question why—with all the obvious danger signs—they didn't stop. The answer is that they did recognize the signs but they chose at each new decision point not to stop. ". . . at some point along the way each individual is fully aware of what's happening and how he or she urges it on, creating the conditions for its continuance. From that point on each one bears responsibility for the developing interaction."[7]

MISCONCEPTIONS ABOUT AFFAIRS

1. "Everyone's doing it." The February 1983 *Ladies Home Journal* reports that 79 percent of the 83,000 women who responded to their questionnaire have never had an affair.[8] Our own studies among Christian women indicate that 80 percent of the women that we surveyed had never been involved in an affair. Obviously, everyone is not doing it.

A 1975 *Redbook* questionnaire and a 1979 *Cosmopolitan* survey both reported significantly higher statistics,[9] which may indicate a difference of readership or that America's conservative element is now becoming more vocal in national polls.

2. "It's possible to separate sex and love." "The argument that sex can be detached from love and marriage is simply not backed up by the biological, psychological, and anthropological evidence. In infancy, we first learn to associate creature comfort and sensuous good feeling with love, and the connection is ineradicably imprinted upon us. As adults, we may be capable at times of having sexual experiences—even, indeed, powerful ones—without any emotional attachment to the partner, but this is the exception, not the rule. The normal tendency—and it has been true in most human societies, not just our own—is for intense sexual experiences to generate emotional ties, and for powerful emotional feelings to arouse sexual desire. That's why the history of extra-marital behavior is filled with stories of a mere romp turning into a great love affair that damages or destroys the marriage."[10]

3. "An affair will meet the need caused by loneliness." It is true that an affair may change the loneliness in the short run. But it *is* something *extra*marital. It is a temporary solution. People fantasize that this temporary solution can be a lifelong satisfaction, but for that to happen the people having the affair must make sure they do not get emotionally involved. "People who function best in a system of sex without intimacy are generally those who have not developed their capacity for feeling in the first place."[11]

Truly solving loneliness requires a deep sharing of lives through the multifaceted experiences of life. That depth and width of sharing cannot be accomplished by a clandestine affair. Ultimately the affair breaks up and the woman is confronted again with her loneliness.

4. "Affairs are fun." Maslow says, "There's a marvelous incandescence. It blinds people to their lovers' faults and reminds them of the days when they were young and carefree.

". . . Then the glow wears off and the real world starts to intrude. People appear more perfect when you don't have to get along with them daily or share the stresses of married life. If the circumstances were reversed, a spouse could easily be as exciting as a lover, and a lover as boring and predictable as a spouse."[12]

5. "At last we have discovered the real thing." This is *not* the real thing. It is a false world of limited scope. Anybody can get psyched up to perform well for a few minutes, hours, or days, but the real world is living day after day in an uptight world with stress and pressure and not enough money and time to go around.

The affair is an artificial world which cuts you off from your friends. If you are involved in an affair, have you taken this guy over to meet your mom yet? Does your Bible study group know about him? And how do you explain to your sixteen-year-old daughter, who wants to run around braless in tight tank tops, that she shouldn't do that, but that it's OK for you to have an extramarital affair?

6. "An affair will strengthen my marriage." This distorted philosophy has been preached by many and even published in a book, *Open Marriage,* by the O'Neill husband-wife team. But our observations and those of other counselors[13] indicate that affairs do not strengthen marriage; in fact, they cause marriages to break.

The philosophies advocated in *Open Marriage* and in another book, *Thy Neighbor's Wife,* have been believed by many, but the believers also have experienced the same sad results as the couples whose broken marriages are recorded in *Thy Neighbor's Wife.*[14]

PROHIBITIONS AGAINST AFFAIRS

Why is it that the Scripture is so negative about affairs? Why, when this new romance may provide relief from monotony, emptiness, loneliness, boredom, restlessness, even depression? Why criticize the affair, when the benefits seem so positive?

In many places the Bible says very simply and directly, "You shall not commit adultery." (For examples, see Exodus 20:14, Matthew 5:27, Matthew 19:18, Mark 10:19, Romans 2:22, Romans 13:9, James 2:11.)

The biblical prohibition against adultery has a bigger meaning than simply "thou shalt not." The commandment is intended to protect the family, to keep it united and intact. Adultery is forbidden in order to minimize the spiraling effects of insecurity caused in children whose parents are having affairs or have divorced.

NO WOMAN IS AN ISLAND

Leanne was in her first year of college when she heard that her mother had left home and was living in an apartment with another man. How could her mother do this to her? Leanne was filled with anger and rage and painful disillusionment that a Christian mother would do this. Her parents' marriage had seemed so good; how could this happen?

Leanne dropped out of college and came home to keep house for her father and to comfort him in his tremendous loss. The kids chose up sides. The two younger ones identified with the mother. The older daughter identified with her father. Now there was war—not only between the parents, but also between the parents and children and among the children.

The same conflict and turmoil was going on in the other man's home, involving him, his wife, and their teenage children. The two having the affair had never counted on all of this disruption, pain, and damage in their families. They thought they could just meet a few personal needs.

SO RIGHT—SO WRONG

Another reason for the strong scriptural prohibitions against adultery is that the people in the affairs themselves are damaged. But how could anything so wonderful be so tremendously damaging?

Chris and Bruce, the Christian workers who had fallen in love, continued to write and call each other. Finally, they were asked by the engaged couple who had been at the four-week training seminar to participate in their marriage. Chris writes, "Bruce met my plane. We laughed and kissed. We drew smiles and stares from others in the airport, which didn't bother either of us. We drove to a motel near the church where the wedding would take place the next day. He came around the car, opened the door for me, and said, 'I didn't ask you if I should get a double room or two singles or what,' and he kissed me. 'You didn't answer my question.' Another kiss.

" 'Yes, I did,' I said.

"And so we got a double room. I remember little of the flight home except for a kind stewardess bringing me a cup of coffee as I sat quietly crying. Bruce told me later that the closer he got to his home, the more slowly he drove, postponing the inevitable. But it was back to work, to more letters, to more phone calls, planning the next times to be together."

THE CONFRONTATION

"Finally another woman who became aware of our affair told us of her intention to tell Bruce's wife. At this point Bruce decided to leave his wife and I decided to leave my family. We drove together to his home. He packed some of his personal things, left his wife and each of his children a message, and then we made the long trip to my home. By the time we arrived, his wife and son were there also. They had discovered where I lived and had chartered a plane to get there by the time that we did.

"In spite of the confrontation, it did not alter our plans. What did happen is that we decided to drive back to his home town so that he could care for his family. He assured me that everything was all right. His son was making housing arrangements for the family since they would, of course, have to leave the parsonage. We checked into a motel and spent the afternoon discussing housing locations for ourselves and checking out possible jobs for both of us. By the time Bruce left in the early evening to meet with the church officials, he seemed very distant, and I was literally shaking with anxiety.

"When he returned to the motel a couple of hours later, my world disintegrated. 'Chris,' he said, 'you know that I love you very, very much.'

" 'Of course, sweetheart, I love you too,' I said.

" 'And you know that I love God very much,' he declared.

"My reply was, 'I couldn't love you if you didn't love God.'

"Then began a rambling discourse about all the guilt he was suddenly feeling . . . maybe it was the way he was raised . . . his anguish over what he had done to both of us. On and on and on. The conclusion was that he could not fulfill his commitment to me but intended to hole up in a room someplace and find a job that paid enough to live on. And what was I to do, having resigned my job and taken leave of my family? I didn't know."

THE AFFAIR FALLS APART

"Thus began several months of pure hell which I'm not sure are finished yet. The tears that began that night did not cease at all for ten days. They flowed like water being poured from a pitcher. I took a bus back to my home town, not so much because I wanted to go there, but because I did not know what else to do. More like a zombie than a human being, I moved through the next few days until my husband and a pastor friend checked me into the psychiatric ward of a local hospital.

"I really didn't care whether I lived or died, but if I could have made a choice, it definitely would have been for death. I could neither eat nor sleep. I had staked my life on the gift God gave me in Bruce, and now that gift was no longer mine.

"The letters and phone calls continued through February. That was a month of anguish for him as his sixteen-year-old daughter announced her pregnancy. He and his family moved to another state to help their daughter through the pregnancy, and our communication stopped. Not an hour passes when he is not on my mind with both love and pain. Meanwhile I have no choice but to continue to go through the motions of living. . . . Indeed life is hell."

The strong scriptural prohibitions against adultery are to protect us from personal hurt and our families from disintegration. The restrictions are intended to prevent damage that spreads like the ever-widening rings when a stone is dropped into a quiet pool of water. Yes, the prohibitions may seem to be going against human need at the time, but in fact, the wisdom is based on human need—long-term human need.

It's important to point out that being sexually attracted to a man is not a violation of the scriptural teaching to not commit adultery. But remember that there are many little steps between the tempting thought that crosses your mind and the actual acts that are so damaging. Jesus carefully warned not to commit adultery with someone in your heart. In other words, don't think you can play the game of committing adultery in the playground of your mind without it some day becoming a reality that you act out.

AFFAIR PREVENTION AND RECOVERY

Affairs tend to take three different directions. There are the one-night stands, somewhat like a spontaneous eruption of sexual passion, which are later confessed. Corrections are made, and the marriage continues.

The second type is the extended affair which lasts perhaps three to six months. Then there is a return to the marriage, usually because the affair is seen in a more realistic light and because the married partners try to work at marriage restoration.

The third type of affair breaks the marriage. This generally involves the husband's discovering his wife's infidelity, his becoming angry, kicking her out, and suing for divorce. All of the messy custody and property division battles are a painful result.

TIMES TO BEWARE

To help prevent affairs, we need to consider when they are most likely. We have discovered from our research that the late twenties and the late thirties currently are likely times for women to experience affairs. The following list of change events might also alert you to times to be especially on guard:

• Pregnancy or childbirth
• Times of bereavement
• Accident or extended illness of a child or a mate
• A job change
• The beginning or ending of a career
• Extensive travel
• Depression because of failure or loss
• Elation because of success
• Quiet Nest time (children all in school)
• Empty Nest time (children gone from the home)

In short, any major change event that alters your psychological or spiritual balance is likely to cause you to need deep emotional caring. If you don't receive this caring through normal, legitimate channels, such as from your mate, family, and/or friends, then you may find that you become vulnerable to an affair.

Affair prevention not only involves being aware of our

potentially vulnerable time, but it also demands that we understand our life needs and then seek to meet those needs through legitimate channels. If you need adventure and some pizzazz in your life, take steps to bring that about, but do it through relationships and activities that are morally and psychologically proper.

GARBAGE IN—GARBAGE OUT

To prevent affairs you need to look carefully into your thought life. It may sound like that old conservative line, but it's common information in the computer industry: GIGO—garbage in, garbage out. What you put into your life and mind is going to come back out. You receive hours of exposure to all kinds of sexual stimuli every day. How much time do you spend in the Scriptures and in quiet meditation with God, allowing him to counteract some of the cultural impact?

Affair prevention also means that you think through your values as you continue to move along through life. What really is important to you? Work toward those goals and values that are truly significant and high on your priority list. Don't allow yourself to be trapped into an affair because you've not been carefully defining your values.

Get into a regular Bible study and sharing group where people are opening themselves to God and to each other and are becoming a mutual support network for what is happening in life. You may not feel comfortable to say to the group, "I'm really being tempted by this attractive guy in church." But you may be able to say to them, "You know, I have some special needs in my life right now—the kids are all off at school, I'm working at a job I don't really like, and I just don't feel I'm as close to people as I need to be." A good small group will fill some of those gaps and will help to diffuse some of your vulnerability toward an affair.

Commit yourself to one female friend and ask her to pray for you and to hold you accountable. If you are especially vulnerable right now, ask this trusted friend to support you by asking how you are doing and to pray for you day by day, asking God for the necessary internal healing.

SMALL STEPS TO START—AND STOP
Remember that affairs start with small steps. To prevent them you also need to take small steps. An affair starts with your need, but it ends with your forgetting who you are. Daily make those small decisions to reduce vulnerability, to strengthen your spiritual and emotional life, and to build a strong support network. If you're married, work on your marriage relationship. Turn down the offers, innuendos, and jokes that may come your way from needy men who are testing to see if you are willing to respond to them in an affair.

Make those decisions daily. You may say, "I don't *want* to make the decisions. I don't want to turn down the flattering care and concern that I'm getting from this man." Then, take the step that you *can* take, which is to ask God to make you *willing* to make the decisions.

Cindy, now thirty-five, gave us the details of her story, a typical scenario of a career woman who had been involved with a married man. The affair had followed the usual sky-rocket beginning, leveling off, and crashing conclusion.

She said she was not really able to let go until she finally prayed, "Lord, take him out of my life and help me not to need him." It was at that point that God began to move him from her and to change the need structure in her life so that she was emotionally able to walk away.

It's not easy to pray that prayer, especially when a person seems so significant to you, but you *must!* An affair is an illegitimate relationship that is unhealthy, emotionally and spiritually, for everybody who's involved in it or because of it. Don't let your needs cause you to forget who you are.

DIVORCE

Many women feel that the way to escape a troubled marriage is through divorce. However, divorce does not usually turn out to be the satisfying solution hoped for.

Morton Hunt reports, "Some years ago . . . I interviewed some 200 people and conducted a questionnaire survey of nearly 400 others; since then . . . I have interviewed many hundreds more. Of them all, I can recall only a handful who did not suffer considerable pain as the result of the marital breakup; many suffered intensely, some to the point of attempting suicide."[15]

The movement toward a divorce is also a progression of small steps. You aren't happily married one day, and the next day, without cause, decide to get divorced. Instead, as in building a brick wall, one painful problem, or brick, is put into the wall and then another and another.

Many women who consider divorce have already gone through some of the earlier stages, such as running away to escape the unpleasantness of their marriages, or being involved in affairs to meet some of their needs. Others have not run away or had affairs but have had many problems in their marriages so that, one way or another, brick walls have been erected.

A surge of divorces has occurred in the middle years. The rate has increased more rapidly among mid-life people than among younger couples. In 1964 the number of divorces granted to persons aged forty-five and older was 164,000; in 1974 it had doubled to 315,000; and in 1980 the rate stood at 1,817,382. In the thirty-five to forty-four age group the number divorced has increased by nearly 60 percent in the past two decades.[16] Some experts are projecting that during the eighties we will see one in every two marriages affected by divorce among the people who live beyond age forty-five.[17]

GAIN AND LOSS

If you're in a painful marriage, your normal human response is to want to reduce the pain, to get away from it. But when you think about a divorce, somehow you have to grab yourself and reasonably think through, "What would I gain and what would I lose?"

Let's look at some of the losses. One woman said, "I have learned the hard way that when I got a divorce I didn't only lose a husband, I lost a whole way of life."[18] Divorce means a whole *change of lifestyle*. Usually, finances are reduced; two separate family units will try to survive on the same general income that they had as one. There's also a loss of the history that you've built with your family, friends, and relatives, especially if you're the one who wants the divorce.

"Very often the divorce, once achieved, sets off a chain reaction with one or both of the individuals concerned. The temporary release may suddenly give way to second thoughts, which lead to many self-doubts and uncertainties about the wisdom of the action which was taken. This, in turn, can lead to the feeling that perhaps a mistake has been made, and it may cause the now self-tormented ex-husband or ex-wife to start making efforts to reconciliations. Sometimes it is too late for the rejected spouse is remarried."[19]

When you total up the losses, be sure to include *loneliness*. You may think your present marriage is difficult, but if you file for divorce and move out, you may find yourself in a very lonely apartment with only TV for company.

The losses must include potential *emotional damage* to you. For example, among Caucasians, those who are divorced have the highest suicide rate.[20] The loneliness can become extremely grinding. One divorced woman writes, "No, I don't miss him—but I do miss having *someone*. And there is no one. Where does one look, at my age, for intelligence, humor, and compassion? Not where I used to look. And I don't know where else to go instead. I believe I have grown immensely. I feel capable of a loving, loyal, dependable relationship—and yet I have not even dated in months! There *must* be someone. I can only wait and hope."[21]

Let's suppose you've had a rotten marriage. Perhaps you've tried leaving a couple of times and it didn't work. Now you finally are in an affair with someone who really loves you, and on the basis of that love, you have decided to get divorced. As you total up the potential losses, it's important to remember that *very few people marry the person* with whom they had an affair before they were divorced.

Morton Hunt found that "only about one-tenth of his interviewees had married, or were planning to marry, the person with whom he or she had an affair. . . . Whereas the romance may have thrived in relation to the intolerable marriage, the dissolution of the marriage forces the spouse and new partner into a new intimacy which causes a new strain. One woman and man who did marry each other had trouble shortly after their wedding and then broke up. His periods of silent withdrawal led her to doubt the validity of his accusations about his first wife and to think that maybe he had shut her out rather than vice versa, as he had said."[22]

We also have known some similar situations and occasionally hear from one or more of the persons involved in such marriages. Lynne, Henry, and Marilyn are an illustration. We knew Lynne and Henry before Henry and Marilyn began having an affair. We had little contact with Henry, but we had a friendship with Lynne through several Christian organizations. We had never met Marilyn, but knew that she was a lonely divorcée whose path daily crossed Henry's. Lynne shared her agony with us after she learned of the affair, and we worked with her for some time in trying to restore her relationship with Henry. But Henry, who was deep into a mid-life crisis, resolutely went about divorcing Lynne and married Marilyn. Neither Henry nor Marilyn knew much about our being involved in trying to help Lynne.

About eighteen months after the second wedding, we received a call from Marilyn who had by this time learned of our work with mid-life people. She felt Henry was in mid-life crisis. She gave her story, unaware that we knew of it from Lynne's side. When she and Henry had "fallen in love," Henry had painted a miserable picture of Lynne, showing her to be incompetent, insecure, and uninterested in meeting his needs or in doing simple household tasks. He complained that she would often spend the whole day in bed, not functioning at all as a wife and mother. "Now," sobbed Marilyn, a formerly strong, capable career woman, "his behavior is driving *me* to be incompetent, insecure, and uninterested in life!"

YOUR KIDS SUFFER TOO

As you total up the losses, count your children's losses. Remember, you can divorce your husband, but never a child. You may temporarily or permanently lose physical contact with your children after a divorce. At first you may not notice much because you are taken up with the excitement of your new life. However, an urgency within parent and child sooner or later erupts into a deep-seated desire to relate to his or her own flesh. Even if you have custody of the children, you have caused a deep loss for them. Your children will never have the basic family unit with their two birth parents, and they may have gigantic adjustments to make in the new situation.

SAME OLD PATTERN

You and your mate chose to marry because of needs in your lives. At the time of marriage, you may not have fully understood each other, but you felt an unconscious attraction to each other. You chose each other on the basis of your needs at that time in your lives. The frightening thing about divorce and the possibility of remarriage is that *you are likely to choose the same kind of person* again unless you have grown a great deal. Unless you understand why you chose your first mate and how you contributed to that first marriage breakup, divorce will not remove future emotional stresses in a new marriage. Out of the first marriage you carry yourself and your own set of needs. Any emotional problems that you have now will probably continue to cause you problems in a future marriage.

IS THE MID-LIFE DIVORCE NECESSARY?

We are in touch with hundreds of mid-life couples whose marriages are in trouble. Some of them, unfortunately, have been told by Christian counselors or pastors that they might as well just give up and separate. You or your husband may be going through mid-life crisis, everything around you may seem unstable and causing you great stress, and your relationship may not seem as meaningful as when you were dating, but that does not mean you should opt for a divorce. We are firmly convinced that many mid-life divorces are unnecessary. Spouses give up on each other and themselves too quickly. If they would hang on a little longer, they could make it through this difficult time.

Sometimes a person will come for counsel, saying that the mate wants out of the marriage but he or she wants to keep it. One of the early questions that we ask is, "Are you really willing to put up with a great deal of stress and do a lot of personal growing and changing over the next three to five years?" To restore a troubled mid-life marriage, somebody has to be willing to commit a lot of energy and time to saving it.

If you happen to be the one who wants to run from your marriage, we'd like to encourage you to hang on for three to five years. Don't just suffer and struggle, but take some specific direction that will change your marriage from being a drag to being a real source of strength.

MARRIAGE RESTORATION

Dr. Paul Meier, a Christian psychiatrist, says, "Out of all the vast array of psychiatric patients that I see (ranging from childhood schizophrenics to senile patients with organic brain syndromes), marital conflict patients are the easiest to help and the most rewarding to work with."[23]

He further points out that incompatibility is too often used as an excuse to leave the marriage. He says, "I can honestly and emphatically say that this excuse is no more than a cop-out used by couples who are too proud and lazy to work out their own hangups. Instead of facing them, they run away by divorcing and remarrying. Then there are four miserable people instead of just two."[24]

Les and Beverly were an attractive mid-life couple whom I had not met before. They had just seated themselves in my (Jim's) office when they explained in very direct terms that if I couldn't help them, they were going to get a divorce. They went on with their blunt explanation that this was their last try.

They said they had read all of the recent marriage manuals and books and listed dozens of titles. They had been through Marriage Encounter and other couple-retreat weekends, plus almost a year of professional counseling, and they still couldn't stand each other.

They explained that before they were married, they couldn't keep their hands off each other. They spent end-

less hours together and would do almost anything just to be with each other a few more minutes. Now, when they were in bed together, they found it repulsive if they inadvertently bumped each other.

Their communication, sex life, and casual talking had essentially dried up. Their marriage was a day-by-day endurance contest. They said they were completely incompatible but that some Christian friends urged them to come to see me.

The first response racing around in my mind was, "Why me? Why not go talk to somebody else? If I don't pull off a miracle and save your marriage, then it'll be my fault." I didn't say that aloud, but I wanted to.

What I did say to them was that I refused to take the responsibility for their marriage breakup or for this counseling session unless they were willing to become active participants. They agreed that during this session they would really work.

THE OLD GLEAM

We talked about two basic matters that hour. The first was what had attracted them to each other years before. Each one of them responded and listed the things that had been so compelling. I found it interesting to see their eyes light up and to watch their little smirks as they recalled their clandestine meetings and the magic and magnetism that had drawn them together.

Next, I had each one tell what was irritating about the other now. The response of each was one of shock and surprise. "You mean that really bothers you?" "Wow, that's such a little thing, I didn't think you ever thought about that." "I didn't realize that was important to you."

The problem was that they had forgotten what had so strongly attracted them to each other, and now they were magnifying a pile of little irritations that became a growing wedge between the two of them. They agreed to make

some small changes in themselves and in their habits and to come to see me again in two weeks.

KEY TO A LOCKED DOOR

They came back with some apprehension, but now they had had a few successes. They had experienced a number of failures, but some of the modifications were starting to work. They didn't see each other in quite as bad a light as before.

During the second session I probed for more irritations, and now some of the real ones started to surface. They were little things that had been swept under the rug for so long that they had become giant bumps.

I had noticed that Beverly would never let Les talk for himself. I would ask him a question and she would always respond. He never got to speak or to express his own feelings. She was always there, the helpful *mother.*

I decided to be fairly direct and told her that when I asked him a question I did not want her to answer for him. When I said that to her, suddenly Les became a new person. He came out of his shell and began to interact in ways that he had not done with her for years. It was as if a key had unlocked the door of communication between them.

As the session went along, I sensed that his traveling job was more than a way to make money; it was a way to escape from her. I looked at him and told him my gut reaction. His face turned white, Beverly jumped in immediately and said, "You know, I've always thought that."

Now the door was ajar for communication, for rethinking his work, for building on the strengths of their past, and eliminating some of the negatives in their current lives.

They came back two weeks later. We continued to work on the basic areas that we had already uncovered, and then I asked them to begin affirming each other at least three times a day. Each was to thank and appreciate the

other, not so much for what that one did as for who he or she was. If he appreciated her because she cooked a fine meal, that was for something she did. If he appreciated her because she was a tender, sympathetic, and caring woman, that was for qualities in her life. Both kinds of affirmation were important, but the qualities of the other one would be more enduring and basic to self-esteem than his or her activities.

After their sixth appointment with me, I didn't see them again until we met unexpectedly in a shopping mall a few months later. They were walking with their arms around each other, acting as if they were newlyweds who couldn't stand being apart. Grinning widely, they told me they had fallen in love with each other again.

REMEMBER, THEY'RE ALL MEN

Sally and I have watched a number of bad marriages be renewed. Yours can experience the same kind of restoration too. Remember that God wants it to work. Also, you should realize that if you do get divorced, you may not find anything better.

"In Fellini's movie *Juliet of the Spirits*, Juliet is unable to allow herself to be seduced by a young and handsome man, and she protects herself from it by having a religious vision. '. . . maybe it's just that the flesh is willing but the spirit's weak, because if you really want the truth, I looked around at what was available and as far as I could see, it would only mean changing the middle-aged bore I already have for somebody else who'll be just as middle-aged and no less boring.' "[25]

WHAT ABOUT REMARRIAGE?

Some of you are saying, "Well, that really sounds great. I wish I had had some solid marriage counseling when my marriage was falling apart. But the reality is that my marriage did fall apart and I'm already divorced. Now what about marrying again?"

For people considering remarriage, several things need to be remembered. First, thoroughly *understand why you married your first partner,* what needs attracted you to him, and why that marriage fell apart. You need to come fully to the point where you can recognize your fault and his, without blaming it all on him. He was not entirely at fault.

Sometimes people say, "Well, he went out and had an affair so the marriage broke up." The question still remains as to why he had an affair. What part did you have in contributing to an atmosphere that made him vulnerable to an affair?

It will be extremely helpful for you to discuss with a close friend, professional counselor, or your pastor, exactly why you got married and why the marriage collapsed so you have a full understanding of who you are and your part in the marriage collapse.

Second, *confess to God your part* in the marriage collapse. Ask him to forgive you, but more than that, ask him to heal you. Ask God to help you grow so that the same error is not repeated.

Suppose that you've identified your fault as being that of a perfectionist who demands much from people and pushes them to the brink of their endurance by repeated nagging. Now that you've identified your part in the marriage breakup, if that's what it was, ask God over the period of the next year or so to help you to mature so that problem will not taint a future marriage.

Third, *allow sufficient time to elapse* between your divorce and any future remarriage. You need a minimum of a year to work through some of the growth process that has to take place in your life and to allow for some of the things to settle down from your past. Don't start looking for another mate until a year has gone by. That doesn't mean that you shouldn't have companionship and friendships. But it does mean that you need to commit yourself to allowing this amount of time to elapse so you can be healed and not make a hasty jump into another marriage. If you move too fast, you will probably unconsciously choose someone very similar to your first husband and thus set up the circumstances for a second divorce.

A side observation: If you've been involved in an affair or an off-and-on-dating relationship with someone before your marriage broke up, remember that the statistics say it's probably not going to work. Our clear, direct advice to you is, "Do not marry anybody with whom you've had an affair before your divorce or anybody with whom you get involved in the first six months to a year after your divorce."

Fourth, *know that your loneliness will make you extremely vulnerable.* Even though you don't feel like it, try to expand the circle of friends you can depend on. The temptation will be to lean on one or two people and then feel guilty when you wear them out. Get into a small Bible study and sharing group and give those people an opportunity to support you during this transition as you heal from the divorce.

Fifth, remember that *God loves you.* You may feel very crummy, unlovable, and worthless. Christians around you may try to reinforce what a "bad girl" you are, but remember that God loves you. He wants you restored and healed and growing.

When you wonder whether or not he loves you, think of this promise from Psalm 89: "If his children forsake my laws and don't obey them, then I will punish them, but I will never completely take away my lovingkindness from them, nor let my promise fail. No, I will not break my covenant; I will not take back one word of what I said" (Psalm 89:30-34).

PART V
EXCITED
ABOUT
SUCCEEDING

Chapter Fourteen

KEEPING UP WITH LIFE'S CLOCKS

Rebecca, who had just turned thirty-six, was crying as she shared with us her feelings about her recent miscarriage. She had been six months into the pregnancy. Once more questions were raised in her mind. Should she try again to become a mother? Was it too late for her? Should she continue with her career? These very painful questions had been handled more than a year ago. Now they were resurrected and crying out for answers all over again.

Rebecca had gone straight through college with her sights clearly fixed on a business career. Dating was only casual for social contact, and marriage was not programmed for her life schedule until she was in her late twenties.

She finished her degree, took a responsible position in a growing firm, and started to climb the corporate ladder. She advanced quickly, and in some ways seemed ahead of her life schedule. Young men her age viewed her with some degree of suspicion and jealousy, and their attitudes tended to keep her more socially isolated. She continued to date casually until at age twenty-nine she met Chad.

They married when she was thirty, and Chad was willing for her to continue her career. In fact, he was pleased to see her becoming successful as she moved up the business ladder.

When she became a vice-president at age thirty-four, she felt an exhilarating sense of accomplishment. Yet she began to feel a desire to slow down the frantic corporate race and to look at some other values. It was then that she and Chad decided to have a child, but unfortunately she had miscarried in the sixth month.

As we talked, the issue that kept recurring was, "I didn't know this was going to happen to me. When I was in my early twenties, I only wanted a career in my life. I did not want children. All of my energies went toward that career through my twenties and half of my thirties. Then suddenly this change has come. I feel very mixed up. Part of me wants to press on to become president of some corporation—to make a real mark in the business world. But the other part of me, that I never realized I had before, wants to be a mother and a homemaker. I don't know what it is—maybe I'm thinking about getting old. Maybe what I really want is to have children and grandchildren who will be there when I'm an old lady. Maybe I just want to leave something more of me in the world than an impact in business. Whatever it is, I didn't expect it to happen to me. I wish someone had told me."

CHANGE? NOT ME!

Hundreds of men and women have shared with us the anxiety of wishing that they had been better prepared to face the middle years. Young adults are a little curious about what might happen in mid-life, but they really don't think there is going to be any value change in their lives. They believe that the mid-life adults who are wrestling with various life issues are inadequate persons who never have had the grip on life that they, the young adults, think they have.

What is it that causes a woman like Rebecca, who had

staunchly declared from adolescence up to mid-life that she did not plan to be a mother, suddenly to make a sharp turn-around and have a desire for children? Why is it that an eighteen-year-old girl and a twenty-two-year-old young woman look at a dating relationship so very differently? Why does a twenty-year-old married woman usually not feel panic if she is not a mother, whereas a childless woman who passes thirty or thirty-five may begin to wrestle seriously with a new set of desires about mothering?

Adults are exceedingly complex, and many researchers and writers over the years have been trying to put their finger on exactly what causes these changes. Researchers such as Charlotte Bühler, who started in the 1930s, Erikson, Havighurst, Kohlberg, Neugarten, Lowenthal, Gould, Levinson, and Knox, among others, have been examining adult development to learn what happens in adult life. As we learn more about the *what* and *why* of changes, adults can be forewarned and able to take appropriate steps to prepare for various aspects of their future.

TO MATURE. . . .

Erikson's stages have been the framework around which many other researchers have worked. He proposes eight stages of development from infancy through late adulthood. Five of the stages are to be completed by adolescence. Early adulthood development then deals with "intimacy," the appropriate giving and receiving of love; middle adulthood settles the issue of "generativity," which is leaving something positive for the world after you are gone; and late adulthood development must handle the task of "integrity," a basic acceptance of one's life as appropriate and meaningful.[1]

As the theory of adult development has progressed, it has tended to become more age related, meaning that certain kinds of things are predicted to happen to you as you reach certain ages. The problem is that human beings are too complex for a simple age-specific theory. We're also finding that people who may not follow normal societal life patterns seem to relate quite differently to life. Therefore, to tie all adult changes to age will not enable us to account for the great variety of human experience.

DIFFERENT LIFE SCHEDULES

A second problem is that men have been the main focus of most adult development study. Some of the studies have then assumed that women are similar. This is not true, however. For example, quite often a woman in her forties and fifties is demonstrating a great deal of assertiveness. She may start a new career and begin to exert leadership and influence in several areas, while the man in that same era of life is starting to mellow. He is focusing on more narrow horizons. She may be just taking off like a rocket while he is winding down and preparing for retirement.

We must realize that each woman is unique and must not be put into some box or category. In fact, recognizing this uniqueness will enable women to more nearly reach their full potential in life and make the kind of contribution that will be significant for them.

With all of that as a backdrop, however, we are aware of various clocks within a woman that continue to tick incessantly. Alarms go off at different times in life as these clocks tick away. The development of a woman is geared to several clocks. All of them are interrelated, and that's why we should not be too simplistic when we talk about what is happening to women at mid-life.

THE GENETIC CLOCK

This clock was set in motion when you were conceived. You carried with you at birth a whole pattern of factors that are going to influence all of your life. Your genetic inheritance determined when you would come into puberty, how difficult your monthly cycles would be, and how many years in life you would be fertile. The genetic clock also decides when your hair will turn gray and when those wrinkles around your eyes and mouth will begin to form.

The genetic clock is a given. To some degree you can control your weight and size, but your genetic clock tells your body when and how to shift weight off your limbs toward your torso. Therefore, as you progress through life, certain processes in you will continue regardless of what you might do to slow them down or alter them.

THE AGE CLOCK

On each birthday your age clock goes off. When you were a little kid it went off with bells and whistles. When you were a teenager, it was sirens. But as you move into the mid-years, you may find that your age clock is tolling slow, deep gongs like a lonely bell in an empty churchyard.

Obviously, an interrelationship exists between the genetic clock and the age clock. As we talk about other clocks, you'll see that they also are interrelated.

The age clock causes each year to have meaning for you and every year to have a history of its own. Each year not only says something about the past, but crossing that milestone also says something about your future.

What's the difference between being thirty-nine years and 364 days old or being forty years old? One day! You haven't changed that much biologically, but that internal age clock is saying, "You have crossed over into another world."

From childhood on, you have been looking at various markers and placing a certain significance on them. "Wow, when I get to be five. . . ." or "When I get to be sixteen or twenty-one or thirty-two." Whatever the markers, you designate a special meaning to those particular years. When you're in the early part of life, you're looking forward to the markers because something new and exciting is going to happen. But as people think of the years after thirty, they usually associate those years with losses.

I (Jim) remember that when I was about sixteen I said to my dad that people over thirty were essentially dead mentally, ought not to be trusted, and simply should be allowed to die. As an adolescent I was attributing negative qualities to life after thirty. As you can imagine, that attitude had a negative impact on me as I moved into my post-thirty years. When you consider the key marker years in your life, you may realize that the positive or negative associations you had for those points have influenced your attitudes and behaviors as you crossed them.

THE CULTURAL CLOCK

Our surrounding culture exerts pressures on us that form another clock. Culture says that at a certain age girls should start school, ride bikes, go to Girl Scouts, have boyfriends, learn to drive, go to college, move out of the parental home, get married, and have children. Different cultures around the world have different times for these events to take place, but we are conditioned to live with the clock of our culture.

The cultural clock may be saying one thing and another clock within us—for example, the genetic clock—may be saying something else. Our oldest daughter, Barbara, did not enter puberty as early as two of her close companions. These two girls could not understand why Barbara was not interested in boys but instead enjoyed walking in the fields, finding a bird's nest, or playing with a frog along a river bank.

One day these two girls came to our house with a big brown grocery bag. They marched up to Barbara's bedroom and took all the "junk" off her dresser—a bird's nest, some pretty rocks, a sling shot, her jackknife, and assorted other items in her collection. They put all these things into the bag and set it in the closet. In their place these friends put out perfume, nail polish, powder, lipstick, mascara— an array of makeup—and said to her, "We're going to make you into a lady!"

This produced a great deal of tension within Barbara. It was very clear that if she did not respond to the cultural clocking, she would lose the friendship of these two girls. But the cultural clock being enforced by these two girls was out of sync with the genetic clock within Barbara's body.

At that time we bought Barbara a record by Sammy Davis, Jr., entitled "I've Got to Be Me." We suggested that she play the record several times a day, listening carefully to the words that emphasized that she must become her own person, not what someone else expected.

Each woman will be affected differently by the cultural clock, but she must deal with it. The cultural clock is a reality and is one of the clocks that incessantly ticks and influences what happens to mid-life women. Maybe your cultural clock said that you were to marry and have children. You may have arrived at mid-life, then, having listened predominantly to this clock and perhaps having ignored some of the other clocks.

THE FAMILY CLOCK

This clock is interrelated with the cultural clock but it has a ticking that is unique. The family clock started ticking way back in your grandparents' lives. Their attitudes toward family influenced your parents and, thus, have influenced you. Yes, the family clock is influenced by the cultural clock, as well as by the other ones, but this clock tells you when you will marry, the kind of person you will marry, how many children you are to have, and how you will raise those children. It also tells you whether you as a woman will integrate marriage and a career, and how you will handle being an aunt, cope with the empty nest, and respond to being a grandparent.

The family clock tells you, in a sense, when you're on schedule and acting appropriately. Our family clock said to our three girls: "Go to college, get married, and combine a family with a career."

THE CAREER CLOCK

Your career clock obviously is interrelated with your cultural, age, and family clocks, but again it has a distinctive ticking of its own. The female models who were important to you when you were young determine how loud or well developed this ticking is. If you were strongly influenced by a woman teacher anytime through school, she became a pattern for you to consider. Her particular life schedule will become a part of your career clock. Your mother and other family members also become part of your career clock development. You probably are today living out a response to your career clock, whether you are deeply involved in a career or in some combination of career with other life commitments.

THE GOD CLOCK

Some people who do not come from a Christian background might want to refer to this as morality. We, however, believe that God is a person who acts on us personally. Within each person is a dimension that can be satisfied only by relating to God. As one moves through life, this call of God comes at many different times and through many different circumstances. God actively calling us is like a clock inside us.

Through the years, we've asked groups of guests in our home when it was that they first became aware of God in a personal way. We've heard many interesting stories from

Christians and from those who have not yet chosen to be Christians about their becoming conscious that God was seeking to penetrate their lives.

In my own life, I (Jim) can remember as a boy walking the campgrounds in Lakeside, Ohio, late at night after youth rallies. I was acutely aware that God was communicating with me. It was frightening and awesome, but at the same time reassuring. I was very conscious of a time framework and accountability as I communicated with God.

During my adolescent years I had a growing sense of God's will and purpose in and through my life. That awareness of God's hand on my life has caused me to respond at different eras of my life in ways that cannot be accounted for just by the genetic clock, the age clock, or any of the other clocks. God is interrelated with all of these other forces, causing direction and decision in my life.

CHANGE EVENTS AND LIFE CLOCKS

We see two kinds of women in big trouble at mid-life. The one woman has responded to only one or two of the clocks related to her life and because she has ignored the others, she has become unbalanced. She is now making a mad dash, trying to reorganize and stablilize her life. The second woman is experiencing too many change events piled on her life at once.

We have talked about the large number and variety of change events that may happen in a woman's life. Every change event (anything that happens to you) affects many of these clocks that we've talked about, and, in turn, all of these clocks affect your change events.

For example, if your parents were divorced because your father deserted your mother when you were a teenage girl, you may hate men, reject marriage, and throw yourself into a competitive career seeking to outdo men.

On the other hand, some of the other forces in your life or clocks, as we're calling them, might have caused you to view that change event very differently. With strong support from your extended family and the culture around you and a relationship to God, you may have looked at your parents' divorce and said, "Well, that's their problem, but I need to move on in the right direction with my life."

Remember that each event that happens to you causes you to make choices and influences your values. Your values also influence each change event that comes into your life. We'll speak more of this in the chapter, "Answering Life's Questions."

TOO MANY ALARMS

Most of the clocks, as they tick away in our lives, are not only telling us what to do but they are also telling us whether we're on or off time. Events that arrive off time can add stress to the call from other clocks in our life, but we may also experience stress from on-time events for which we are unprepared. Problems are also caused by the events themselves and the increased number of events, anticipated or unanticipated.

In mid-life a woman faces her own personal change events, plus the trauma of her adolescent children's change events and the potentially dangerous changes in her mid-life husband. Also, she may be dealing with aging parents who need her time and emotional commitment.

What is happening to the mid-life woman is like having an alarm clock set in every room in the house and suddenly they all go off at once. She runs frantically from one room to the next, shutting them off as they buzz and gong and clang. She barely gets one shut off and leaves that room to quiet others when the alarm she has just silenced goes off again. The dog starts barking, the family members all start yelling, and she feels trapped in a maze of unreasonable confusion.

BUT THERE'S HOPE

We both have been there. We have experienced the desperation, the confusion, and the fear of the future, as each of us went through mid-life crisis. We had a deep sense of inadequacy, and we wondered if God or any other person understood or cared about what was happening.

We've each made it through, and you will too. God *is* alive and cares for you. There *is* life after your mid-life crisis, but you are not going to be the same woman. Your perception of yourself, your family, your friends, your career, and of God are going to be different, because your values are in the process of changing and that value change will produce a more mature, sensitive, stable, and peaceful woman—you.

Chapter Fifteen

ANSWERING
LIFE'S QUESTIONS

A few months ago we received a letter from a friend whom we had known well when she was a young married woman. After she gave us general news, she said, "It's good to know you are there—especially as I approach forty with phenomenal speed. My 'baby' has two years after this before she enters eighth grade—that's high school here. I realize there's precious little time for personal or family goals—sometimes I feel like 'I haven't done anything yet.' Whoever would have guessed the price so many options would extract in terms of frustration over unrealistic expectations and demands. I am really not as frustrated as that sounds. Especially on days when I'm free to write and chip away at the hunk of as yet unrealized and still unformed dream that sits like lead inside me and that I run into in the dark. . . . Now if somebody could just advise me as to how to slow down the clock. . . ."

TIME RUNS OUT

When we were children, we felt that time stretched out forever. Time was indefinite and vague.

Time has a very different meaning when we are in mid-

life. We realize time is limited and it becomes strangely important to us. We assign it a higher value in our lives. We realize that time is worth more, because we're sensing that we've lived a big chunk of our lives. Time doesn't stretch endlessly before us as if we were standing at the crest of a mountain, just ready to ski down. We realize that we've skiied halfway down the mountain and our ski run will come to an end too soon.

At mid-life our values come sharply under scrutiny. What are the things to which we have given priority? What gets our time, our money, our energy, and our love? And how did we choose to put them in the order they are in?

DON'T MISS YOUR SPECIAL TIME

Reconsidering life and its values and priorities is the most important task of your mid-life passage. Don't try to avoid this thinking and redefinition process. You are skiing down the mountain of life. It *is* going to end, and only you can determine how profitably to live your life.

Some women who are confronted by many change events and who hear the incessant ticking of their life clocks are tempted to play more tennis, exercise more, have more parties, go to more conferences, buy more clothes, or get a new hair style. Those activities may be helpful for your self-image and mental health, but if they are causing you to avoid thinking about your life values and priorities, then you're fooling yourself and setting yourself up for a fall.

Now is the time in your life to seek the truth about who you are, what you want to do with your life, who you will love and let love you, and what mission you want to accomplish in life. The temptation will be to try to hush the questions that are going around inside your head, but they should not be hushed.

Jesus used an illustration that was commonly known in

his day when he explained the disastrous process of trying to keep new truth inside old structures. He said that we can't put new wine into old wine skins. In that day wine was stored in an animal skin flask. As it fermented, the new skin would stretch with the expanding wine and then the skin would harden and become brittle. If you tried to reuse the skin jug, the new fermenting wine would cause the skin to crack and all the wine would run out.

MIDCOURSE CORRECTION

The same is true of your life. The old structures, life forms, and values may not fit you now. Some of your priorities may be the same as before, but some will be discarded and new ones added.

Mid-life is one of the times when a great many events force a reassessment of life. The reevaluation isn't caused just because a person turns thirty-six or thirty-nine, nor is it caused by culture, genetics, career, or family. It isn't even caused by a stale marriage or some other traumatic loss in life. The reassessment seems to happen because of a combination of several of these factors which converge at the midpoint of life.

The crucial issue is how you value each of these events in your life and what happens inside you as a person. When our youngest daughter, Becki, had her left leg amputated about mid-thigh at age sixteen, she responded optimistically and viewed the amputation as something that God allowed and was going to use for her benefit and God's glory.

Why is it that some people react positively to a difficult situation and others respond negatively with depression, anger, or giving up? The answer is found in their value system—in how they perceive themselves, the world around them, and God. If the amputee views herself as having lost her worth and importance, she will feel depressed. If, on the other hand, she feels she is still the same person, only—as Becki says—seventeen pounds lighter, then there isn't any great change in her outward response.

The way you respond to the change events in mid-life will be determined by your previous value structure and the choices you've made all through life. And, in turn, the responses, choices, and decisions that you make now at mid-life are going to restructure your value system, so that as new change events come at the next stage in life, you will respond on the basis of this new system that you are now establishing.

MID-LIFE QUESTIONS

The questioning in mid-life is a common experience and is essential to the process of redefining our values and priorities. All kinds of questions spill out, such as, "Who am I?" "Now that I've come this far, was it worth it?" "What is life all about anyway?" "Am I living the life that I want to live for the next five, ten, or twenty years?" "What am I accomplishing with my life?" "Do I want to live in this neighborhood?" "Do I want to be in this family?" "Do I want to keep working or change careers?" "What do I really get from my husband, children, work, friends, community?" "What do I give to all of these people and organizations?"

Not only is it important to ask these questions, but it's important to decide how you will divide your energy and time among all the priorities of your life. Remember that you will experience an emotional crisis if the choices you make and the activities you live out are not in line with your inner value system—that is, your life characteristics, wishes, needs, goals, feelings, your *real self.*

Mid-life questions seem to group into four basic areas: the meaning of life, the choice of environment, decisions about relationships, and the self as a person. First are the *meaning-of-life* questions. We may question why we were born, why we exist, what is important in life, and how it all fits together.

Perhaps you've heard the story about a man who was digging a ditch. Someone asked him why he was doing that. The man responded, "So I can earn money."

"Why do you want to earn money?"

"So I can buy meat," the man answered.

"Why do you want meat?"

"So I can be strong."

"Why do you want to be strong?"

"So I'll be able to dig this ditch."

Do you ever feel as if your life goes around in a circle like that? There's got to be more to living than just endless activities that feed on themselves.

The second grouping of questions falls into the category of *our world and our environment.* We reevaluate why we live in this country with this government, in this state, in this neighborhood, in this house. We think about why we go to this church, shop at this supermarket, and so on. We want to pick the best fit for us in these matters.

The third area concerns our *relationships.* Whom shall I love and whom shall I let love me? With whom shall I be interdependent? Jesus had various circles of friends. There were the three close disciples, Peter, James, and John, and then the rest of the Twelve. In addition to that, he had selected seventy disciples, and a large crowd of other disciples always followed him. He had different levels of commitment to each circle of friends.

By the time we get to mid-life, we quite often realize that our friendships sometimes have been built for political purposes and on the basis of obligations. Our relationships may not reflect who we are at this era of our life and may be out of balance.

To be healthy, you need three distinctly different types of relationships. The diagram illustrates these. The circle on the right stands for YOU with your gifts, abilities, needs, and desires—the real you. Circle One has an arrow pointing to YOU. You need relationships with people who mostly give to you, enrich you, build you up, and who don't take anything in return. Obviously, this is going to be God and some other significant people, such as a teacher, leader, pastor, counselor, or special friend or relative—someone who nourishes you through Scripture, books, Christian radio and television programs, conversation, or kind acts.

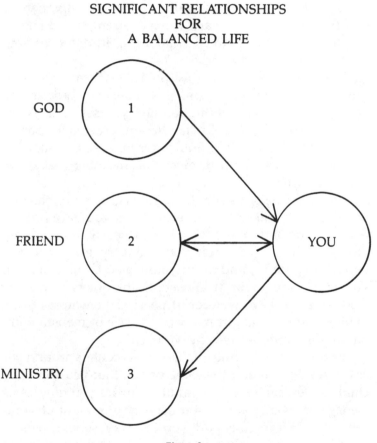

SIGNIFICANT RELATIONSHIPS
FOR
A BALANCED LIFE

Figure 2

Notice that an arrow goes from Circle Two toward YOU and an arrow returns from YOU toward Circle Two. This is a peer relationship. You build and strengthen some person emotionally and spiritually as much as that person builds and strengthens you. It's fun to be with someone like this. You spend a lot of time talking, listening, and sharing. Yet when you leave each other, even though you have given, shared, listened, and cared a lot, you feel nourished and built up. In a true peer relationship, each one goes away feeling he or she has gained from the relationship. God has planned that in the sharing of two lives, a supernatural occurrence takes place. Each receives strength and energy. You must have this kind of relationship in order for your life to be whole and complete.

Next, notice that an arrow points from YOU to Circle Three. Circle Three represents your ministry. These are the people and causes to whom you give yourself. This is one of your purposes in life. Circle Three represents the part of the world that is enriched and better because of you. Ministry in the lives of others gives you meaning that is beyond yourself.

When any one of these relationships gets out of balance, the other ones will suffer. For example, if you have no peer relationships and very few relationships with significant others, such as God, then your ministry to people will become dry, sterile, and a duty motivated by obligation. If you only have input from significant others, including God, and you have wonderful peer relationships, but no ministry, you are caught in a vicious cycle of me-ism without any life purpose beyond yourself.

The fourth area of mid-life questions centers around *you as a person.* You're not the same person that you were as a child, adolescent, or young adult. Who are you now? As a teenager or young adult, you may have thought of yourself as the life of the party or the very serious person. Maybe you were a flirt or philosopher. Did you think of yourself as a leader or a leaner? The question is, who are you now? With the life experience that you've had and the growth you've experienced, you're not the same person. But who are you?

You may experience some degree of pain or fear as you begin to ask the mid-life questions. You're afraid that if you dig around too much, you might turn over a rock and find some ugly bugs there. What if you discover that you're a hostile person or overly sensitive to criticism? What if you're too passive, afraid to take risks, or too controlled by other people? What if you find out you're aggressive or greedy, or sometimes act helpless, or don't really love people but just manipulate them? What if you are . . . and on and on goes the list. What if you do learn some hard things about yourself? Remember that whatever you are has been an open secret to God all along and he still loves you unconditionally.

A SMOOTH ROAD

A transition is made up of three stages. First is the awareness stage. Quite often awareness is triggered by some change event. Perhaps you feel a sense of irritation or, at least, an awareness of seeing that there is something more in life. For example, you may decide that it's time for you to go back to work part-time. But before you made the decision to go back to work, there was some pressure, some nagging sense of need or unfulfillment that caused you to make that decision.

The second stage is the one of disruption. In order for you to go back to work, you have to break up the old lifestyle and start a new one. A mild to severe amount of disruption or confusion occurs in the process of moving from one lifestyle to your new lifestyle of work.

The third stage is the resolution stage with some ups and downs. When you are comfortably adjusted to your new life experience, you will easily define yourself in that role and capably carry it out. You feel settled again.

There are many transitions in our normal day-to-day experience that we may not even identify as transitions;

for example, buying a new dress. First there is that sense of need, that feeling of incompleteness that causes you to go through the activity of buying. Going to buy the dress is somewhat of a disruption in your schedule and your budget. Finally there is the resolution—you are satisfied with the dress, it fits well, you look sharp, and nobody killed you for spending all that money.

Many major transitions occur in life, such as puberty, leaving home, finishing college, events all through life which we'll consider later in this chapter. You need to realize that the major life transitions will come, whether you choose for them to come or not. You move inexorably from being a child to an adolescent to a young adult to a mid-life adult to a mellow adult and to an aging adult. Each of these transitions will demand a value redefinition of your life structure. You have no choice about whether the transitions come, *but* the values that result from each transitional experience *are* your decision.

WET OR DRY?

We are often asked, "What is the difference between a transition and a crisis?" A transition is a move from one settled state through a moderate amount of disruption to a second settled state or resolution. A crisis has a greater degree of disruption and usually some sort of breakdown, so that the person in crisis is not able to function in some area of life as she had previously.

For instance, imagine yourself standing on a dock on the edge of a beautiful little lake. There is a gentle breeze blowing and tiny ripples cross the surface of the water. You're invited by a friend to go for a canoe ride. You've never been in a canoe before, so you are instructed by your friend to step carefully from the dock into the exact center of the canoe. If you step on one side or the other, the canoe will tip over immediately. You want very much to please your friend by going on the ride. It looks as if it would be fun to be out on the lake along with the other canoeists. Since you've never gone canoeing before, you decide to take the risk. Stage one in the crisis is the same as stage one in the transition: there is a desire for something different.

One foot is placed in the center of the canoe. Your other foot is still on the dock. You're in the middle of a transition and everything is going along well. There is some disruption because part of your weight is in the canoe and part is still on the solid dock. Now, if you can carefully bring your other leg into the canoe, keep your balance in the center, and quietly sit down, you'll be all right—you've made a smooth transition.

A crisis, however, is when you have one foot in the center of the canoe, the other foot on the dock and slowly the canoe begins to separate from the dock. Your legs are spread ever wider. Soon there is no control left. You make a mad grab backward for the pier, but too much of your weight is out over the water. In you go! In the process, the canoe tips over too. That's a crisis! Instead of moving from one stable position to a second stable position with only a minor disruption of fear and anxiety, you didn't make it. Instead you went into the drink.

As many people pass through normal transitions, they tend to experience some part of the passage as a calm transition and other parts as a severe crisis. It's possible, you see, to be having a severe identity crisis—Who am I? What am I going to accomplish in my life?—and, at the same time, have a very supportive and strong marriage. Or the opposite is possible. In the mid-years it is quite likely that some events will be handled smoothly as a normal transition and others will be handled rather poorly. You'll fall flat on your face or into the lake. Both a crisis and transition can be profitable in our lives, because they force us to think about our value system and reorganize our priority of life energy use.

ALL OF LIFE IN FOCUS

One of the common things that happens with us human beings is that we try to avoid *pain* at the same time we are drawn toward *pleasure*. We need to add a third "p" by pointing out that our lives ought to be marked with *purpose*.

If we have purpose in our lives, we're able to put pain and pleasure into proper perspective. We'll be able to see the profit in pain and, at the same time, not feel guilty about enjoying pleasure. *Perspective* gives us that balance. But you can't really have perspective without a purpose or a reason for living. Again we're back to values and back to living a balanced life.

James 1:2b-4 (Conway Free Paraphrase) sums it up this way: "People, jump for joy when a variety of trials and tests come into your life, because these very trials and tests produce stability, and this process of trials and tests which produce stability will bring about the ultimate result of maturity."

The point of the account is that we should be grateful when pain and trials come to our life, not for the pain or trials themselves, but because of the changes they work in us. The troubles produce stability, the ability to stay under stress. Pain can have a positive benefit in us and produce something in us that pleasure never can.

GOD IS NOT A KILLJOY

On the other hand, many Christian women are afraid to enjoy themselves. They have cast themselves in the role of pain only. The more pain and hardship they have, the more effective their lives are, they think. These women imagine God to be just about as mean as Satan, only dressed in white clothes instead of red. They see him leaning over the banister of heaven, hollering down, "Aha, I saw you laughing down there. Cut that out, you're not supposed to have any fun in life."

The picture of God revealed in the Bible is one of balance, with serious times of judgment; times of counsel—the arm-around-the-shoulder type; the friend that sticks closer than a brother; and the God who loves us very deeply and who laughs and rejoices over us.

" 'Cheer up, don't be afraid. For the Lord your God has arrived to live among you. He is a mighty Savior. He will give you victory. He will rejoice over you in great gladness; he will love you and not accuse you.' Is that a joyous choir I hear? No, it is the Lord himself exulting over you in happy song" (Zephaniah 3:16-18).

God uses both the crisis and the smoother transition to bring about growth in your life. He wants you to have a purpose and a direction. He wants you to have perspective, to be able to understand and evaluate what life is about, who you are, and how you fit into that life.

VALUE REDEFINITION CYCLE

The values that you hold today—that is, the worth, the importance that you have given to each area, event, and experience in your life—are values that you have built up from many small choices over many years. You didn't make one choice for all time. You kept on reassessing choices and giving them more or less importance as you reevaluated them.

The following diagram should help you see that your values continue to be redefined by your choices or decisions, by your actions, and by the events that result. In turn, those redefined values affect how you think of yourself and your world around you. So, each time a change event comes along, the event not only affects you, but you interpret the event through your value system.

Suppose that you wear glasses, and you're outside on a bright, sunny day. You can choose not to use your sunglasses or not even to use your regular glasses but you see the world as a blur. Or you can use your regular glasses and see the world clearly for a moment, but you have to partially close your eyes because of the sun's intensity. Or you can put on your sunglasses and see things clearly with relaxed eyes. Your glasses help you to see the world more clearly, but the bright day also influences your choice of glasses. Your choices also affect how you see the world. You are not a victim of your life events.

Now let's walk through the value redefinition cycle.

Notice Point One. From conception on, you have been receiving input into your life that is going to influence how you will face future change events. All of your childhood experiences; your relationships with your parents, relatives, and friends; and your school experiences were part of a value system that was given to you. This childhood value system, formed also by the small choices that you made, has brought you to late adolescence or early young adulthood thinking of yourself, life, and God in a certain way (Point Two). We'll pick up the story, imagining that you are facing one of life's major change events—to marry or not.

MR. WONDERFUL

At Point Three you met a wonderful man. You made the choice of that man over others on the basis of the values that you had accumulated thus far in life (Point Four). This change event will be a very powerful and life changing event. You will never be the same. Your values influenced your selection of this man, but now your relationship with this man will also influence your value system. Here's how it works.

You made a decision to marry this man (Point Five). That choice, as you can see from the chart, resulted in actions, events, and redefined values. You not only made a choice but you acted on that choice; that is, you actually married him. (See Point Six.) Because of the decision you

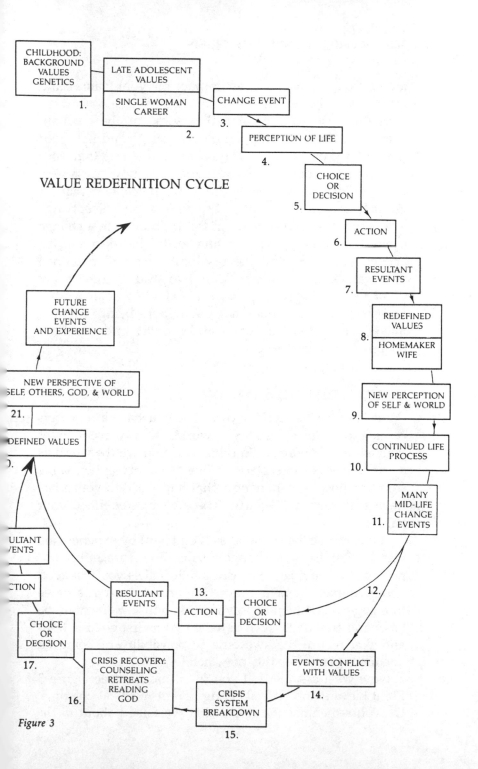

VALUE REDEFINITION CYCLE

Figure 3

made, your actions had an impact on your values and influenced other events.

In this case we'll assume that some of the resultant events are that you dropped out of college and had your first child (Point Seven). The consequence was that your values were redefined (Point Eight). You now are a very different person with a different life perception than at Point Four, which was an early young adult perception.

You see, it all started back at Point Three with a change event and your decision relating to it. That decision, the actions you took, and the resultant event all redefined your values. Look back at Point Two. Your values at that point were strongly emphasizing a single woman with a career. Now your values have shifted to being a home-maker, caring for a husband and a child, and you have dropped the career role.

YOU'RE DIFFERENT NOW

Point Nine on the cycle shows that you have a new per-ception of yourself and the world. Your perception of yourself is as a wife and mother, and you see the world as a friendly, enjoyable place to live. That perception came from the positive experiences that happened in your mar-riage and your child's birth. These events redefined your values.

You continue the life process (Point Ten) by experiencing literally hundreds of change events. Some are rather mi-nor, such as buying a new dress that makes you feel good about yourself; some are more important, such as a move to a larger apartment or to your first house. Some may be large and traumatic, such as when your first child is born and you realize the awesome responsibility of being an adequate parent for this new, helpless life.

Now we'll assume that you're in mid-life (see Figure 3 Point Eleven) and several change events come at one time. Do you remember the clocks that we talked about in the earlier chapter? At mid-life they all seem to go off at once. You're worried about getting older, gray-haired, and over-weight. You wonder if you're losing your sexual appeal. Time is running out before you get things accomplished. Your children don't seem to need you anymore, and the culture is pushing you aside. You may feel you are not quite with it in the career market. Your husband may be preoccupied in his own mad dash to success and your marriage may be going to pot. On top of all this, you discover that your oldest daughter has been fooling around with drinking and sex, and your mother has be-come extremely dependent on you because of your fa-ther's recent stroke. (That's enough to kill off anyone!)

TRANSITION OR CRISIS

At Point Twelve there are two separate paths. One arrow leads down toward crisis, the other one follows the normal flow of choice, decision, action, and resultant events to-ward redefined values. The normal flow marked by Point Thirteen indicates that even though there are many change events, they were assimilated as you went through this transition. Probably you were growing and maturing as a person all along, and each of the earlier choices and decisions helped to prepare you for this onslaught of sev-eral change events.

But look at Point Fourteen. There are many change events that are *conflicting with your changing value system.* Each event is a jolting experience that sends you into confusion and crisis (Point Fifteen). (Conflict between our values and the change events results in crisis.)

Remember that any time there are multiple change events that are out of step with your previous value sys-tem, a crisis will be produced. That's why we keep empha-sizing the importance of being reflective, thinking about your life, and not being afraid to wrestle with questions. It is better to face questions and life events, redefine the events, and let the events redefine you and your value system than to allow a crisis to build up.

Most people in a crisis don't need someone to tell them that they are in a crisis. They already know that their world seems to be coming apart. There are people, however, who refuse to change their direction while they are in a crisis, hoping that things will get better automatically without any thought or activity on their part.

When you get into a crisis, the important thing to do is to discover the several causes that have triggered the crisis and how your value system is being forced to be redefined. Next, take one small area and work through it, asking who you are, who you want to be, and how you can accomplish the necessary changes.

For example, you may feel overly stressed by trying to meet all of the needs of your husband, children, and career. What you really want to do is just run away. Try now to discover the root causes. In this case, there is too much pressure and stress. You have accepted too much responsibility for other people's lives and your reflex action is to escape.

By carefully looking at the situation, you may discover that what you can do is to reduce some of your responsibilities by letting each family member be more accountable for himself and herself. At the same time, do some restorative things for yourself, such as going for a walk, biking, skiing, window shopping, reading a good book, having coffee with a friend, or attending a special seminar or retreat.

WARNING SIGNS

If you are wondering about some of the early signs of crisis, let me refer you to the following list of the symptoms of stress overload. If one or two of these things are happening in your life, you are beginning to pick up stress overload. If several are happening, you probably are on the edge of a crisis. This list is from a book called *Stress/Unstress,* written by Keith W. Sehnert, M.D.

• Decision-making becomes difficult (both major and minor kinds).
• Excessive daydreaming or fantasizing about "getting away from it all."
• Increased use of cigarettes and/or alcohol.
• Thoughts trail off while speaking or writing.
• Excessive worrying about all things.
• Sudden outbursts of temper and hostility.
• Paranoid ideas and mistrust of friends and family.
• Forgetfulness for appointments, deadlines, dates.
• Frequent spells of brooding and feeling of inadequacy.
• Reversals in usual behavior.[1]

Crisis means that there has been a breakdown of the system (Point Fifteen). Crisis may be indicated by many different kinds of activities or thinking, such as depression, involvement with alcohol, an affair, or inability to concentrate. Any abrupt life change would indicate a breaking down of your life system and that your personality is trying to compensate.

RECOVERY—AT LAST

Some of the normal process in a crisis ultimately will be helpful in getting a person through it (Point Sixteen). For example, many people in crisis want to be alone. Sometimes they sleep or spend a lot of time just thinking. These activities can be very helpful. Extra rest can help equip you to handle problems better. Time away from people will give you perspective that will be one of the ingredients for recovery from the crisis.

Allowing God to nourish you physically and emotionally, as he did Elijah (1 Kings 19:1-18), is also important. We have found that listening to music and reading Christian biographies and Scripture are rebuilding to us. Sometimes we simply leaf through several books of the Bible, reading verses of God's love and care that we've underlined through the years. Other times we carefully study sections such as Ephesians 1 and 2. Being in the woods or by a lake or seashore is also therapeutic for us.

Crisis recovery, however, often requires more than just being alone or getting more rest. We must also think through each of our values or we may not really recover from the crisis. It's helpful to be able to talk to a close trusted friend or a professional counselor.

You need the times when you are with other people to be unstressful and pleasant. You may find that you have trouble going to some kinds of social events if they are likely to produce pressure on you.

In crisis recovery it's important to understand the source of the stress and then to make deliberate choices that will move you away from the crisis and back toward redefining values. At Point Seventeen, you are started back on the path again. You make decisions related to the change events that caused your life to experience crisis. Perhaps you decide to return to school and to work on your marriage.

You now carry out appropriate actions in line with those decisions, such as starting a refresher course or going to a marriage enrichment retreat (Point Eighteen). At Point Nineteen there are events that result from your action. You take a part-time job or you spend additional time away with your husband for a weekend.

THE REDEFINED YOU

When you reach Point Twenty you are back to redefined values. If you went through the crisis route, you are a different person. You still may think of yourself as a mother and wife, but perhaps now you have elevated career to be equal with the other two or even more important. You probably have a new understanding of your family and the place of each member. If you are single, you may have come to a fresh acceptance of your singleness, a clearer understanding of friends, and perhaps a refocusing of your career. Your redefined values now give you a different perspective on yourself, other people, God, and the world (Point Twenty-one).

You have gone through a unique series of experiences, whichever route you took, and you are a unique person with a new outlook. This unique perspective is going to cause you to react differently from any other woman, even though you both may experience the same future change events, such as the deaths of your husbands or someone else very important to you.

Life is filled with thousands of change events, both minor and major, and many times we go through the process we have described here. Our values are continually redefined, and it is our value system and the perspective we receive from our values that cause us to react uniquely to each change event that happens in life.

SAME VALUE QUESTIONS, DIFFERENT LIFE PERSPECTIVE

As we've said, there is much discussion today in professional circles about how adults develop and how their values change. By values, we mean the worth that you assign to each area of your thinking and life. Some researchers believe that adult development should be considered in the same way that we study child development. We expect a child's motor skills to develop before his speech skills. We expect a child to be able to think concretely before he can think abstractly.

This sequential model has been used to study adult development and to learn what is happening at mid-life. As a result, many authorities are trying to determine in what order events come and which ones cause a mid-life crisis. Some suggest that the major cause is aging itself; others blame it on the culture and, interestingly, some experts in adult development don't believe that anyone has a crisis at all.

Maybe we need to look at the whole life span from a totally different perspective. Could it be that our value system is the key to understanding adult development? It is noteworthy that many of the same values come up for rethinking several different times in our lives.

For example, when you were about age two, you were wrestling with your self-identity. Yes, you wanted to be close to your mother and father, but you also wanted to be an individual. That battle for individual identity and independence is why that age is called the "terrible twos."

The change event of starting to school forced you to redefine your values, and you had to ask yourself, "Who am I? Who is my family? What are my interests? How do my family's values fit into this school's values?"

"WHEN I BECAME A WOMAN. . . ."

When you came to puberty, your breasts began to develop, you started your menstrual cycle, and men began to look at you differently. You were looking at yourself in a different way too. Again you were forced to rethink, "Who am I? What is life all about? How do I relate to people? What kind of person do I want to be? Do my family's values fit my life now?"

As you started to date, you wrestled again with values in the same basic areas. Moving into your own apartment, starting work, or going to college also demanded a reconsideration of your definition of yourself. Every promotion in your career or milestone in your education forced a reevaluation of who you were in the light of these change events.

The choice to marry or not, to have children or not, to have a career and the kind it would be, or whatever combination of roles you chose, also forced you to rethink your values. As we've already pointed out, your values determined how you reacted to each event of life.

THE NEVER-ENDING PROCESS

Now you're at mid-life, and you're considering the same values that were there in infant form when you were a child. "Who am I? Whom shall I love? Whom shall I let love me? With whom shall I be interdependent? What shall I do with my life? What is the meaning of life? Who is God and how does he relate to me?"

When you were an adolescent girl and wondering who you were, you probably thought once you got it figured out, you'd be fixed for the rest of your life. The truth is that every change event that comes along in life forces you to reconsider your value structure and identity.

Some authorities who have had a strong influence on our understanding of adults have suggested, for example, that we really don't become generative, or concerned about a younger generation and helping to bring them along, until we reach mid-life. Do you remember, however, that when you were a little girl, you were wrestling with this same value? At times you were very protective of a younger brother or sister, and of course, at other times you weren't concerned at all. Maybe during college you were big sister to a freshman girl and helped her to learn the ropes. That's all part of this same quality of generativity.

SAME BUT DIFFERENT

The point of all of this is to tell you not to be discouraged because you're having to rethink your values. Reevaluating is a normal process in life. Every change event causes this process to take place, and the process will continue right up to the moment of your death.

Perhaps a way to illustrate this might be for you to think with me (Jim) about a lake that was very important in my childhood and teen years. It is Rex Lake, near Akron, Ohio.

When I came into the world, Rex Lake was already there. As a baby and a young child, I sat on the shore looking out at the lake and its different moods and settings. There were times when the lake was very still, times when it had waves, and times when the sun made a giant path across the whole lake, all the way over to me. I was seeing the lake from my viewpoint on the shore. When we were children we also considered life's values from a child-sized view.

As I got into grade school, but before I could swim, I was allowed to walk along the side of the lake and explore from Sandy Beach (about 200 yards to the west of our cottage) to the channel (about 200 yards to the east). I was also able to go out on the dock. I could now look at the lake from those several new vantage points.

I learned to swim in that lake and then was permitted to take the rowboat or the canoe into the water. Now I could roam anywhere I wanted around the lake. My brother, sisters, and I had great fun on hot summer days, turtle hunting, fishing, exploring the island, and checking out that mysterious "other side" of the lake. I was able to pick blueberries along the bank and apples from an abandoned apple orchard on the other side. Yes, my world was expanding, but the lake was still the same lake. So it is with values. We are, as we grow older, still exploring the *same values*, but we are looking at them from a *different perspective*.

ENLARGED PERCEPTION

When I became a teenager, I was able to venture through the channel into the other lakes. A whole chain of lakes were there to investigate. New beaches, inlets, and coves were waiting to be explored. That's when I first saw a sailboat, and I immediately fell in love with sailing.

During those years I was also allowed to take the small motorboat and go aquaplaning on Rex Lake. I swam the entire mile length of that lake several times each summer. It was the same lake, but now I was more a master of it. Life's value issues are nearly always the same, but from each age and each change event in life we look at those values systems differently, and those values change us.

Not only was I seeing the lake differently as I grew older, but the lake also was changing me. To this day that lake has caused me to feel a strong pull toward water, sailing, swimming, the sun, and to enjoy all of the things God has made. Our value system changes us as much as we change our value system.

In the late teens and the young adult era, the lake took on a romantic dimension, with a streak of moonlight coming all across the lake to meet me while I paddled quietly in the canoe with a pretty young woman seated in front of me. I was seeing the same lake through different eyes. I had a deeper understanding of the lake and its meaning, just as life experience gives us a deeper understanding of our value system and the kind of people that we are becoming.

MYSTERIOUS YET MAGNIFICENT

John Powell in *Fully Human, Fully Alive* says, "There is no painless entrance into a new and fully human life."[2] Each transition in life can be to some degree an upsetting experience. There is a time of uncertainty, maybe even fear.

A few days ago we took some friends to Laguna Beach on the ocean. We wanted them to enjoy a good climb on the rocks, but when we got down to the shore from the grassy cliff above, the tide was high. We could not get around one of the rocky points to explore a cave we knew was just beyond that point. We discovered, however, that just for a moment while a wave was out, we could go over the rocks quickly to a high spot, wait there while a wave was in, and when that wave went out, move rapidly across the exposed rocks to another high point. Finally we got around the point and into the mysterious little cave.

From the cave there was a magnificent view of the surf crashing against the rocks right in front of us and the sun setting behind Catalina Island. If we had not been willing to make those dashes between the waves, we could not have been able to experience that special little cave and sunset. From the top of the cliff one wouldn't even know that a cave existed.

Life is like that. Each change event puts us for some time in a precarious situation, and we realize again, "There is no painless entrance into a new and fully human life."

ALLOW LIFE TO QUESTION YOU

Doug (real name), one of our close friends in Illinois, repeatedly asked me (Jim), "Do you enjoy what you're doing?" Or he would rephrase his question, "Why are you doing what you're doing?" Doug was challenging my value system and wanting me to rethink some areas of my life.

The psychiatrist Viktor Frankl said, "Let life question you."[3] Let the events of life challenge your values instead of looking at the events as enemies that are disturbing your smooth life process. See change events as an opportunity for your values to be challenged and to mature.

Allow yourself to be questioned by every event and person you meet in your daily life. "The needy, unattractive person asks me how much I can love. The death of a dear one asks me what I really believe about death and how profitably I can confront loss and loneliness. A beautiful day or a beautiful person asks me how capable I am of enjoyment. Solitude asks me if I really like myself and enjoy my own company. A good joke asks me if I have a sense of humor. A very different type person from a background very dissimilar to my own asks me if I am capable of empathy and understanding. Success and failure ask me to define my ideas of success and failure. Suffering asks me if I really believe I can grow through adversity. Negative criticism directed to me asks me about my sensitivities and self-confidence. The devotion and commitment of another to me asks me if I will let myself be loved."[4]

My friend Doug was asking me these questions when I was a busy pastor, and my response to him was, "Well, these people have all these needs; somebody has to help them." However, it was this very distorted anxiety to meet the needs of every person who crossed my path that partially caused my own mid-life crisis. Because I had not been willing to change much as the events of life questioned me, I soon found myself in a trap with my value system out of step with many of my change events. This resulted in my mid-life crisis.

I (Sally) feel that the trauma I experienced as I began my transition into mid-life also came from a mismatch of values and change events. The difference for me, however, was not that I had been *unwilling* to change, but that I was *unaware* I needed to. My generation of women had little preparation for mid-life, and I went from year to year without a refining of my value system. When I was confronted with the need to think, I didn't even know I needed to, much less *how.*

CHOOSING TO GROW AT MID-LIFE

You are the person you are today because of a series of events and choices you have made along through life. The way to work through a mid-life crisis is to realize that there are certain ingredients you need in your life now and that you need to systematically tackle each one of the troubling change events to bring about a satisfactory resolution.

The following may help you grow and change:

1. Spend time reflecting on who you are as a person, where you've come from, your past value system, and the events that are taking place in your life now, so that you can carefully think through the options that are before you. Reflection time gives you the opportunity to think carefully about what your next decisions will be and how those decisions will impact on action, events, and your redefined values.

2. Have a group of other people with whom you can talk. Sometimes talk one-to-one with another person; at other times be in a group where you can discuss change events that are important to all of you. Other people give you an opportunity to test what you have been thinking in your personal reflection time. Talking with others also lets you ventilate your feelings and allows you to hear how other people react to the same change event you're going through.

3. Get ideas and information from sources other than yourself. You need to know about mid-life and the change events that you are going through. Reading can be helpful, along with group discussions with other people. Reading the Bible provides both information and perspective. Unless you get outside input, you are likely just to stew in your own juices, which could lead you into depression.

4. Allow God to be involved. The first three ingredients will be more effective if you allow God to be the center of each one.

Suppose that one sunny day, you sail a boat out of Newport Harbor in California, into the ocean, and along the coast. You enjoy sailing north with the fantastic view of the coastal cities in the Los Angeles Basin, that magnificent sight of the mountains in the backdrop, a salt breeze in your face, and that deep, clear, blue ocean all around you. About 2:30 in the afternoon, as you move up the coast, you notice that Los Angeles is slipping into the distance and you decide it's time to turn around. As you do, you also notice that the wind is starting to fall off. Even though you're heading back south, by three o'clock it is dead calm. Your boat doesn't have a motor and you're almost helpless as you wait for the wind to come up.

Now, darkness begins to settle in and a gentle breeze does pick up, but so does panic. It's dark out there. You can see the city lights of Los Angeles and you know that somewhere south of there is the Newport Harbor, but where exactly? You keep sailing south. It's got to be here somewhere. If only somebody were with you who knew where the harbor was and how to get into it in the dark. It isn't a problem of no wind now, it's the problem of how to use the wind to go in the right direction.

Let us put it to you bluntly. God is the one who has created you. He's been through life with millions of people, and he's the one who can give you insights for your life now that are absolutely crucial. To use our sailing analogy, God wants to come on board into your life, and he wants to steer you. Ask him to do that.

Let's think in practical terms of here and now. When you get up in the morning, say to him, "God, the world seems to be spinning around. I'm not sure where I'm going. I'm not sure how to get there. Use the events surrounding me and bring people and ideas across my path to help me go in the right direction." Then, spend some time reading from the Scripture. If it's your first time, you might like to start your Bible reading with the Gospel of John. You don't have to read it all in one day, but take a chapter or a few verses at a time. Specifically say to God, "Give me new insights that will help me to go the right way."

When you finish John, start at the beginning of the New Testament and read all the way up to the Book of Revelation. Then you might like to start reading the Psalms and the Proverbs. Every day say, "God, you've been there before; give me the ideas and insights I need. Bring the people I need into my life. Help me to think the right ideas as I quietly think and reflect." What you're asking God to do is to become the manager of your life or, in sailing terms, the captain.

We have sailed at night in a gentle breeze with the moon coming across the water. There is a stillness and a beauty about night sailing that can't be duplicated in daylight— as long as you know where you're going. The difference is knowing where you are going. And God can give you that perspective and that peace.

Chapter Sixteen

PREVENTING A CRISIS

"How can I prevent a mid-life crisis from happening to me?" is the most common question we are asked by young adults or early mid-life people.

We point out that everyone is going to experience a mid-life *transition,* but this transition can be very positive as you think through the values of your life for the next life stages. In the long run it's not going to be profitable to suppress your feelings and your value questions during the mid-life transition. You will be a healthier person if you think through your life and its purpose.

However, we can make some suggestions that will lessen the intensity of your transition, so that your mid-life transition is a process in which you can more easily absorb several change events without a crisis occurring.

DISCOVER SEED PROBLEMS

Vickie is a woman in her early thirties who is married and has four children. Her life clearly shows some of the seed problems that could grow into a crisis in her late thirties.

She is a very intelligent woman who did well academi-

cally during college. She is a high achiever, somewhat of a
perfectionist, and is extremely adept socially. She is a
warm person, committed to people and to God. She was a
leader on her campus, in her sorority, and in a major
Christian campus group. She also was strongly affected by
the Women's Movement and definitely wanted to have a
career.

During her last year of college in California she met a
graduate student and fell deeply in love with him. They
were married after her graduation. He encouraged her
development as a woman and urged her to exercise her
leadership ability.

They both attended graduate school. Mark earned a
degree that prepared him for pastoral ministry and Vickie
earned a master's degree in developmental psychology
from a state university. While Mark finished his degree,
Vickie continued in a career direction and grew strongly
sympathetic to biblical feminism.

UNFULFILLED NEED SEED
After Mark's graduation, they took a position with a para-
church organization working with students. Mark and
Vickie had understood that Vickie would be equally involved in ministry and thus be fulfilled in her own career
direction. This was not the case, however. The people in
her organization and her supervisors tended to see her
more in the role of homemaker. Since she was not paid
separately, they saw her only as a significant support person to her husband.

Vickie felt a deep resentment and almost a sense of
betrayal toward the employers and somewhat toward her
husband. She wrestled long and hard with this frustrated
career direction, trying to fill her needs with short-term,
unpaid opportunities that supported her husband's ministry.

In her late twenties Vickie had a growing desire to have
a child. It may have been part of the late twenties assess-

ment and wanting to get settled into the community, or it may have been a growing compensation from her frustration with the lack of career involvement in her life. Four children were born in rapid succession, and now at age thirty-four she is pregnant again. The last three pregnancies were unplanned. She does not indicate at all that she is entering mid-life transition nor a crisis—but the seeds are there.

COMPETITION SEED

More seeds of a future crisis are seen in their recent move to a church in a Texas university city where Mark is the senior pastor with major oversight of preaching, counseling, and the healthy direction of the church. At age thirty-seven Mark has a strong need to make this church successful, and he will likely give a great deal of energy and concern to his ministry. He will probably divert time and energy from his family as he tries to establish a significant ministry before he is forty.

The suburban community into which they have moved is strongly affected by the local university and by financial opulence. Vickie feels that she is in competition with the young, attractive female students at the university and with the fashionable community women who are able to buy expensive clothes that are beyond her meager budget.

Because she is pregnant again, she is putting on weight. She feels she is an unsuccessful competitor with the university students and the women of the town. The responsibility of her active children is almost overwhelming. Her husband is preoccupied with succeeding in his career. There are also the smoldering embers of her own unfulfilled career.

On top of all of this, they have decided that they must not have any more children, so Vickie will have sterilization surgery after this fifth child's birth. She is experiencing loss. Her age and three unplanned children are now forcing a decision on her that she feels will take away a dimension of womanness. Other birth control measures have failed, so she knows the surgery is necessary, but she feels sad.

FATIGUE SEED
Even though Vickie does not yet show the signs of mid-life crisis, she is beginning to hint in those directions with phrases such as, "It's difficult to compete with other women in this community." Or, "I'm tired of carrying everybody in the family and meeting all of their emotional needs." "What about my career?" It's only a few short steps to where she may be saying, "I'm tired of being everyone's support. It's got to stop. I'm burned out. It's time for my needs to be met!"

If you are hoping to prevent or reduce a mid-life crisis, the first thing you must do is recognize the potential seeds that may grow into a mid-life crisis. Identifying those means that you think back to your adolescent and young adult years and remember the *dreams* you had then. Are they being fulfilled now in your life? Areas of your dreams that have not or are not being fulfilled will likely cause you some problems, unless your value system has changed so those dreams are no longer important to you.

Seeds of mid-life crisis can also be found as you evaluate the *stresses* in your life. What are the areas or experiences that are causing you to feel burned out, abused, or exploited?

You may find mid-life crisis seeds as you think through areas of *competition*. Are you trying to compete with the younger generation, or with women who are in an exciting career, or women who get to be full-time homemakers? The drive toward competition indicates an unsatisfied area of your life.

Think through any part of your life that has been affected by *loss*. Accumulated losses have the potential of bringing about a mid-life crisis.

COMMUNICATE YOUR NEEDS

The second aspect for preventing or reducing a mid-life crisis is to educate the people around you. Tell those who are significant to you what is happening in your life. You need to communicate very directly and specifically where you sense there is potential danger. If you're not married, you may need to be talking with close, intimate friends, especially if you sense in recent months a growing urgency to mother and nurture.

Friends can be alerted to help you think through the emotional and logical concerns that you are wrestling with. If you don't share and educate people to your need, your bottled-up desires may become explosive. Your new longings may cause you to make some decisions out of haste and panic that may bring about long-term sadness.

Verbalizing your needs and some of the potential mid-life crisis seeds you've discovered will be an education for your friends and will help you clarify who you are. Your friends may also help you answer the question, "Now, given this situation, what do I do?"

COMPENSATE

The third important aspect to lessen or prevent a mid-life crisis is to compensate. Compensation means that which you do to make up a deficit or a lack you sense in your life.

Look again at the illustration of Vickie, the thirty-four-year-old mentioned earlier. How can she start to compensate so she can head off a crisis?

Let's assume that she's already thought through the potential seeds of her own mid-life crisis. Let's assume also that she has extensively reflected on what values are important for her at this time in her life. Suppose that she has started educating her husband, her children, and other significant people around her about her needs. Now let's

think of a deliberate plan of action that she might follow
to compensate or more accurately meet some of her needs
so that she can lessen or prevent a mid-life crisis.

CAREER REENTRY

One thing Vickie might work on would be to plan with her
husband her own career reentry. Additional continuing
education or skill updating might be needed so the reentry
would be an easy transition.

Five children are going to produce a great deal of parenting responsibility. Thus another compensation area
might be for her husband, Mark, to carry more of the
parenting responsibility. This request is likely to be very
difficult because he is deeply committed in a heavy output
of energy for his own career. If he can understand that ten
years from now he will wish he had put more time into his
children, he may be willing to shift some of his time
priority to parenting his family instead of just parenting
the church.

TIME FOR THE MARRIAGE

Another important area for her to adjust is time for the
two of them in their marriage. With heavy career and
parenting responsibilities, they're likely to ignore their
couple relationship. They need time with each other. Perhaps after the children have gone to bed they can sit with
a cup of coffee and talk. Maybe once a month they could
spend time together answering the question, "How is our
marriage doing?" They also need fun times, going out
together.

CHILDREN PITCH IN

Parents need to involve children in the compensation process by teaching them to assume more responsibility. The
family is a team working together. Mom and Dad are not
their servants. We all serve each other. Sometimes children
don't realize the pressure their parents are under. Often

they don't fully grasp it by just being told. They may have to be put on their own to some degree so that if they don't do their task the whole family suffers. They need to learn that Mom and Dad are not going to jump in and do their job for them.

Grade school children can easily assume responsibility for preparing simple meals, setting the table, and cleaning up afterward. They can also do portions of the house-cleaning and the yard work under supervision of their parents. Older children can help more.

A NEW LOOK

Vickie is feeling a strong competition with younger or more fashionable women. Another compensation for her might be a spa membership to help her get back into shape after the fifth child is born. If the membership is provided now, she will feel that she can be in control of her life and soon be able to feel better about herself.

Compensation may also include a look at the family budget. Perhaps a shift of some funds would enable Vickie to buy one classy outfit with several changeable accessories. Then she would feel comfortable in her role as a leader in her church and community.

SUPPORTIVE FRIENDS

Regular discussion with close women friends her age as well as with older women will give her the opportunity to rethink the gains and the losses she has experienced thus far in her life. These close friends can be very significant as they provide stability for her during these potentially dangerous value redefinition years. Talking with friends will also help to diffuse some of the stress and will give her an accountability relationship, so that she does not feel she is experiencing life on her own.

The purpose of compensation is to try to bring control back into your life, to offer options and alternatives, and to meet your needs. The common cry of women in mid-life crisis is that things have become so bad that they are out of control. Therefore the suggestions we have just made are targeted toward restoring choice and control to Vickie—and to you.

BALANCE

Preventing or lessening a mid-life crisis demands that you strive for balance in all of your life. You were created by God as a multifaceted person. If you ignore one area, it will become the squeaking wheel that cries out for oil.

If you have decided to follow God's gifting in your life and entered a career, you also need to realize that you must meet the other aspects of your personality. All of your energy must not be focused only on your career.

If you are a single career woman, you need to develop such things as your living quarters. Do they really speak of who you are as a person and do they meet your emotional needs so that you are rebuilt by being there? Where you live needs to be a place where you feel "at home." Your career cannot substitute for your need of deep, interpersonal relationships. Keep balancing your life so that friendships are continuing to develop in depth as well as number.

ROLE BALANCE

Another important way to keep your life balanced is to have a ministry with people. Try to have your ministry in some area that is different from your work. Think of a ministry such as working with underprivileged kids, hearing-impaired people, or at a halfway house for people who've had brain trauma. Whatever your particular career or homemaking pattern, try to keep a balance by having a ministry of a different type and pace.

Sometimes women are trapped into working more hours than men do when they start to push into middle or upper management. There is a terrible male chauvinism in business that says, "Women don't really want to work and don't really want to be in leadership." The woman pushing for upper management levels has to prove her abilities and commitment. Remember not to be so desperate in proving yourself that you get your total life out of balance.

In the February 11, 1983, issue of *The Denver Post*, an article entitled "Women at Mid-Life Shatter Stereotypes" reports a study showing that women need two basic elements in their lives. One is "mastery (feeling important and worthwhile, with a sense of self-esteem and control)," and the second is "pleasure (finding life enjoyable, measured by happiness, satisfaction and optimism)."[1]

The researchers who evaluated 300 mid-life women indicated that the people who showed the highest degree of satisfaction in life were the women who were married, with children, and in high prestige jobs.[2]

LIFE SPAN BALANCE
It's desirable to seek balance as a continuous experience in your life, but it may not always be possible. There may have been times—for example, when you were in school—that your life was unbalanced with heavy commitments to studies. There may be other times in your life—such as when you first had a child—that the balance of your life shifted to meet the needs of that child. Other directions and choices can also temporarily unbalance your life, but the goal is to get back into equilibrium as soon as possible.

Do you remember when you were a kid on a teeter-totter? You were OK as long as the teeter-totter was balanced and the board was going up and down smoothly. But sometimes two kids would jump on the other end of the teeter-totter, and you'd find yourself way up in the air. Pretty soon you'd start sliding down the board toward the middle. It's the same with life. You can tolerate being out of balance for a little while, but you must work to get the balance back as soon as possible or else everything starts to slide off the board.

Gail Sheehy surveyed 60,000 people, evaluating among

other things, their well-being in life. Regarding women, she says, "the women in their forties and fifties who came out at the top of my well-being scale were mostly women who had made commitments to marriage, career, and motherhood, all before the end of their twenties. They did not postpone. Usually theirs were *serial commitments;* sometimes they waited to have children until they passed 30. If there was a trade-off, it was that for the most part the highest-well-being women were not extraordinary successes in a professional sense. Few of them had gained much public recognition. Probably they had resisted devoting to their work the kind of time and absorption required to make a bigger mark."[3]

Sheehy further points out, "By contrast the lowest-satisfaction women in this generation group had followed the more traditional path of postponing outside work until their families were fully established."[4] When we ask, "How can we prevent or reduce the intensity of a mid-life crisis?" a part of that answer must be, "By living a balanced life." Remember you don't have to do everything at one time in your life.

THE FUTURE GIVES BALANCE
Another dimension of the balanced life is hope for the future. You've lived in the past and accomplished certain goals, yet there were areas that didn't go as you planned. Now you are at mid-life, making the necessary adjustments. An orientation toward the future will help you to realize that the best years of your life—having it all together, with physical strength, wisdom, and life experience—are just ahead of you.

You see, youth are slaves of their dreams and old women often live with their past and regrets. It is the mid-life woman who has all the pieces of the puzzle and whose life can make a real difference. That pull of the future productive years will help to give your life balance at this crucial time.

SPIRITUAL GROWTH

The fifth major area for reducing or preventing a mid-life crisis is your personal spiritual life. You need more than simply involvement with a church; you must know God in a personal way. We will call it having a walk with God.

WALKING WITH GOD

We are describing a personal relationship with God as a walk because it is an on-going experience, not just a decision you make once in your life because of panic or a problem. Perhaps these four basic concepts will help you.

1. *Facing God.* Knowing God in a personal way means that you allow him to confront you about your personal life and the way you've lived your life. Facing God means you confess to him the things that he brings to your attention in your past or present life that are wrong. Confession means that you say the same about your own sin and error that God says about them. In other words, confession is agreeing with God about what was or is wrong. (See 1 John 1:9.)

2. *Forgiveness.* A second aspect of walking with God is to ask for forgiveness. In essence, you say, "God, I know I was wrong, please forgive me." (See Psalm 51.)

Sometimes we find women who ask God for forgiveness but never really face God in honesty and confess their sin. Or we see the other side, the repeated confessing of sin but never receiving forgiveness. You need both to confess your sin to God frankly and then accept his forgiveness. You can walk away from your past because of God's forgiveness. He has removed it totally from you. He has forgotten it as well as forgiven it. (See Psalm 103.)

The biggest sin you need to face God with is not some evil action from your past, but rather that you've kept him at arm's length from you. You've said, "God, you stay up there in heaven and I'll stay down here on earth, and we'll both do our own thing."

Face God about the separation and distance that you've allowed to continue between yourself and God. Ask him to forgive you, to come into your life and to become part of all that you do and think. Jesus, who is God, says very simply, "Look! I have been standing at the door and I am constantly knocking. If anyone hears Me calling [her] and opens the door, I will come in and fellowship with [her] and [she] with Me" (Revelation 3:20).

So, walking with God means that you have faced God with your past by confessing your sins to him and you've asked his forgiveness. Now you have given him control of your life.

3. *Communication.* Communication with God means that you talk with him through the normal process of your day. It is more than just spending an hour in church on Sunday morning or what happens in your small Bible study group. Communication is the moment-by-moment inter-action with a friend. You share life together and are open to his promptings and leadings. "What do you think about this, God?" "OK, I'm for that! Thanks, God!"

During each day you ought to spend some time just quietly reading the Bible for yourself. As you begin read-ing, ask God to guide you into truth (John 16:13). Jesus promises to reveal himself to those who obey him and who love him (John 14:21, 23). God wants to have a personal relationship with you. He will reveal himself more and more, day by day, as you allow that process to take place.

So then, communication with God means that you share with him what's happening day by day and that you're open to his speaking to you through the Scriptures and through prayer.

Some people ask, "How does God speak to you?" Think of it this way: As you read the Bible, look for ideas or phrases that jump out at you—those phrases that become important for your personal life right now. Then try to incorporate those into your life as you go along that day.

Thus, God speaks to you through sections of Scripture that he selects and through impressions that he gives you as you read and reflect.

4. *Trust.* Another aspect of walking with God is that you rely on God. In the Psalms a beautiful phrase tells us what God wants in his relationship with us: "I want you to trust me in your times of trouble, so I can rescue you, and you can give me glory" (Psalm 50:15). Believing in God means trusting him with our life situations, but the question always comes, "*Can* I trust God?" Or, even more, "*Will* I trust God?"

Dick, an engaged student, wanted some help because his fiancée, Pam, was being dangerously harassed by her former boyfriend, Ralph. Dick was extremely distressed as he asked me (Jim) what to do. Dick said that Pam had told Ralph that their relationship was all over. She explained that she was engaged to Dick and she didn't want to talk to Ralph anymore. Pam's family had also explained this to Ralph. He had even been confronted by other friends of the family as well as by Dick himself.

Now Dick asked, "Should I get a restraining order against Ralph? Should we move away? (Although Ralph *has* threatened to follow.) He's a very violent man. I'm afraid he's going to do one of us harm. In the past he's gotten drunk when he's been despondent and he's almost like a wild man."

I explained to Dick that a restraining order was not going to keep Ralph from harming anyone; in fact, it would probably make him angrier. I told him that there was not much use in going to him again because, as Pam's fiancé, he was viewed as the enemy.

I said, "You need somebody who is a friend, who can get inside of him and appeal to him." Well, Dick assured me there was just no one like that.

I told him that my suggestion might sound strange and not very professional as a counselor, but I would suggest that he gather six or eight friends together to pray that

God would change this ex-boyfriend's heart. Dick looked at me incredulously. How could I suggest such a dumb, impractical thing as that with all of my counseling degrees? Wasn't there something else he could do?

I said to him, "Remember, you're studying to be a pastor. Not many months down the road you're going to be confronted with the same kind of problem from many different life situations, problems where you are helpless in your own strength. Now is a good time for you to learn to believe God, to depend totally on him, to 'trust me in your times of trouble so I can rescue you' [Psalm 50:14]."

He said, "I do believe in prayer, but this is just not going to work. You don't know this guy." I replied, "Well, at least I'm going to be praying, and I'd encourage you to get your friends to pray."

About two weeks later Dick stopped me and said, "You'll never believe what happened! Ralph's mother got hold of Ralph and told him flat out that the romance with Pam was over and he should stop bothering her and her new fiancé." I asked Dick, "Who told her to do that?" He smiled and said, "Maybe God did it in response to our prayers."

You see, walking with God means that in the tough times, when everything seems impossible, you believe God. It's easy for us, Jim and Sally the married couple, to believe in God and think he is great when everything is going wonderfully well in our lives. But the real test is when we've just had a fight and we're angry with each other. When we don't feel like making up and don't want to pray together, then the question is, "Do I really believe in God now?"

Maybe you've just been passed over for a promotion at work. You were the logical one to get it, but because of some inter-office politics you were passed over. In times like that, can we still believe the verse, "And we know that all that happens to us is working for our good if we love God and are fitting into his plans" (Romans 8:28)? In other

words, believing God is really putting our lives in his hands and trusting him with *whatever* happens.

5. *Let God be God.* Walking with God also means that we allow God to be God. You see, Dick's problem was that he wanted to take things into his own hands to control the situation. We are creatures who enjoy being in control.

Letting God be God means that you recognize that you are the servant and he is God. Sometimes we treat God as if he were a genie in a bottle. We think we can rub the little magic bottle called prayer, and God will pop out and say, "What is your wish?"

Walking with God means that you allow him to be sovereign and in absolute control in your life. You yield that right to him.

LET GOD BE MYSTERIOUS

Letting God be God also means that you allow him to be, to some degree, mysterious or unknowable. He knows things that we don't know. We are only finite human beings; he is the eternal God, the Creator who made us and everything in the universe. It is true that God wants to reveal himself to us; in fact, the Bible says that revealing God to us was part of what Jesus did as he came into the world: "Anyone who has seen Me has seen the Father . . . I am in the Father and the Father is in Me" (John 14:9-11).

However, Scripture also says that God and men don't think and function on the same level: "Neither are my thoughts the same as yours! For just as the heavens are higher than the earth, so are my ways higher than yours, and my thoughts than yours" (Isaiah 55:8-9).

When you walk with God, therefore, you acknowledge that you are the servant and he is the Lord, who knows more than you do. At the same time, you acknowledge that he is God who loves you and wants the very best for you: "For I know the plans I have for you, says the Lord. They are plans for good and not for evil, to give you a future and a hope" (Jeremiah 29:11).

Whatever you may be going through now in your life, God's purpose is to use it for your maturing. His purpose is also that you will have a future and a hope. God is not going to abandon you. But he doesn't promise to eliminate difficulties from your life. Remember that classic section of Scripture, Psalm 23, which says, "Even when walking through the dark valley of death I will not be afraid" (Psalm 23:4). It isn't saying that if we walk with God we don't have to go through the valley, but he promises to go through the valley with us whatever those valleys of our lives may be.

An outstanding woman is the subject of Proverbs 31. Some of the qualities of her life were her walk with God and her confidence in God for whatever the future held. The Bible describes her: "She is a woman of strength and dignity, and has no fear of old age" (Proverbs 31:25).

The mid-life woman who walks with God, facing him frankly with her past and her present, confessing her sin, accepting his forgiveness, communicating openly and responsively with him, believing him, and allowing him to be sovereign in her life, will be given the qualities of "strength and dignity" which will give her a hope and a confidence for whatever the future holds.

These lines, written by a single career woman, express some of the struggles that she faces in life and yet expresses her deep sense of God being in control of her life.

Sometimes I feel like a stream, flowing, hidden in the woods,
beautiful if anyone would look through the trees to see.
But left alone to stumble on and on across the rocks.

But God arranged my course, set
all the stones in place, put the trees
to shelter and hide.

So let me race on, sometimes still, sometimes bubbling,
to that place where He will collect me
into the ocean of His love.[5]

Chapter Seventeen
HELPING
A WOMAN IN CRISIS

You can't do it on your own. You were designed by God to be in relationship with other people. We all were designed to help each other. Only as we help one another do we become fully human.

For a moment, think back over the issues we have been considering. None of these is successfully handled without other people. We've talked about career, family, personal identity, and the various value questions that will come at mid-life. We've also talked about experiencing traumatic losses, depression, sagging self-esteem, and the impact of culture and physical aging. All of these require that other people be involved to help you work through this stressful time to become a stronger, more mature you.

In many places the Scriptures speak about our need to be involved with each other. Sometimes we are described as stones in a building, each one fitted to the other, supporting the other, and building on the other. But perhaps the best image of our interrelatedness, our needing each other, is that of the body. The body has many parts, yet each performs an important service for other members of the body: "Now God gives us many kinds of special abilities . . . the Holy Spirit displays God's power through each of us as a means of helping the entire church" (1 Corinthians 12:4-7).

This same chapter goes on to remind us that each part of the body is important. We can never say that we don't need each other: "The eye can never say to the hand, 'I don't need you.' The head can't say to the feet, 'I don't need you. . . .'

"If one part suffers, all parts suffer with it, and if one part is honored, all the parts are glad. . . . Now, here is what I am trying to say: All of you together are the one body of Christ and each one of you is a separate and necessary part of it" (1 Corinthians 12:21, 26, 27).

God intends that we help one another. He wants us to use the gifts and abilities he has given us to strengthen one another. We're not intended to make it on our own. We really do need one another.

EVERYONE'S ALWAYS SUPER

If we listen in on conversations at the average church, we will hear mostly positive stories of how great things are going for each person. Before, during, and after the service, as well as in Sunday school classes, it's the same dialogue: "How are you?" "Fine." "How are things going?" "Great."

Now a question: If God has given everybody abilities to help one another, how are we ever going to help if we don't know the needs? Suppose now that God has given to me (Sally) the gifts of wisdom, discernment, and counsel. If I never know of your need, I will not have an opportunity to exercise my gifts and you miss receiving valuable help God intended you to have.

Only as you begin to share your needs and your life struggles with other people can they use their gifts. You may never have thought of it this way, but when you don't let people know of your needs, you're cheating them out of the opportunity of putting their spiritual gifts and abilities into action. When you share problems, you are not imposing on your fellow body members, you are giving them the opportunity to grow as Christians, to exercise their abilities, and to live out the biblical admonitions to help others.

From now on, let people help you! Forget all those excuses that keep you away from people: "They're too busy." "My problems are too big." "I don't want to be a bother." "I'll work it out myself." Instead, give the rest of the body of Christ an opportunity to use their gifts and to strengthen you.

If you smash your little finger, your whole body reacts in pain. In the same way, when you're a wounded person, people around you and the body of Christ, in particular, suffer. So loosen up and let the body help you. That's the way God built us.

Now we want to focus our attention specifically on several different individuals or groups of people who can help. These next pages are specifically targeted as coaching guides for people who will be helping the woman go through mid-life crisis.

THE EMPLOYER HELPS

The question asked by many employers is, "Why should I help a woman who is going through mid-life crisis? I am concerned about my bottom line—profitability."

The answer is very selfish: "No man is an island." Without your employees, you can't make it. Employees provide your "profitability." If you are seen as an employer who simply chews up people and spits them out, then you have a suspicious group of employees who are not really committed to you or your product. They are working for money. That's a dangerous group to have as your employees.

Reaching out in concern for the individual development and problems of your employees expresses that you care.

In turn, they care for you and your organization. You become a team rather than competitors.

One of our students, Mel, had an impossible boss, who was always demanding blood from everyone. The student said, "I couldn't believe that one man could be so abominable, so self-seeking, so unwilling to give an inch." But Mel quickly changed his mind.

He went on to say, "One Christmas all of his employees wrapped several packages with the loveliest of gift paper, bows and all; and left them anonymously on this man's desk. The card said, 'From your crew.' The boxes were empty.

"I never met a man who earned his hate so well. Then one day while talking to me, he told me that he was a Christian."

Employer, you can help by becoming more sensitive to the needs of the people around you. Provide opportunities for them to talk. Let them ventilate problems they have with the job. They also need to talk about things they're wrestling with in their own personal lives.

If you have women employees in their thirties or forties, it would be helpful to give them this book, *Women in Midlife Crisis*, and one by Richard Bolles entitled *The Three Boxes of Life*.[1] Giving them a fresh flower for their desks would help, but a book or a pamphlet will probably have more impact. A book keeps saying for you, "I'm concerned for my people."

HER FRIENDS HELP

During the mid-years there is a shuffling of friends. Because we're changing and developing different interests and needs, we outgrow people or they outgrow us. It's normal to have a reshuffling of friends at this time in life. If you're a friend of someone going through mid-life crisis, you need to realize that she is likely to shuffle you out of her life unless you really understand her as a person and seek to meet her changing needs.

Mid-life is an era in life when time is at a premium. You may feel that you're being shuffled out of a woman's life when, in reality, she just doesn't have much time for people, period.

Sometimes you may feel that you're just being put off. This happens commonly when a person is going through some traumatic change in her value system and she's not sure how you'll react to the new values.

I (Sally) remember on one occasion saying to a mid-life woman, who was obviously showing mid-life crisis stress, that I'd be glad to sit down and chat with her some time. She assured me that everything was OK. I saw her on another occasion a few weeks later and she still seemed stressed. I said to her that both Jim and I had been in mid-life crisis. "It's not fun, but we've learned some things and perhaps could be of help—even if just to listen." Her response was, "Thanks a lot. It's really good to know that people like you who care are around, but there's really no problem."

I knew there was a problem, so I pressed again the next time we met. This time she said, "I sense that *you* have a need to talk to *me*, so let's go talk." She threw up some trial balloons. Then she found that it was OK to trust me and began to share some of her inside struggles and heavy decisions. When a friend puts you off, be caring, sensitive, gentle, and try to understand her needs—and keep coming back to help.

A study of women and their friendships concluded that "having a confidante eases major life adjustments to all ages. A confidante can support us, validate our beliefs, and act as a 'sounding board' when we need to 'let off steam.' "[2]

Being a friend to a woman going through mid-life crisis is very difficult because you feel like you're walking on eggs all the time. You may decide to do nothing. You may put off talking to her. Sometimes you may put it off even when the person is giving all kinds of unspoken or spoken signs. You may say, "I don't have time," or "I don't know how to help," or "Maybe she will reject me as a friend." But please don't put off helping until some better day.

The late Billy Rose told this story: "Two sisters in their twenties were bequeathed twenty-five thousand dollars when their father died.

"After the funeral the girls began wondering what they should do. Marie, the younger one, said, 'I'd like to do some traveling and see a little of the world.' But Hortense said, 'We mustn't throw our money away foolishly.'

"So the sisters purchased a general store in their village and enlarged it. During the next few years they built it into the most popular store in the area. One day a car drove up and a couple of good-looking men came in to buy some fishing gear. They engaged in some mild flirtation with the sisters and then drove away.

"Marie studied her features in a mirror and then turned to her sister, 'Let's close the store for a couple of months this winter and visit some resorts.' But Hortense shook her head. 'People would take their business elsewhere.'

"Ten years later the sisters had accumulated enough money to take care of them the rest of their lives. 'Come on,' said Marie, 'let's sell the store and start enjoying life. Let's go to California, Mexico, or Bermuda. We might even meet a couple of fellows and get married.' But Hortense said, 'We can't sell now—nobody would pay what the store is worth.' About that time a competitor opened a store across the street, and the sisters buckled down for the next five years to run him out of business.

"But one night Marie, who was then fifty, slipped on the ice and struck her head against a fire hydrant. The following day she died. Hortense never returned to the store. She held the most elaborate funeral ever seen in the area, sold the store, and went into seclusion.

"The following spring she made an unusual request. She asked permission to remove Marie's body to California. When permission was granted she had the coffin flown out and went along to supervise reburial. Then she moved into a resort hotel not far away.

"The following year she obtained another disinterment permit and this time had the coffin flown to Mexico City. A few months later she had it flown to Bermuda. In this grim manner she and her sister finally took the trips they had always planned."[3]

The story is a rather bizarre one, but perhaps it drives home the point. If you're really going to be a friend, take some risks *now!*

THE CHURCH HELPS

People in mid-life crisis are often disappointed with their churches because they see them as uncaring institutions which carry out their own programs. The people in the pews often are used for fulfilling the dreams of the leaders and do not have their needs met.

When a church decides to minister to mid-life people, the first step must be to *understand* the unique time of life and the special needs that mid-life people have. The second step flows naturally, which is to *design programs* to meet the needs of mid-life people. Perhaps a church can plan educational classes during the week or on Sundays that will face the problems common to this age group.

Classes could be offered to discuss the unique anxieties of the unmarried career woman, the married career woman who has chosen not to have children, the homemaker, and the person who is trying to do it all—marriage, children, and full time career. Classes could also be available on the needs of children at this age in life, how to help husbands with career and their potential mid-life crisis, American values of a house in the suburb and two cars in the garage, or how to live with a reduced lifestyle. Whatever the topics, they can be handled in a variety of ways, specifically aimed at meeting the needs of mid-life women.

Pastors often think only of a Sunday morning class. But what about a luncheon meeting to discuss women's financial concerns? There could be a weekend away for women only. Maybe the weekend should be for women in individual categories—never married, single-parent, married without children, married with children, divorced, or widowed. The point is, women are not just women, they are unique people with unique needs. The programs should be structured to meet those unique needs.

Churches commonly have couples' retreats. Sometimes they are heavy teaching times. Why not build them primarily for "R 'n R" to encourage couples to build their marital relationship? Make the sessions you do have low keyed and yet building toward a strengthened marriage.

Perhaps the pastor needs to speak more frequently on women's concerns. Scripture is full of help for women, as well as illustrations for women to model. If women are used in a brief sharing time in the morning service, their importance to the body will be demonstrated. Their sharing can be an encouragement to other women who are struggling at mid-life.

HER EXTENDED FAMILY HELPS

In the article entitled "What Do Women Use Friends For?" the researcher reports, "Relatives were not usually considered 'best friends' by the women in this study. On the average, only 25 percent of all close friends were relatives."[4]

That's not very good news for the woman in mid-life crisis nor for the extended family. In other words, extended families are not really being the support mechanism they ought to be for the mid-life woman.

Part of the problem, no doubt, is that the extended family is more spread out than it used to be. But the bigger problem seems to be that we don't work at understanding each other. We assume that because we are blood relatives there is automatic understanding. That's not at all true.

Understanding requires that we listen, spend time, and are nonjudgmental, kind, and open to each other. In short, understanding means that we are as concerned for our extended family members as we are for our other friends.

In recent years we (Jim and Sally) have renewed our efforts to strengthen relationships with all our extended family. We always had been close to some of our family, but we had lots of people around us in the churches that we served, so we really didn't feel a need for all our family. But as we have continued to age through the middle years, we are aware of a growing urgency to reach out to our extended family. It takes time and effort, but mostly caring.

You could start by identifying members in your extended family who may be going through mid-life crisis or some other stress in their lives. Drop them a note of encouragement every now and then, call them on the phone, and remember them in prayer. Perhaps you can send them books or articles that have been helpful to you. Start to rebuild the bridges so that you can minister to these few people in the world who are related to you by blood.

CHILDREN CAN HELP

In other parts of the book we've talked about how children can assume a greater responsibility for some of the work at the home. We think that's important, and it's one way children can express concern for their mom who may be struggling with mid-life crisis.

Another important way that children or adolescents can help is to begin thinking about caring for their parents. If you're an adolescent who is reading this section of the book, let us ask why you are able to be so concerned about some of your friends at school? Sometimes you even cry over their problems. Try reaching out, understanding, and caring about your mom's problems with the same intensity.

Or let's ask another question: "How old do you think you have to be in order to start understanding life from your parents' perspective and trying to help them?" In other words, at what age do you think you'll become their equal?

You need to start now, learning to understand and care for your parents, because being their friend and peer will help you to become a mature young adult. It is this ability to give love to another person (that is, understanding their needs and then taking care and concern from your life and giving it to them) that will help you to advance toward maturity.

Let's think for a moment about some of your mom's needs and how you can meet them. She is probably a little overweight, so don't make fun of her. Be a help to her as she tries to lose some weight. Maybe you can encourage her in her efforts to exercise and to watch what she eats.

She probably also feels insecure in her marriage. You can talk up your mother to your dad, telling him what a great person she is. Remind him tactfully how fortunate he is to be married to her and how great they are as a couple. You can also let your mom know the good things you see in your dad. She may need the reminder now!

She may also be struggling with her career, wondering how she's going to fit it all together. Tell her how proud you are to have a mom who is really a mover, a thinker, and involved in life. Tell her that you don't mind some things undone at home and show that you're willing to pitch in and help.

Another of her struggles may be with her age, feeling that she's getting old. You can build her up and encourage her. Talk about how wise she is and how you wish you knew all that she knows. Let her know she's at the prime of life and has it all together. Tell her that you want her to teach you everything she knows.

If you would find at least three things a day to compliment your mom about, and if you would assure her of your regular prayer, it will be a great encouragement to her. This kind of caring will also change you because you'll suddenly find yourself growing up.

HER HUSBAND IS THE KEY

Helping your wife through mid-life crisis may be one of the most demanding things you've ever had to do in your life. If you've thought it's been difficult to figure her out in the past, you may find it even harder now. She may have giant mood swings and obvious instability. She may express insecurity about herself, her values, your marriage relationship, and even life itself. If you're going to help, you've got to hang on, even though you may feel many times as if you're on a giant roller coaster.

As you help, remember that it's OK for your wife to be going through this time. It's important for you to understand and read about mid-life crisis so you're ready to be the supportive person she needs.

It's also crucial for you to realize that it's all right, in fact, very positive, for her to spend some time crying. A helpful article entitled "Weep with Those Who Weep"[5] talks about some of the positive things you can do to help a person who is struggling with life and who needs to cry.

Try saying to your wife, "It's OK for you to cry, honey." Give her the warm acceptance she needs. Give her the permission to cry either in front of you or privately. If you're with her when she cries, reach out and touch her, put your arm around her. You don't need to say any words.

After she's done crying, you need to be ready to listen. She's probably ready to talk now. Listening has a primary purpose of understanding the other person and helping her to ventilate her feelings. Be careful not to be defensive.

Sometimes a cup of coffee or tea at this time will help her calm down and will give her more objectivity as she shares with you some of the feelings she has been having.

STRONG AND GENTLE
Joyce Landorf has written a good little book to husbands, entitled *Tough and Tender.*[6] She says these are the two qualities that women look for in men. Women like men to

be strong in themselves and know where they're going. They want men to be strong for their wives, yet be sensitive, caring, and hurt when they hurt.

During your wife's mid-life crisis you will need to be strong in yourself. We're not talking about being macho or pumping iron. We're talking about being emotionally and spiritually strong, being well-rested, and really being in tune with yourself. You need to have an emotional reserve so that you can give to your wife. You must be sure that you're not so exhausted with your job that you have nothing left for her.

She needs to see you as a strong spiritual person who is walking with God. You may want to read that section on walking with God in Chapter 16. Your wife needs you to be trusting God and praying for her. She needs you to be strong for her when she can't be strong for herself.

Sometimes strength will mean that you help her put things into perspective, refocus her energies, and think through her values. As you help her refocus, it's important not only to be tough, but also to be tender.

NEW MARRIAGE PERSPECTIVE

The following article by Jim Sanderson is a touching example of a husband trying to reorient his wife. He does a great job. He's a little bit too gruff in the process but he also has some soft, tender parts to him. (Jim Sanderson is a nationally syndicated newspaper columnist and the author of the book *How to Raise Your Kids to Stand on Their Own Two Feet.**)

"The morning after the wedding she found herself standing in her nightgown in the doorway of her daughter's room experiencing the void. *I almost feel as if she's died,* the woman thought wryly. *Stop it. She's on her honeymoon, surely some of the happiest days of her life.*

"But, later, as she packed away some childhood artifacts

*This column reprinted through the courtesy of Sun Features, Inc. © 1982, all rights reserved.

to be put in the attic for the grandchildren, the hollowness returned. Her daughter was not planning any babies right away. It would be a long time before she might need a grandmother's help.

"The woman heard the question echoing in her head again: Of what use am I, really? What's my function now? She became angry at herself for permitting the question, in this form, and the anger diffused toward her husband.

"Riding home in the car after the wedding, they'd had the worst fight in their marriage. 'You're actually glad they're all gone,' she had cried out.

" 'Of course. It's over. We've done our job,' he had said.

" 'What's over?' she had flared. 'You sound as if you're planning to cut our children right out of your life.' She had known at the time that she was overstating; obviously he loved the kids.

"But finally he had said those bitter words: 'You became a different woman with the first baby. All those years you were a mother first and a wife second. Sometimes I felt I was at the bottom of your list, right after the dog.'

"Outrageous and cruel. Not true. Not true at all. He'd had too much champagne, and now suddenly he was like a wounded little boy: 'You never had time for me. Your mind was always somewhere else. If a child sneezed you were out of my arms in a flash, like a mother bear defending her cubs in mortal danger.'

"Sex, that was it. 'Yes, that is it,' he had said. But also when we were talking, or not talking. Or trying to do something together as adults, just the two of us. Evenings out, we'd talk about the kids. I couldn't get you off it. And we never took a vacation on our own.'

" 'I thought you loved our family vacations,' she had cried.

" 'I did. I do,' he had groaned. 'What's the use? A man can't ever fight Motherhood—all that virtue.'

" 'What do you want from me?' she had finally asked in a small, tight voice.

" 'I want us to be lovers again, the way we were before the kids came. There's only the two of us now. We've got the rest of our lives to live together, alone, and it's got to get better than it has been—or else.'

"Suddenly now, just thinking about that brutal threat, she became weak and had to sit down. Yet, it happened all the time: men and their mid-life crises. Looking for young bodies, young women to flatter their egos.

"And, yes, in all those frenzied months of the wedding preparations, he had become distant. Maybe he already had a mistress. She tried to think when they had last made love. Was it possible that something terrible was about to happen to her?

"No, surely not. Surely he knew how much she loved and respected him. He'd looked so sad that morning when he'd left for work, so tired. He wasn't a young man anymore. But he's right, she thought, I can be a better wife to him. If it isn't too late.

"At the bottom of her despair that morning in the kitchen she unscrewed her jar of instant coffee, and found inside his scrawled note: 'Dear Wife, grow old with me. The best is yet to be, the last of life, for which the first was made.—Robert Browning & Your Husband'

"She read it again and again. Then, when she had exhausted her tears, she reached eagerly for the phone to begin her new life."[7]

THE GAME PLAN

Maybe some practical coaching tips might help you to work more effectively with your wife during her mid-life crisis. These ideas are in brief form. More extensive information is given in a book entitled *You and Your Husband's Mid-Life Crisis* by Sally Conway.[8] If you would read that book, and reverse the roles, you'll find a lot of help to get you through this difficult time in your wife's life, your life, and your marriage. Think through these tips:

1. Understand mid-life crisis. Understand the feelings

and the causes behind it. Understand the confusion she feels. Understand that it is a short segment of life; it's not going to go on forever. Understand what you can do to help her through this time.

If you've read only this section of this book, we would encourage you to read the whole book so that you get a good handle on what a woman's mid-life crisis is all about.

2. Your wife needs space. She needs time to be alone, but at some times she also needs to be dragged out of those low periods of depression. Look for a balance in your relationship with her. Give her time to be reflective, go on walks by herself, ride a bike, or wander through the shopping mall. But there are times when the two of you need to be together. In those together times, don't push her with words such as, "Now, let's be reasonable, let's be logical." Instead, ask, "What are you feeling?" or "Talk to me about your confusion."

3. Build her self-image. All of the suggestions that we made earlier in this chapter to your children could also be used by you. Think of positive ways to meet her special needs at this time. At least three times during the day express verbal appreciation to her. Congratulate her and thank her for who she is. Be careful not to thank her only for the things she does, but also thank her for the quality of person she is.

If you say thanks for doing your laundry, that's important but you could hire that out. When you say thank you for being a kind and sensitive person who cares for hurting people, that's something you can't buy. That's a quality of her person, and that's what you want to reinforce.

4. Be attractive to her. How about getting rid of that extra twenty pounds that you've put on since you were married? Maybe you could work on that muscle tone. Remember that male bodies are going to be more important to her right now, especially if she's wondering if she has any sexual appeal.

Dress attractively. What kind of clothes does she like to

see you in? Wear those. You can be attractive to her by doing some crazy stuff together that might not be part of your normal routine. Plan some special weekends. Surprise her with a special little gift. Be sexy. Flirt with her. Make some passes at her. Start touching her more often. Look for more times and creative ways to have sex. Build your attractiveness on the same things that drew you together at first, as well as according to her needs now.

5. Encourage her blooming. The next chapter, "Blooming at Mid-Life," should become your guidebook for practical ways to help her during this time.

You are the most important person to help her through mid-life crisis. She will either love you more for your care and understanding or want to be away from you because you "blew it."

Understand her needs and adapt to meet those needs. Don't wait, because tomorrow you might not have a marriage. Your wife might be singing the Laura Branigan song, "Solitaire." This song is the story of a guy who was always gone, leaving his wife home alone to play solitaire. She needed him and tried so hard to please him—but he didn't need her. He just did what he wanted—he didn't care.

Now life has turned. He wants her, but she's on the run. It had taken some time, but she had become accustomed to living without him. Now he finds he loves her, but "it's a little too late."

The song ends as she defiantly sings the pathetic words, "Don't wait up, babe, because I won't be there."[9]

Chapter Eighteen
BLOOMING AT MID-LIFE

"For is it not possible that middle-age can be looked upon as a period of second flowering, second growth, even a kind of second adolescence?"[1]

Mid-life reevaluation can be extremely positive for a woman. A realigning of her values and priorities can cause her to bloom and be productive for a new season in her life. She has new freedoms and much life experience to use now for a fresh surge of fruitfulness. Her success will depend largely upon whether she emphasizes her assets or her liabilities.

A TALE OF THREE WOMEN

There are three kinds of women at mid-life. The first is one marked by "despair and disgust." She feels tremendously sorry for herself because life seems to have handed her a pile of difficulties. When you listen to her story, you have to agree with her that her life has been very hard.

The woman in despair feels helpless. She is a woman without hope and she is determined to live in her sour, withdrawn life. She's like a rosebud that has come to full size but started too late in the season. The cold, early winter winds never allow the bud to open and blossom.

The difference between the late season rosebud and a mid-life woman is that the woman has a choice to stay in the pit of despair or to bloom. People all around her have had as difficult experiences as she has and have bloomed in spite of their stresses. If you're one of those people caught in despair, you can bloom—you *must* bloom!

The second kind of woman is the one who has decided to "grin and bear it." She is not lost in despair but she believes that she will never really come into her flowering. This woman says, "I'm stuck in this bad situation with a job I hate, a marriage that doesn't satsify, and kids that don't obey me." When she's asked if she has given up, she'll say no, she hasn't given up. Ask her if she believes it can be any better. "No, it will always be the same."

If you're just trying to hold out until you die, you need to realize that instead, you can bloom—you *must* bloom!

The third woman has chosen to "bloom at mid-life." That doesn't mean that she didn't accomplish anything in her adolescence or young adulthood, but this woman views each section of life as a crucial time to grow and mature. She looks back on the past and says, "That was good" or "That was bad," and she goes on to ask, "Where do I go from here?" and "How can I make the most of what I have?" She is more than a survivor.

The growing mid-life woman knows how to sort out the good from her past, add new dimensions to her mid-life years, and create a whole new maturity.

CREATIVE RISKING

Our daughters have a real gift from God, or maybe it's from poverty. They are able to take junk and make it look great in a room. When we say junk, we're not talking about antiques, we're talking about *junk*. They mix together old burlap bags, rusty cans, growing plants, used chairs, wooden crates, things scavenged from old barns, and special handmade things they've created. The result is a warm, homey, living environment that says to everyone entering the room, "You're welcome here."

The growing mid-life woman is not held back by obstacles such as a poor marriage, a job that isn't right, little money, limited education, an imperfect body, or by thinking it's too late in life. Instead, she asks, "What do I have and what can I do with it now?" She makes something good even out of the junk of life.

Blooming can be a frightening experience because it means something that was not there before is now going to develop. It means leaving the safe places and ways of the past. Even if the past was uncomfortable, at least it was familiar. Now you're going to launch into something new and different.

Blooming, launching, or creating something new in your life is always frightening, but it's also frightening to stay where you are. Remember the times you've been afraid in the past—perhaps when you left grade school, or puberty, your first date, your first job, or the first time you faced death. Life is filled with frightening experiences. If we face the challenge, we grow. Then we look back and are grateful.

If a sailboat stays in the harbor, it's very safe. There's no risk. But remember that sailboats were not made to stay in harbors. There's no risk if you stay in the old personality of the young adult woman, but you'll miss the flowering. You'll miss the emerging of the new mid-life butterfly, that new, more complete you.

FORCES THAT CAUSE MID-LIFE BLOOMING AND FLOWERING

Several factors will be assisting you to bloom at mid-life. Most of these forces will exert pressure for your growth without your conscious effort.

THE COMMAND GENERATION

Fortune magazine, September 1981, reported some of the advantages for mid-life people:

- Less than 2 percent of mid-lifers were victims of violent crime in 1978 versus more than 6 percent of the unfortunate twenty-to-twenty-four slot.
- The mid-life unemployment rate in 1979 was only 3 percent versus an average of 6.8 percent for everyone else.
- Only 8 percent of the mid-life people were below the poverty line in 1978 versus 12 percent for everyone else.
- Among year-round full time workers, mid-life women earn about 9 percent more than other women.[2]

The middle generation in the United States holds the control over power, wealth, and prestige. The people in the middle generation are the decision makers. Even though society reveres youth, it is controlled by mid-life people.

By the time a woman reaches forty, she has an advantage over the twenty-year-old woman because of having twice as much life experience to draw on. You can remember when you were a young woman and walked into a room full of strangers, you wished you could just disappear into the wall. Or remember how you had difficulty looking people in the eyes, especially if they were persons who were in authority or who were attractive to you? Think about the time when you applied for your first summer job, or when you wished for courage to talk to a teacher about your low grade. Remember when you needed to confront the boss on your first job when it was time for a raise, and you just let it go by? Twenty years of life experience helps you to look at life a little differently and handle some of the issues more gracefully than when you were a teenager.

This sense of being a more experienced person and part of the command generation will be part of the push or force helping you to bloom and flower. You feel a sense that you are in charge, you can do it, you've got the experience, the background. Now you're ready to take off and become a more fully-developed woman at mid-life.

ASSERTIVENESS

There is a natural growth of assertiveness that takes place in women at mid-life. Men, after mid-life, tend to become more mellow, less authoritative, less domineering, less aggressive, and less interested in conquering the world around them. Women, on the other hand, become more aggressive and more assertive than when they were young. They are less likely to conform and more likely to dominate. Carl Jung observes, "Woman . . . allows her unused supply of masculinity to become active."[3]

A fascinating study done some years ago explored this idea of the exchange in men and women. Over a hundred people were asked to make up a story about a picture showing a younger couple and an older couple. They were asked to assign an age to each of the four people, to give a general description of each of them, and, finally, to describe what they thought the figures in the picture were feeling about each other.

"Most striking was the fact that, with increasing age of respondents, the old man and old woman reversed roles in regard to authority in the family. For younger men and women . . . the old man was seen as the authority figure. For older men and women . . . the old woman was in the dominant role, and the old man, no matter what other qualities were ascribed to him, was seen as submissive."[4]

Along with other studies which show this to be true,[5] you probably know from your own experience more older women than men who are assertive. Or if you know their history, you know how they've changed so that the men are now more affiliative and the women more assertive than when they were younger.

This quality of assertiveness is going to help you flower

and bloom. It doesn't mean that you have to become aggressive and obnoxious, but it does mean that God has built into you an urgency that will help you to develop into a more expansive person at mid-life.

LIFE EXPERIENCES

Every experience you have in life is like being given another crayon with a slightly different color than all the rest to use in creating a picture. Each new color allows you to expand the shading, the tone, the richness.

The mid-life woman knows a lot about being a career woman if that's the direction she has chosen. She not only has the skills, she also knows the little games, the politics, the times to be quiet, the times to make suggestions. She has learned how to plant ideas in people's minds, how to ask for raises, how to handle men with sex on the brain and arms like octopus tentacles.

If she chose the mother direction, she knows about being up all night with a child running a high fever. She has learned how to sing quietly at bedtime and cheer wildly at games. She has learned how to say no, and she has learned how to listen as she sits on her child's bed late at night and lets the sad or happy stories pour out.

After all these years of managing a family, she has administration and coordination skills galore. She knows how to balance budgets and meals. She is a travel agent, scorekeeper, public relations agent, and still keeps clean clothes in everyone's drawers.

The mid-life woman has it all over the girl at age twenty. Yes, the twenty-year-old has a firmer body, but she doesn't have the life experience to make her as indispensable as you are. All that life experience is going to help you to blossom, to grow, to become that great mid-life woman that God wants you to be.

MID-LIFE CRISIS

Mid-life pressures and problems that have caused you to think and reevaluate are giving you a great opportunity.

This can be either a Renaissance or the Dark Ages. It can become a time of growth or a time of retreating.

Think of some people you know who are in their sixties or seventies. Now, pick out the ones who are especially optimistic and growing, who seem to enjoy life. They're fun people. You want to be around them. We both have relatives who are like that. Our girls have always enjoyed them and looked for opportunities to be with them. Invariably these are the people who made choices to bloom and grow all through their lives.

We also have relatives and friends who are just the opposite. They are depressing to be around. They crab and complain about everything in life. We often think, "If we're miserable just being around them, think how miserable they must be living with themselves."

I (Sally) have an aunt named Marie (real name). She's not had an easy life, but she's made life nicer for those who know her.

She was the oldest daughter in a family of seven children. After graduation from high school, she taught in country schools. She lost her money in the Depression and didn't get to go to college. She has fought a chronic, life-threatening disease all her life.

She married a kind, loving man, but they were poor. I remember that they always seemed to have fun together and my aunt could "make something out of nothing," whether it was a meal or a new pair of drapes.

She was told by doctors not to have children because of her health, but she had two sons anyway. They grew to be men, worthy of the pride she had for them, but then one was suddenly snatched by death when his military plane crashed.

In a few short years her husband died a painful death from cancer. His business partner did some maneuvering so that there was little or nothing left in the estate for my aunt. She was in her late fifties, nearly broke, without a "trade," and her only surviving son was married and living with his family several hundred miles away.

Those are some of the facts about Aunt Marie. More of the facts are that after my uncle's death, she went to college and received a degree in library science. She taught in city schools for a few years, and then due to an unfortunate political situation, she was not rehired one year. Where does a woman somewhere around age seventy go to apply for a new teaching position? She didn't find a teaching job that year, so guess what she did. She managed an airport! You see, despite some physical barriers, she had taken flying lessons and had become a pilot. She also had the skills to manage a small town's air terminal. Then she taught several more years at a rural school in a sparsely populated region of western Nebraska. I can tell you that those kids are some of the best educated in the nation right now.

Her son finally convinced her to move from the sand, cactus, and winter snows to be nearer his family, so she now cares for her own home and garden in a Denver suburb. Has she retired? No. Besides motherly and grandmotherly roles with her nearby family, she spends several hours a week tutoring adults in English. Furthermore, she is collaborating with her son in a writing venture.

More facts about Aunt Marie are that she is a delight to be around, she is loved by all who know her, and she is a model of courage and optimism. All my memories of her are the kind that cheer and uplift me. Obviously, she made choices at every point in her life that caused her to be a woman we enjoyed then and now.

You have the opportunity now at mid-life to decide what the rest of your life is going to be. Are you going to end up being a grouchy, old lady, making yourself and everyone else miserable from now until you die? Or are you going to use this mid-life crisis to be a positive reevaluation time? Will you discard some of the bad stuff from your past and add new, exciting and positive things for your future? Your mid-life crisis can be a force that will cause blooming to take place in your life.

ENOUGH IS ENOUGH

It is usually at mid-life that people begin, for the first time in their lives, to say, "That's enough. I'll let go of it. I'll quit pushing. I have enough success. I am rich enough or thin enough. I've achieved enough in that area."

When we come to the point where we're able to say, "That's enough," it means that we're willing to let go. We're willing to shift our priorities and take on some new directions. At mid-life, the woman is able to say, "I've had enough of being the little girl, even the young adult girl; I'm ready to be the mid-life woman, mature, poised, knowing who I am and where I'm going."

Mid-life is also when a person can say, "That's enough of the exploitation. I'm through allowing others to take advantage of me. It's time for me to look at myself in a different light. Enough is enough!" Being able to say, "Enough," perhaps for the first time, enables you to start this new blooming and flowering of your life.

ABILITY TO SYNTHESIZE

Certain parts of your intellectual capacity, such as your memory, started going downhill at about age seventeen. But there are other dimensions of your intellect, such as your ability to synthesize—make sense out of the pieces of life—that increase into your late fifties. Now, if you try to survive on just the memory part of your intellect, you'll be fighting a losing battle, just as you will fight a losing battle trying to keep your body looking young, your hair from turning gray, or wrinkles from forming on your face. You must move in the direction of your strengths and away from the things that you are losing. The areas that are losses are in your youthful body. What is growing is your wisdom.

It always looks as if the girls' basketball coach is just sitting there on the bench. The girls are the ones who are doing the job and playing the game. That's not true. The girls on the court are the players being directed by the coach. The coach, in a sense, is really playing the game. She has learned to go with her brains and wisdom; she doesn't have to play the game with her muscles anymore.

As you come into mid-life, God has given you the ability to make sense out of life. The adolescent or young adult is able to understand pieces of life, but they do not understand how the pieces fit together. As a mid-life woman, you're no longer asking the question, "What is it worth?" You're now asking, "What is worthy?" You're able to pull the pieces together to give worthy directions to your life.

You may not have realized it before, but you are growing in wisdom. That wisdom that you've been accumulating from life experience, your growing assertiveness, your mid-life crisis, and your ability to say that enough is enough—all these are a growing gift from God that you didn't have when you were twenty years of age. He has been building these into you to help you in this blooming and flowering era of your life.

We hope you'll take advantage of all that God has poured into you and you'll respond the same way the Apostle Paul did: "But whatever I am now it is all because God poured out such kindness and grace upon me—and not without results: . . . actually I wasn't doing it, but God working in me, to bless me" (1 Corinthians 15:10).

ATTITUDES FOR BLOOMING

Cathy was an attractive mid-life woman. She sat on the rock wall with her legs crossed and her toe bouncing up and down nervously. "I just don't like what's happening," she said. "I don't like what's happening to me. I don't like what's happening to Duane. I saw this same ugly thing happen with my parents.

"I remember when I was thirteen, my parents used to fight a lot. I don't mean hitting, just words. It wasn't that I was afraid that they were going to leave each other but I just wanted them to love each other. Now it's happening to us.

"The big thing, I guess, is that Duane is following his dad's pattern. He just keeps getting pushed at work and he keeps doing what they want him to do. He's like a puppet on a string, or maybe like a donkey following a carrot—a little more time, a little more sacrifice, and you'll get the next promotion.

"We've already had five major moves. They've not necessarily been up either. And each time I've had to give up some friends. This last time, I told Duane I wasn't going to move again. I didn't like what was happening to me. I was almost afraid of making friends for fear I'd lose them, and yet I need people.

"I told Duane I didn't like what was happening between us. We never had any time to talk, never had any time for fun. I didn't like the way our marriage was going.

"I told him that it was time for me. I'd followed him all over the country for his job and his promotions, but now it was time for me. It was time for me to be able to finish my education, to work on my career. There were some things that I wanted to do before I died and I didn't like living in this lousy, dry marriage and being dragged all over the country losing friends."

All the mid-life forces were at work inside of Cathy, causing her to look back over her life, to evaluate, and to look ahead.

The question we need to consider is, "How can I bloom?" How do you make it happen? How can you move from where you are now in your emotional and spiritual development to becoming that mature, mid-life woman who has it all together? Several attitudes need to become part of your life and thinking so you can move to a new level of maturity.

LIFE EVALUATION
You need to examine where you have been and where you want to go. It's like riding a bike up a hill on a country road. You get to the top, stop for a moment to catch your breath, and look back over where you've been. It was a

hard climb. It's a great view backward, but you also look forward to where you're going. Stopping to reflect on where you've been and where you want to go are both crucial.

Cathy had reflected on where her marriage had been. She compared it to her parents' marriage. She was looking at her own goals, aspirations, and dreams that she had in her twenties, and she realized that she hadn't arrived yet. Now was the time to reset some goals and directions to change priorities, so that Duane's company would not control their lives.

Think back over your life. Where have you been? What have you liked or not liked about it? Perhaps it would be helpful to take a big sheet of paper and jot down the really great and growing experiences and the events and relationships that were crummy. Write down your accomplishments and the goals and dreams not yet fulfilled.

NEW LIFE FOCUS

Second, you need to think differently about yourself and life in general. Most young adult women think of themselves as young, and they also tend to be body-oriented. Many mid-life women are still trying to be young and to compete with twenty-year-old women in their bodies.

Focus less on your body and more on your mature understanding of life, the wisdom that God has given you, the life experiences you have, and the fact that you belong to a command generation.

Stop focusing on the young adult woman as the prize commodity. Start thinking about her as she really is. The twenty-year-old woman has a firm body but many times she is socially inept, feels awkward, and doesn't have skills developed for a career, for mothering, for being a wife. She has a long way to go to learn as much about life as you already know.

Change your thinking about what you have. You know the old story about half a pie in a pie plate. The pessimist says, "Oh, too bad, half of the pie is gone." The optimist says, "Wow, half the pie's left!" Think in terms of what you have to offer to your career, your family, friends, the community, the world, and to God.

GOODBYE, COCOON

A third important attitude is that of shedding the past. You need to walk away from some of the experiences and attitudes of the past. Forget them. The Apostle Paul said, "I am still not all I should be but I am bringing all my energies to bear on this one thing: Forgetting the past and looking forward to what lies ahead . . ." (Philippians 3:13).

For you to become a mature, mid-life woman, growing and flowering, you need to leave some of that "stuff." Forget the failures of the past, forget the things you can't change. So you've made some bad choices, some things have happened in your life that you're ashamed of; you wish you could change some things, but you can't. Tell God—simply and directly in prayer. That's what forgiveness is all about. Ask him to forgive you; then walk away from it because he has forgiven you. Christ died to forgive you. Accept it!

Before you were born, you lived in a different world. It was a safe, secure place inside your mother. But you could never become a real person, develop to your full size, or experience breathing life until you were born. Moving from being a young adult to a mid-life adult may be as difficult as passing through the birth canal. But you need to shed that past world and leave it behind. Yes, you'll want to take the good stuff with you—you'll always take God with you—but there's much that you just need to "let go."

Anne Morrow Lindbergh has said, "Perhaps middle age is, or should be, a period of shedding shells; the shell of ambition, the shell of material accumulation and possessions, the shell of the ego. Perhaps one can shed at this stage of life, as one sheds in beach-living, one's pride, one's false ambitions, one's mask, one's armor.

"Was that armor not put on to protect one from the competitive world? If one ceases to compete, does one need it? Perhaps one can, at last, in middle age, if not earlier, be completely oneself? And what a liberation that would be!"[6]

DECISION TIME
Fourth, remember that blooming is a choice. It demands bravery. Blooming involves risk. You may experience instability, but always, *always* there is choice!

Sometimes it appears that people are forced into things, but ultimately it comes down to their decision to follow one path or another. It is a privilege to have a choice. The opportunity should not be taken lightly. It is also a responsibility to make the right choice. Choose to grow. Choose to bloom. Choose to be different.

ACTIONS FOR BLOOMING

Your new attitudes are going to have an impact on actions. Reinforce your new attitudes by taking on new behavior. Attitudes will change actions. As you act out new directions, you will stabilize the new attitudes. Each strengthens the other.

DREAM, DREAM, DREAM
One new behavior that you should notice and encourage is daydreaming. Set aside some quiet time for reflection. Daydreaming is not negative but is an activity that creative people identify as strategically important for the formation of new ideas and directions.

Daydreaming is a time when you allow your mind to flow in several different directions. You allow yourself to think about putting things together in different combinations, various alternatives, and new possibilities. "Think tank" sessions or brainstorming are forms of active daydreaming, where any thought that comes up is allowed to be considered. None is rejected at the beginning. The attitude of being open helps you to get a better perspective on the past and on the future with dozens of different possibilities.

In spiritual terms, quiet meditation with God is a form of daydreaming. You think over with God who you are, what the Scripture means to you, and how you should fit into life. Encourage daydreaming or creative thinking every day by finding some time to go for a little walk, ride your bike, sit quietly somewhere in the house, or as you drop off to sleep.

ACCENTUATE THE POSITIVE

Second, identify your gifts and abilities. What are the things that you really do well? What are the talents that you have? Make a list. And after you've made the list, rank order the items so you can see which are your strongest abilities and gifts.

Be sure you also identify your spiritual gifts. As you think through your gifts, ask yourself how these abilities are being used to help people.

When you reflect on your gifts and abilities, ask God to help you focus on a ministry or a people-helping direction that will use your talents and gifts to make a difference in the world. Your blooming will never be complete unless you identify your abilities and focus them under God's guidance to help people and change the world.

Ruth (real name) was a normal, mid-life middle-class white woman, sitting in a typical evangelical church that was not much aware of the great social issues swirling in the United States in the late sixties. During a morning message, God challenged her to consider her own personal ministry. What could she do in the world that would make a difference? She began to pray, asking God specifically to guide her.

God gave her a deep burden for the poor Black people in her community. She began by taking food and clothes to them. Then she listened to their accounts of poverty and injustice. She heard stories about slumlords who didn't care and rents that were higher than in middle-class communities. She saw families with several children, sleeping in one room, and with no running water. She also became acquainted with women who didn't know how to read, write, or care for their families.

Now she understood God's calling in her life. She began to mobilize other people to pray with her for these forgotten people who were living only a few blocks from her home. Soon people were bringing canned and boxed food to the church every week. One room of the church became a storehouse from which used clothes were distributed. She also found inexpensive kitchen appliances and furniture for the Black families.

She, her husband, and their task force started confronting landlords and appealing to the city council. They began to cause waves. Ruth's mission was making a difference.

Whenever anyone of their group took food, clothes, or other help to a home, they were to sit, listen, learn, and share in the Black family's lives. Ruth started meetings with the women—a combination of Bible study, reading, and homemaking skills classes. These grew in number so that several were formed. Soon there was a need to change the direction slightly and include husbands and couples. Ruth began discipling couples to teach other couples. Some of those couples have become staff members of local Black churches.

God was laying the burden on other people through Ruth's prayer and concern, so that other churches and organizations became involved. Today many needs are being met in the Black community because of one woman's obedience to her mission.

You're at a crucial time in your life now. Ask God to give

you a special ministry that will change the world around you. We have often asked ourselves what would happen if every Christian had a ministry that was as effective as Ruth's. Wow! Our world would be different.

WHERE'S THE TARGET?
A third action that is part of your blooming process is to set goals. Goals may be short range, just for today, but you'll also want to set some longer-range goals.

Goals should be very specific, but as you make them specific, you also need to be tolerant with yourself for any miscalculations. Remember also that general goals are harder to measure for success.

Ruth's first goal was to be open to God and to seek his wisdom for what her ministry should be. Then her goals began to flow out of the insight God was giving her. You don't have to call them goals if you don't want to. I don't think Ruth ever set out "goals," as such. She just said, "This is what I want to do for people. This is what I think we ought to do as a church. And here's how I'd like to get people helping themselves."

When we had a missions conference in our church a few years ago, the youth group asked us (Jim and Sally) to talk about some of our overseas travels. They were a typically bored teen group, preoccupied with their own self-image struggles and their developing sexuality. Could they be challenged?

We talked about the needs of the world in some specific places where we'd been. Then I (Jim) said, "You teens know more about the Bible than many of the people who are serving as pastors overseas." That blew them away. I suggested, "Why don't you take a summer off and go overseas and teach some people? Why not go door to door and share your faith? How about helping missionaries with work projects?"

The questions flew. Was it possible? Could they really do it? "Yes," I told them, "you can do almost anything if you set out what you want to do and then bite off small pieces toward accomplishing your goal."

The result was that they took the bait and spent a year and a half in preparation. They learned the major theological background for why we were Christians so that they could answer questions. They learned how to share their faith with strangers. They learned how to work with missionaries and identified their special needs. They learned about Venezuela, the country chosen for the mission. They learned to speak and sing in Spanish. They learned to sing as a group for the first time, and some learned to play the guitar. They wrote a drama, and memorized it in English and Spanish. They learned how to pray. They learned how to raise money and believe God.

We spent a month together in Venezuela. In two of the several towns we visited, we went to every home, door to door, sharing the gospel. In both towns Bible study groups sprang up. In other towns we went door to door in highrise apartment buildings. Again, ministries grew. We sang in the public plazas, gave the drama, and showed Christian movies. Venezuelan young people were always teamed with our teens.

Missionary lives, as well as Venezuelan lives, were changed. One missionary said, "I've never led another person to Christ. Kevin [real name] was talking to this young Venezuelan, and because he couldn't speak Spanish very well, he couldn't go any farther than explaining the Four Spiritual Laws. He turned to me and said, 'You do it.' Believe it or not, I led that young man and two others with him to the Lord."

The outcome was that about a hundred people made decisions for Christ. Small Bible study groups were started in several places. Work projects were carried out at two different sites with all the interior walls painted in one large Bible institute. The biggest benefit was the spiritual growth in the lives of those young teens. Without goals it never would have happened.

Growth and change are not going to happen in your life unless you set some goals. Base your goals on who you are and what you feel strongly about. A good test is to ask yourself, "If I could do anything I wanted in the world to minister to people, what would I do?" Other good questions are, "What is it that I feel strongly about? What is it that really disgusts me and I would like to change if I could?" "What would I really like to do for other people?" Your responses to these questions should give you some insight. Then set some goals that will put feet to your insight.

As you keep acting on your goals, you will continually change as a person. Life is made of many small choices, and each choice you make brings new change events into your life and changes you as a person.

NEW ADVENTURES
A fourth new action that will help this blooming and flowering of your life is to try new adventures.

WHY NOT . . .
• Develop your painting or pencil sketching?
• Write a book?
• Learn to play a musical instrument?
• Attend a live performance of a symphony?
• Visit Niagara Falls?
• Take up serious photography?
• Ride a donkey to the bottom of the Grand Canyon?
• Learn to fly?
• Go to a live, major league sports event?
• Attend a church service very different from yours?
• Learn to skin dive?
• Take a canoe and backpacking trip?
• Dig for clams?
• Learn to sail?
• Visit a coal mine?
• Sleep out overnight in a sleeping bag?

- Visit a seminary?
- Work at a school for the blind?
- Invite a missionary to stay in your house for a week?
- Serve on a jury?
- Ride in a police car with a policewoman?
- Write a letter to your Congressman?
- Visit a halfway house for alcoholics?
- Invite in some of your neighbors who've never been in your home?
- Visit a retirement home?

The list is endless. Do something different. Expose yourself to different aspects of life that are not in your common pathway. Get to know people from different countries and different cultures who live in our country. Talk with someone who is a more mature Christian than you are; talk to someone who is an atheist.

Remember, every change event in your life changes you and influences your value system. All these new adventures will help this process of your becoming a mature mid-life woman. Who knows, out of all of your new adventures, God may help you to see a special ministry that's going to change your world, as well as you.

CRACK THOSE BOOKS
A fifth major action that you might want to consider during this blooming era of your life is to go back to school. All kinds of educational opportunities are offered by high schools, community colleges, and four-year colleges and universities. Classes are offered in the evening, grouped on weekends, or during intensive two-week sessions, to fit the busy schedule of the mid-life adult.

Some women return to school to improve their skills and abilities so that they can be more effective in their career. Others want to learn new skills. Perhaps you'd like to learn tailoring, home repairs, car maintenance, sculpturing, painting, weaving, to play an instrument, sing, act, or dance. Classes that can help you grow in all of these areas are probably offered in your community.

Other people take continuing education courses to improve their inner selves. Most churches have small Bible study groups where people meet together to help each other grow. Other organizations in your community may offer growth opportunities, such as your hospital offering sessions on mid-life or a mental health clinic offering marriage enrichment or divorce prevention seminars.

Added to all of the seminars that are available, there are the media. If you would listen, for example, to Chuck Swindoll's program, "Insight for Living," and study along in the guidebooks, you would find yourself growing at a faster pace than you believed possible. He will lead you in a very warm and human way through important sections of Scripture and apply them to everyday life. Or, listen to Dr. James Dobson's "Focus on the Family" or to David and Karen Mains' "Chapel of the Air" as a regular diet to stimulate the growth in your personal or family life.

Perhaps the educational side of you can be expanded by a trip to your local bookstore. Ask for suggestions about the most important books they have in the area in which you want to grow. If you read six to eight pages a day, you can cover an average book in a month. Think of the difference that would take place in your life because of the stimulation and growth you would get from reading twelve outstanding books in a year.

THE PHYSICAL PACKAGE

Another help in your blooming process is to give some special attention to your body. You are a package with three parts: physical, psychological, and spiritual. If you allow your body to run down, you are going to be affected psychologically and spiritually.

Sleep. Start with a proper amount of sleep. Obviously, each woman requires a different amount according to her individual needs. Sometimes women have been so busy

during their twenties and early thirties that they've tried to
save time by sleeping less. Try getting an extra half hour a
day. If there's an improvement in your overall outlook in
life, it's a good indication that your body needs that extra
half hour.

If you have trouble dropping off to sleep at night, try a
warm cup of cocoa. The chocolate will turn on your happiness juices and the milk produces chemicals that somewhat tranquilize you.

Dr. Joyce Brothers recommends an occasional extended
period of time when the body can dictate how much sleep
to get. Every four or five months, when her husband is out
of town, she plans to stay in bed for about thirty-six hours.
Friday night she gets everything around her bed, such as
the radio, TV, telephone, and lots of reading materials. The
refrigerator is stocked with yogurt, fruit, cottage cheese,
and lots of juices. Then she just does whatever her body
wants her to. If she feels like reading, watching TV, or
sleeping, she does. She says, "I sleep and wake and don't
worry about whether I'm awake in the middle of the night
or asleep in the middle of the day. I just relax and do
nothing."[7]

We can hear the laughter coming from all of you who
are saying, "If only I had that luxury!" With a little bit of
planning, you can do it too. You have to plan ahead.
Eliminate all other obligations. If you have children, arrange for them to have a little vacation with some friends
at the same time. If you're married, you might want to do
the special time together as a couple. You don't even have
to leave home. Just put the car in the garage, pull down all
the blinds, turn your telephone off, and put an old rolled
up newspaper in the driveway so it looks as if nobody's
home.

Eat. Another ingredient for caring for your physical
body is to eat correctly. You may have feelings of physical
fatigue or a lack of drive and energy at certain times of the
day. Many times the mid-life woman, in her determination

to lose weight, eats an unbalanced diet. A poor diet can result in some physical and emotional responses such as fatigue, depression, and lack of motivation.

It is important to read some information on nutrition and learn how to stay healthy and feel well through a proper diet. Many such books are available, and each seems to have a particular emphasis, pet slogan, or out-and-out gimmick. As we have checked them, we see that it is best to choose a book with general information and then use your common sense and willpower about correct eating. Avoid fads and strange, unproven procedures, but do get excited about eating right to feel right.

Exercise. Try to work physical exercise into your daily routine. The fact that you're tired at the end of the day from a lot of work at the office or from caring for your home and family does not mean that you've had good exercise.

"A nine-year study of 575 paired brothers, one of whom had stayed in Ireland and the other had emigrated to the United States, showed the rate of heart attack to be higher in the United States, and the research sought to discover what differences might account for this. By using brothers, the factors of constitutional differences were minimized. Every possible fact was considered—nutrition, activity, types of work, degree of tension, living arrangements, etc. . . . only one factor had been found to be consistently different, namely, the amount of exercise."[8]

Good exercise means about twenty minutes of activity that will force your heart and lungs to work hard. It means stressing as many of your muscle groups and moving as many of your joints as possible. Whatever kind of exercise will accomplish that for you, at least three times a week, is good exercise.

You'll exercise more easily if you choose an activity that's fun for you. Maybe that's biking, jogging, swimming, or working out with a jazzercize record on your own or in a class. A good brisk walk or an enthusiastic sexual experience with your husband can provide exercise that your body desperately needs.

Exercise will help to keep your muscles in tone so that your weight is not tending to become flab around your middle. Exercise increases your capacity to endure physical stress. You'll be able to go longer in the day without that sagging feeling. Exercise also changes your body chemistry so you can handle emotional stress better and helps to break the cycle of depression. Exercise will also help keep your weight down.

When we think of all the positive aspects of exercise, we wonder why we don't do more. Our usual response is, "We're too busy." That's why it's so crucial to try to build exercise into our normal routine. As we mentioned before, for the past several years we two have practiced an almost daily custom of taking a brisk walk together. It's an opportunity to exercise as we communicate with each other about what's happening in us as persons. We do other fun things for exercise but some of them are none of your business!

RELATE

Another activity to enable you to bloom is to build and maintain more personal relationships. The stimulation of meaningful friendships is essential for growth.

In *Pathfinders* Gail Sheehy tells of interviewing 106 professional or managerial women. She asked them to draw three lines on a graph. The first was to show their achievement ups and downs from age five through fifty in five year increments. The second portrayed their interpersonal relationships over the same period of time. They were to chart the positive, close, harmonious relationships as the highs and the negative, isolated times as the lows on the graph. The third line was to show their overall life satisfaction.

Sheehy comments on the findings by saying, "A statisti-

cal analysis of the 106 charts from this group was startling. The achievement line was consistently high for these
professional women. But it was their affiliation [friendship]
line that was closer by a significant degree to their overall
life satisfaction line. Although most of their efforts were
being directed toward achievement, their zest for life was
much more profoundly affected by their relationships with
people."[9]

These women were finding significance in achievement,
but their life satisfaction was measured by their relationships. Therefore, be careful that you don't think of your
blooming as only achievement-focused. Real blooming
that will provide a deep life satisfaction must be tied to
satisfying interpersonal relationships. Your blooming
should include deepening your friendships and increasing
their number.

Sometimes in the busyness of the late twenties and the
thirties, women develop only surface relationships and
often very few of those. Your full development as a mature
mid-life woman needs deep interpersonal relationships. In
the opening chapters of the book of Genesis, God says, in
essence, "I created mankind with needs." People need each
other. Mankind was designed incomplete, needing companionship. We are basically lonely creatures who need the
warmth of interpersonal associations.

Friendships take time and energy but they can no longer
be put off for some other day. Think of two or three people
with whom you really hit it off. How can those relationships be deepened? Think of concrete steps you can take
to make that happen.

Some women renew letter correspondence with women
friends from their past. Other women determine to spend
more time with their maturing adolescent children, helping that relationship grow to a peer friendship. Some
spend more time with their husbands or other relatives
who are significant in their lives. Others join small Bible
study groups. Perhaps some of the other dimensions of

your life that are blooming, such as education, will put you into contact with people who may become significant friends for you.

PUTTING IT ALL TOGETHER

We started the book by telling you a little bit about Sally's mid-life crisis. We don't want to leave you wondering what happened to her. Also, I (Jim) want you to see some of the blooming that has taken place in her life since then.

The years of her mid-life crisis were difficult years for me as well. I felt, somehow, that I was failing her, and we had no clear direction as to how to work through a mid-life crisis. In fact, we didn't know there was such a thing. At the time, we went through a lot by trial and error, but in retrospect, I can see an overall pattern of Sally emerging as a very different, more confident, witty, and insightful woman, bearing a large impact on thousands of people across the United States.

An outgrowth of her mid-life crisis was that she returned to finish the last two years of college before it was commonly accepted for women her age to do so. It was kind of a jolt for her to go back to the university campus, where she was in the minority. On one occasion when students were waiting outside the classroom for the first day of class, Sally walked up and all the students ran to the door, assuming that she was the teacher, who had the key to the door.

During those two years, God expanded her interest in writing. She took some writing courses and became a witty writer. One piece, written in jest, was a letter to the chancellor of the University of Illinois. This was during the early seventies, when students were restless and minority groups were often pressing their demands. Sally facetiously demanded equal rights for a certain 141 (out of a total of 35,000) minority students—the undergraduate students over age thirty-five.

She asked, first of all, that the university population of people over thirty-five be increased to equal the same percentage as the population in the state of Illinois (a demand often made by other minority groups).

She also demanded that courses such as "How to Live with Your Teenager 101," "Caring for Your Aging Parents 216," "Coping with Menopause 263," and "Planning for Retirement 333," be added to the curriculum.

She further demanded that there be "elevators in all buildings, motorized sidewalks, reserved-at-the-door parking spaces, upholstered seats with footrests in all classrooms, and telephones in each classroom so that we may keep in touch with our families." Among other requests, she also asked for lounges equipped with "corn pad and Poligrip vending machines."

We observed a humorous blossoming in Sally that none of us had seen before.

Sally graduated with her bachelor's degree the same spring that our oldest daughter graduated from high school. We all went to Sally's graduation and waved proudly as she stood in her cap and gown. Her degree was in elementary education, but her focus was on helping children with reading disabilities.

She took a job as a reading specialist in a local school. She taught kids how to read, but she also helped them to grow with positive self-images. Some of those kids still write her letters every Christmas, thanking her for her contribution to their lives.

Sally has been deeply involved in all the articles I have written and in my first major book. In 1979, in response to hundreds of letters from wives of mid-life men, she wrote her first major book, *You and Your Husband's Mid-Life Crisis*.

Sally was soon thrust into ministering in workshops and conferences all over the country. She was on radio and television talk shows. God was enlarging her communication skills so that her impact would reach far beyond a single local church. The same year that her book came out, she returned to the university to work on a master's degree in human development.

In the summer of 1981 we moved to California, and Sally was invited to be an adjunct instructor at Talbot Theological Seminary where she has taught at both the master's and the doctoral level.

What does the future hold as Sally continues to bloom? She will probably write more books, be involved in many more conferences, and share her knowledge and experience through various media opportunities. She will also continue to help our three daughters blossom as leaders in their own fields.

She delights in the role of being a grandmother—the joy of training and coaching another generation. She enjoys teaching graduate men and women who are preparing for full time ministry and has a burden for pastors' wives and families because of her twenty-five years as a pastor's wife.

Sally's mid-life crisis changed her. She has become more assertive and more goal-oriented, and at the same time, she has become more keenly aware of people's hurts. She is more sensitive. She more easily jumps to the rescue of people who are exploited or misunderstood.

Her walk with God is an experience that she fosters day by day in a quiet time alone with him. It's not a childish faith; it's the faith of a mature woman who has wrestled with life's unanswerable questions and found God walking with her through the valley.

Sally's life is the fulfillment of the Psalmist's words, "Where is the [woman] who fears the Lord? God will teach [her] how to choose the best. [She] shall live within God's circle of blessing, and [her] children shall inherit the earth. Friendship with God is reserved for those who reverence him. With them alone he shares the secrets of his promises" (Psalm 25:12-14).

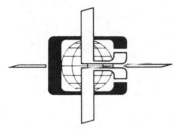

Jim and Sally Conway
have started an organization,
Christian Living Resources,
to minister to the mid-life family
around the world through
    counseling,
    radio programs,
    and conferences.
If you would like
more information about any
    publications,
    media,
    or counseling,
write to:
    Christian Living Resources
    P. O. Box 3790
    Fullerton, CA 92634

Notes

CHAPTER 1, COLLISION OF EXPECTATIONS AND REALITY

1. Helen Passwater, unpublished poem, printed with permission.
2. Joan Israel, "Confessions of a 45-Year-Old Feminist," in *Looking Ahead*, Lillian E. Troll, et al, eds. (Englewood Cliffs, NJ: Prentice-Hall, 1977), p. 65.
3. Ibid., p. 66.
4. Ibid., p. 67.
5. Ibid., p. 68.
6. Thomas A. Desmond, "America's Unknown Middle-Agers," *New York Times Magazine*, July 29, 1956.
7. Gloria Heidi, *Winning the Age Game* (Garden City, NY: A & W Visual Library, 1976), p. 3.
8. Gail Sheehy, *Passages* (New York: Dutton, 1976), pp. 378-383.
9. Bernice L. Neugarten, "The Awareness of Middle Age," in *Personality in Middle and Late Life*, Bernice L. Neugarten, ed. (New York: Atherton Press, 1964), p. 93.
10. Abraham Maslow et al., "A Clinically-Derived Test for Measuring Psychological Security-Insecurity," *Journal of General Psychology*, 33 (July 1945), pp. 24-41.
11. Lillian E. Troll, "Poor, Dumb, and Ugly," in *Looking Ahead*, Lillian E. Troll, et al, eds. (Englewood Cliffs, NJ: Prentice-Hall, 1977), p. 6.
12. Janet Harris, *The Prime of Ms. America* (New York: New American Library, 1976), pp. 11, 14.
13. Jules Henry, "Forty-year-old Jitters in Married Urban Women," in *The Challenge to Women* by Seymour M. Farber and Roger H. L. Wilson, eds. (New York: Basic Books, Inc., 1966), p. 152.
14. Ibid., p. 153.
15. Ibid., p. 163.
16. Maggie Scarf, *Unfinished Business* (Garden City, NY: Doubleday and Company, Inc., 1980), p. 1.
17. Iris Sangiuliano, *In Her Time* (New York: Morrow, 1978) pp. 130-132.
18. Joel and Lois Davitz, *Making It from Forty to Fifty* (New York: Random House, 1976), p. xvi.

CHAPTER 2, THE HOMEMAKER RUNS DRY

1. Anne W. Simon, *The New Years: A New Middle Age* (New York: Knopf, 1968), p. 183.
2. Jane Price, *You're Not Too Old to Have a Baby* (New York: Farrar, Strauss, Giroux, 1977).
3. Anne Statham Macke, George W. Bohrnstedt, and Ilene N. Bernstein, "Housewives' Self-Esteem and Their Husbands' Success: The Myth of Vicarious Involvement," *Journal of Marriage and the Family* (February 1979), pp. 52, 54.
4. Ibid., p. 56.
5. Davitz, pp. 210, 211.
6. Sheehy, pp. 382, 383.
7. Ibid., p. 383.
8. Sonya Rhodes with Josleen Wilson, " 'I'm Sick of Being Supermom!' The Story of a Woman's Revolt," *Woman's Day* (February 10, 1981), p. 65. (Excerpted from the book *Surviving Family Life*, same authors, G. P. Putnam's Sons, 1981).
9. Ibid., p. 90.
10. Ibid.
11. Ibid.
12. Judith Abelew Birnbaum, "Life Patterns and Self-Esteem in Gifted Family-Oriented and Career-Committed Women," in *Women and Achievement* by Martha Tamara Shuch Mednick, Sandra Schwartz Tangri, and Lois Wladis Hoffman, eds. (New York: John Wiley and Sons, 1975), p. 418.
13. Ibid.

CHAPTER 3, THE PROFESSIONAL SHIFTS DREAMS

1. Carl Jung, *Modern Man in Search of a Soul* (New York: Harcourt, Brace, and World, Inc., 1933), p. 108.
2. Betty Friedan, "The Myth," *Family Weekly* (November 8, 1981), p. 10.
3. Ibid.
4. Kari Torjesen Malcolm, *Women at the Crossroads* (Downers Grove, IL: InterVarsity Press, 1982), pp. 85-133, 209-212.
5. Bernice and Morton Hunt, *Prime Time* (New York: Stein and Day, 1975), pp. 29, 30.
6. "More women study to be physicians," *The Register* (Orange County, CA: December 27, 1982).
7. Hunt, p. 51.
8. Paul Tournier, *The Gift of Feeling* (Atlanta: John Knox Press, 1981).
9. Friedan, p. 10.
10. Ibid., p. 11.
11. M. Kuhn, "How Mates Are Sorted," in *Family, Marriage, and Parenthood*, H. Becker, R. Hill, eds. (Boston: D. C. Heath and Co., 1955).
12. P. Stein, *Single in America* (Englewood Cliffs, NJ: Prentice-Hall, 1976).
13. *Ladies Home Journal*, 1961.
14. Barbara Ehrenreich and Deidre English, *For Her Own Good* (Garden City, NY: Anchor Press/Doubleday, 1979), p. 294.
15. Quoted in Ehrenreich and English, p. 295.
16. Erik Erikson, *Adulthood* (New York: W. W. Norton, 1978).
17. Mel Roman and Patricia E. Raley, *The Indelible Family* (New York: Rawson Wade Publishers, 1980), pp. 91-117.
18. Beth Ann Krier, "Surviving the Crisis of Spinsterhood," *Los Angeles Times* (June 26, 1981), reporting on Nancy Peterson's book *Our Lives for Ourselves, Women Who Have Never Married*.

19. Carin Rubenstein, "Real Men Don't Earn Less Than Their Wives," *Psychology Today*, 16:11 (November 1982), p. 38.

CHAPTER 4, WONDER WOMAN TRIES IT ALL

1. Women's Bureau of the Federal Department of Labor quoted in *Christian Women at Work* by Patricia Ward and Martha Stout (Grand Rapids, MI: Zondervan Publishing House, 1981), p. 11; Bureau of Labor Statistics, quoted in *The Two-Paycheck Marriage* by Caroline Bird (New York: Pocket Book, 1979), pp. 4-6; *Information Please Atlas and Year Book*, 36th edition (New York: Simon and Schuster, 1982), p. 54.
2. Gloria Norris and JoAnn Miller, "The New Mother: Juggling Her Job, Her Family, Her Guilt," *Family Weekly* (May 11, 1980), p. 4.
3. Fred Feretti, "Poll: Women Execs Pay Price for Success," *The Register* (Orange County, CA, June 1, 1982), p. B8.
4. Elaine Fantle Shimberg, "The Ultimate Merger: Double Career Marriage," *National Forum*, LXI:4 (Fall 1981), p. 13.
5. Dana V. Hiller and William W. Philliber, "Predicting Marital and Career Success Among Dual-worker Couples," *Journal of Marriage and the Family* (February 1982), pp. 53, 57.
6. Bird, front page [no number].
7. Bird, pp. 99-118.
8. Helen Gurley Brown, *Having It All* (New York: Simon and Schuster, 1982).
9. Ward and Stout, p. 52.
10. Ehrenreich and English, pp. 8, 9.
11. Eda J. LeShan, *The Wonderful Crisis of Middle Age* (New York: David McKay, 1973), p. 47.
12. Patricia Gundry, *The Complete Woman* (Garden City, NY: Doubleday and Company, Inc., 1981).
13. Bird, pp. 41-67.
14. Quoted in "How to be More Successful," John E. Gibson, *Family Weekly* (May 1, 1977).
15. Bird, p. 42.
16. Ibid., p. 43.
17. Linda J. Beckman and Betsy Bosak Houser, "The Consequences of Childlessness on the Social-Psychological Well-Being of Older Women," *Journal of Gerontology* 37:2 (1982), p. 246.

CHAPTER 5, CULTURE'S CREATION

1. *Ladies Home Journal*, August 1919.
2. Ibid.
3. Harris, p. 43.
4. *Statistical Abstracts of U.S.*, "Current Population Reports," series P20, #320, 1978, p. 39, table #45.
5. Wallace Denton, *What's Happening to Our Families?* (Philadelphia: Westminster Press, 1963).
6. Quoted in Hunt, p. 19.
7. Smiley Blanton, *Now or Never* (Englewood Cliffs, NJ: Prentice-Hall, 1959), p. 250.
8. Simon, p. 41.
9. Florence Perkell Hoffman, "Effects of a Youth Culture on Feelings and Attitudes of the Middle Woman," Ph.D. Dissertation, Walden University, December 1978.

10. Phil Pastoret, Newspaper Enterprise Association in *Reader's Digest* 11:668 (December 1977), p. 122.
11. M. Abrioux and H. W. Zingle, "An Exploration of the Marital and Life Satisfactions of Middle-aged Husbands and Wives," *Canadian Counsellor* 13:2 (January 1979), pp. 85-93; R. O. Blood and D. M. Wolfe, *Husbands and Wives: The Dynamics of Married Living* (Glencoe, IL: Free Press, 1960); J. J. Locke and K. M. Wallace, "Short Marital-adjustment and Prediction Tests: Their Reliability and Validity," *Journal of Marriage and the Family*, 28 (February 1966), pp. 44-48; B. C. Rollins and K. L. Cannon, "Marital Satisfaction Over the Family Life Cycle: A Reevaluation," *Journal of Marriage and the Family* (May 1974), pp. 271-282.
12. LeShan, pp. 51, 52.
13. Ibid., pp. 43-46.
14. Jerry Greenwald, *Be the Person You Were Meant to Be* (New York: Dell, 1973), p. 19.
15. Quoted in Fritz Perls and John O. Stevens, *Gestalt Therapy Verbatim* (Lafayette, CA: Real People Press, 1969), p. 4.
16. Greenwald, p. 10.
17. Abrioux and Zingle; Macke, Bohrenstedt, and Bernstein; Lillian B. Rubin, *Women of a Certain Age: The Midlife Search for Self* (New York: Harper and Row, 1979).
18. Judith Bardwick, "Middle Age and a Sense of Future," *Merrill-Palmer Quarterly*, April 1978, 24, (2), pp. 129-138.

CHAPTER 6, THE STALE MARRIAGE
1. Rollins and Cannon, p. 271.
2. Hunt, pp. 60, 61.
3. Elizabeth Mehren, "Shattering Myths of Sanctity of Home," *Los Angeles Times*, Part V (January 26, 1983).
4. Ibid.
5. Ibid.
6. Ibid.
7. Jack London, "In a Far Country," *Great Short Works* (New York: Harper and Row Publishers, 1965).
8. Barbara L. Fisher, Paul R. Giblin, and Margaret H. Hoopes, "Healthy Family Functioning: What Therapists Say and What Families Want," *Journal of Marriage and Family Therapy* (July 1982), pp. 273, 274.
9. Virginia Satir, *People-Making* (Palo Alto, CA: Science and Behavior Books, Inc., 1972).
10. Jerry and Barbara Cook, *Choosing to Love* (Ventura, CA: Regal Books, 1982), p. 57. Used by permission.
11. Ibid., pp. 66-68.

CHAPTER 7, HER HUSBAND'S OWN CRISIS
1. Avery Corman, "The Old Neighborhood," *Flightime* Magazine, (LA East West Network, Inc., January 1981), p. 15.
2. Quoted in Peter Chew, *The Inner World of the Middle-Aged Man* (New York: Macmillan, 1976), p. 113.
3. Edmond Bergler, *The Revolt of the Middle Aged Man* (New York: A. A. Wyn, 1954).
4. Barbara R. Fried, *The Middle-Age Crisis* (New York: Harper and Row, 1967), p. 15.
5. Daniel Levinson, et al., *The Seasons of a Man's Life* (New York: A. Knopf, 1978; New York: Ballantine Books, 1979), pp. 8, 199.

6. Jim Conway, *Men in Mid-Life Crisis* (Elgin, IL: David C. Cook, 1978), p. 67.
7. Estelle Fuchs, *The Second Season* (Garden City, NY: Anchor/Doubleday, 1977), p. 31.
8. Sangiuliano, pp. 119, 120.
9. Quoted in Chew, p. 72.

CHAPTER 8, THE PAIN OF PARENTING
1. Neugarten, 1968b, pp. 94, 95; Abrioux and Zingle; Marjorie Lowenthal and David Chiriboga, "Transition to the Empty Nest: Crisis, Challenge, or Relief?" *Archives of General Psychiatry,* January 1972, 26, pp. 8-14.
2. LeShan, pp. 15, 16.
3. National Center for Health Statistics.
4. Fried, p. 75.
5. Simon, pp. 6, 7.
6. Chew, p. 77.
7. Quoted in Bergler, p. 281.
8. Quoted in Chew, p. 83.
9. Sheehy, p. 424.
10. Davitz, p. 188.

CHAPTER 9, TOO MUCH TOO FAST
1. Carol B. Aslanian and Henry B. Brickell, *Americans in Transition* (New York: College Entrance Examination Board, 1980).
2. Bernice Neugarten, "Dynamics of Transition to Old Age," *Journal of Geriatric Psychiatry* (1970), p. 86.
3. Roger L. Gould, "Phases of Adult Life," *American Journal of Psychiatry,* 129:5 (November 1972), p. 528.
4. Josh Greenfeld, "A Dramatic Sense of Age . . . A Sudden Sniff of Death," *Today's Health* (March 1973), p. 46.
5. U.S. Bureau of the Census, "Marital Status and Living Arrangements: March 1977" (Washington, D.C.: Government Publishing Office, 1977).
6. David A. Chiriboga, "Adaptation to Marital Separation in Later and Earlier Life," *Journal of Gerontology,* 37:1 (1982), p. 11.
7. Judith S. Wallerstein and Joan B. Kelly, "California's Children of Divorce," *Psychology Today* (January 1980), p. 67.
8. Ibid., p. 74, 75.
9. E. O. Fisher, "A Guide to Divorce Counseling," *The Family Coordinator,* 22:1 (1973), p. 55.

CHAPTER 10, THE MARKS OF TIME
1. Fried, p. 81.
2. Simon, p. 158.
3. Lillian E. Troll, *Early and Middle Adulthood: The Best Is Yet to Be—Maybe* (Monterey, CA: Brooks/Cole Publishing Co., 1975), pp. 20-23.
4. Susan Sontag, "The Double Standard of Aging," *Saturday Review of the Society* (September 23, 1972).
5. Simon, p. 35.
6. Joyce Brothers, *Better than Ever* (New York: Simon and Schuster, 1975), pp. 19, 20.
7. Troll, *Early and Middle Adulthood,* pp. 22, 23.
8. Leslie Aldridge Westoff, *Breaking Out of the Middle-Age Trap* (New York: New American Library, 1980), p. 42.

9. Nancy Stahl, Universal Press Syndicate in *Reader's Digest*, 111:668 (December 1977), p. 122.
10. Troll, *Early and Middle Adulthood*, pp. 22, 23.
11. Quoted in Heidi, pp. 96, 97.
12. Ibid., p. 97.
13. Brothers, p. 29.
14. "How to Stay Slender for Life," condensed from *Executive Health* in *Reader's Digest*, October 1982, pp. 117-120.
15. Ruth Weg, "More than Wrinkles," in *Looking Ahead*, Lillian E. Troll, et al., eds. (Englewood Cliffs, NJ: Prentice-Hall, 1977), p. 32.
16. Bruno Hans Geba, *Vitality Training for Older Adults: A Positive Approach to Growing Old* (New York: Random House, 1974), p. 9.
17. Ollie Pocs, et al., "Is There Sex After 40?" *Psychology Today*, 11 (June 1977), p. 54.
18. Heidi, p. 4.
19. Paul Chapman, M.D., "Hormone Imbalance," tape-recorded interview, *Focus on the Family* radio program, 41 East Foothill Boulevard, Arcadia, CA, 1982; Robert B. Greenblatt, M.D. and Charles Weller, M.D., "The Endocrine Glands," *Family Medicine Guide* (New York: Better Homes and Gardens Books, 1964).
20. Kevin McKean, "Estrogen 'Safe' in Short Term," *The Champaign-Urbana News-Gazette* (July 17, 1979), p. A-2; Chapman taped interview.
21. Hunt, p. 167.
22. Alice Lake, "An Honest Report on Breast Cancer," condensed from *Redbook* in *Reader's Digest* (September 1982); Hunt, pp. 168, 169; Westoff, p. 45.
23. Carol A. Nowak, "Does Youthfulness Equal Attractiveness?" in *Looking Ahead*, Troll, et al. eds. (Englewood Cliffs, NJ: Prentice-Hall, 1977), p. 59.
24. Ibid., p. 63.
25. Brothers, p. 135.
26. LeShan, pp. 63, 64.

CHAPTER 11, DEFEATED BY A SAGGING SELF-ESTEEM
1. Sangiuliano, p. 238.
2. H. N. Mischel, "Sex Bias in the Evaluation of Professional Achievements," *Journal of Educational Psychology*, 66 (1974), pp. 157-166.
3. David A. Seamands, "Perfectionism: Fraught with Fruits of Self-Destruction," *Psychology Today* (April 10, 1981), p. 24.
4. Helen Haiman Joseph poem, "The Mask."
5. Brothers, pp. 27-159.
6. Alan B. Knox, *Adult Development and Learning* (San Francisco: Jossey-Bass Publishers, 1977), p. 489.
7. Cecil G. Osborne, *The Art of Learning to Love Yourself* (Grand Rapids, MI: Zondervan, 1976), pp. 99-123.
8. Ardis Whitman, "The Awesome Power to Be Ourselves," *Reader's Digest*, (January 1983), p. 80.
9. David D. Burns, "The Perfectionist's Script for Self-Defeat," *Psychology Today* (November 1980), p. 38.
10. Ibid., p. 46.
11. Ibid.
12. Ibid.
13. Ibid.

14. Ibid., p. 52.
15. Quoted in *49 and Holding,* "Who Am I?" pp. 36, 37.

CHAPTER 12, TRAPPED BY DEPRESSION
1. Phyllis Chesler, *Women and Madness* (Garden City, NY: Doubleday and Company, Inc., 1972), pp. 39, 40.
2. Margaret Williams Crockett, "Depression in Middle-Aged Women," *The Journal of Pastoral Care,* 31:1 (March 1977), p. 48.
3. Scarf, p. 2.
4. Crockett, p. 48.
5. Pauline B. Bart, "Depression in Middle-Aged Women," in *Women in Sexist Society,* Vivian Gornick and Barbara Moran, eds. (New York: Basic Books, 1971), p. 110.
6. Robert Lee and Marjorie Casebier, *The Spouse Gap* (New York: Abingdon Press, 1971), p. 155.
7. Robert N. Butler, "Prospects for Middle-Aged Women," *Women in Midlife—Security and Fulfillment* (Part I), A Compendium of Papers Submitted to the Select Committee on Aging and the Subcommittee on Retirement Income and Employment, U.S. House of Representatives, Ninety-fifth Congress, Second Session, December 1978, Comm. Pub. No. 95-170, p. 330.
8. Crockett, p. 53.
9. Susan Seliger, "Go ahead, cry your eyes out!" *The Register* (Orange County, CA, January 19, 1982), D1.

CHAPTER 13, TEMPTED TO ESCAPE
1. Sheehy, p. 382.
2. Ibid., p. 383.
3. Mel White, *Lust: The Other Side of Love* (Old Tappan, NJ: Fleming H. Revell Co., 1978), pp. 18, 19.
4. *Playboy,* September 20, 1976.
5. Maggie Scarf, "The Promiscuous Woman," *Psychology Today* (July 1980), p. 83.
6. Lewis Smedes, *Sex for Christians* (Grand Rapids, MI: William B. Eerdmans Publishing Company, 1976), pp. 168-169.
7. Dwight Small, *How Should I Love You?* (San Francisco: Harper and Row, 1979), p. 123.
8. Ellen Frank and Sondra Forsyth Enos, "The Lovelife of the American Wife," *Ladies Home Journal* (February 1983), pp. 72, 73.
9. As quoted by John Leo, in "Sex and the Married Woman," *Time* (January 31, 1983), p. 80.
10. Hunt, pp. 93, 94.
11. Rollo May, "The Promiscuity Trap," *Reader's Digest* (January 1982), p. 88.
12. As quoted by Alice Fleming in "Six Myths About Extramarital Affairs," *Reader's Digest* (October 1982), p. 67.
13. Alan Loy McGinnis, *The Romance Factor* (San Francisco: Harper and Row Publishers, 1982), pp. 153-155.
14. Gay Talese, *Thy Neighbor's Wife* (New York: Dell, 1980); Nena O'Neill and George O'Neill, *Open Marriage* (New York: M. Evans and Company, 1972).
15. Hunt, p. 186.
16. U. S. Departments of Commerce; and Health, Education, and Welfare reported in *U. S. News and World Report* (December 20, 1976).

17. "Surge in Divorces: New Crisis in Middle Age," *U. S. News and World Report* (December 20, 1976), p. 56.
18. Davitz, p. 180.
19. Rose N. Franzblau, *The Middle Generation* (New York: Holt, 1971), p. 153.
20. Lee and Casebier, p. 175.
21. Morton Hunt, *The Affair* (New York: New American Library, 1969), p. 253.
22. Ibid.
23. Paul D. Meier, "Is Divorce Ever Necessary?" *Christian Medical Society Journal*, VII:1 (Winter 1976), p. 4.
24. Ibid.
25. Fried, pp. 40, 41.

CHAPTER 14, KEEPING UP WITH LIFE'S CLOCKS

1. Erik Erikson, *Childhood and Society* (New York: W. W. Norton, 1950).

CHAPTER 15, ANSWERING LIFE'S QUESTIONS

1. Keith W. Sehnert, *Stress/Unstress* (Minneapolis: Augsburg Publishing House, 1981), pp. 74, 75.
2. John Powell, *Fully Human, Fully Alive* (Niles, IL: Argus Communications, 1976), p. 87.
3. Quoted in Powell, p. 90.
4. Ibid., p. 92.

CHAPTER 16, PREVENTING A CRISIS

1. Linda Matchan, "Women at Mid-life Shatter Stereotypes," *The Denver Post* (February 22, 1983), p. 2-E.
2. Ibid.
3. Gail Sheehy, *Pathfinders* (New York: Bantam Books, 1982), p. 165.
4. Ibid.
5. Unpublished poem used by permission.

CHAPTER 17, HELPING A WOMAN IN CRISIS

1. Richard Bolles, *The Three Boxes of Life* (San Francisco: Ten Speed Press, 1978).
2. Sandra E. Gibbs Candy, "What Do Women Use Friends For?" *Looking Ahead*, Lillian E. Troll, et al., eds. (Englewood Cliffs, NJ: Prentice-Hall, 1977), p. 108.
3. Robert Peterson, *New Life Begins at Forty* (New York: Trident Press, 1967), pp. 135, 136.
4. Gibbs, p. 107.
5. Judith F. Van Heukelem, "Weep with Those Who Weep," *Journal of Psychology and Theology* (Summer 1979) 7:2, pp. 83-91.
6. Joyce Landorf, *Tough and Tender* (Old Tappan, NJ: Fleming H. Revell, 1975).
7. Jim Sanderson, "Now That the Kids Have Grown," *Los Angeles Times* (December 15, 1982), p. V-8.
8. Sally Conway, *You and Your Husband's Mid-Life Crisis* (Elgin, IL: David C. Cook Publishing Company, 1980).
9. Laura Branigan, "Solitaire," BRANIGAN 2 Album, Atlantic Recording Corporation, 75 Rockefeller Plaza, New York, NY 10019.

CHAPTER 18, BLOOMING AT MID-LIFE
1. Fried, p. 8.
2. Daniel Seligman, "Keeping Up," *Fortune* (September 7, 1981), p. 37.
3. Quoted in Chew, p. 10.
4. Bernice L. Neugarten and David L. Gutmann, "Age-Sex Roles and Personality in Middle Age: A Thematic Apperception Study," *Middle Age and Aging*, Bernice L. Neugarten (Chicago: University of Chicago Press, 1975), p. 71.
5. Henry Grunebaum, "Middle Age and Marriage: Affiliative Men and Assertive Women," *The American Journal of Family Therapy*, 7:3 (Fall 1979), pp. 46-50.
6. Anne Morrow Lindbergh, *Gift from the Sea* (New York: Vintage Books, 1965), pp. 84, 85.
7. Brothers, p. 118.
8. LeShan, pp. 102, 103.
9. Sheehy, *Pathfinders*, p. 150.

Suggested Reading

WOMANHOOD

Fix, Janet with Levitt, Zola. *For Singles Only*. Old Tappan, NJ: Fleming H. Revell Company, 1978.

Gundry, Patricia. *The Complete Woman*. Garden City, NY: Doubleday and Company, Inc., 1981.

Hendricks, Jeanne. *Afternoon*. Nashville, TN: Thomas Nelson Publishers, 1979.

Landorf, Joyce. *Change Points*. Old Tappan, NJ: Fleming H. Revell Company, 1981.

Malcolm, Kari Torjesen. *Women at the Crossroads*. Downers Grove, IL: InterVarsity Press, 1982.

Ortlund, Anne. *Disciplines of the Beautiful Woman*. Waco, TX: Word Books, 1977.

Pape, Dorothy R. *In Search of God's Ideal Woman*. Downers Grove, IL: InterVarsity Press, 1976.

Swindoll, Luci. *Wide My World, Narrow My Bed*. Portland, OR: Multnomah Press, 1982.

MARRIAGE

Bustanoby, Andre. *But I Didn't Want a Divorce*. Grand Rapids, MI: Zondervan, 1978.

Cook, Jerry and Barbara. *Choosing to Love*. Ventura, CA: Regal Books, 1982.

Dobson, James. *What Wives Wish Their Husbands Knew About Women*. Wheaton, IL: Tyndale House, 1975.

Guernsey, Dennis. *Thoroughly Married*. Waco, TX: Word Books, 1977.

Gundry, Patricia. *Heirs Together*. Grand Rapids: MI: Zondervan, 1980.

Kilgore, James E. *Try Marriage Before Divorce*. Waco, TX: Word Books, 1978.

McGinnis, Alan Loy. *The Romance Factor*. San Francisco: Harper and Row Publishers, 1982.

Miles, Herbert J. and Fern Harrington. *Husband-Wife Equality*. Old Tappan, NJ: Fleming H. Revell, 1978.

Smedes, Lewis. *Sex for Christians*. Grand Rapids, MI: William B. Eerdmans Publishing Company, 1976.

Swindoll, Charles R. *Strike the Original Match.* Portland, OR: Multnomah Press, 1980.
Thatcher, Floyd and Harriett. *Long Term Marriage.* Waco, TX: Word Books, 1980.
Tournier, Paul. *The Gift of Feeling.* Atlanta: John Knox Press, 1981.
Wheat, Ed. and Wheat, Gaye. *Intended for Pleasure.* Old Tappan, NJ: Fleming H. Revell Company, 1977.
Wright, H. Norman. *Pillars of Marriage.* Glendale, CA: Regal Books, 1979.
Wright, H. Norman. *Seasons of a Marriage.* Ventura, CA: Regal Books, 1982.

CHILDREN AND FAMILY
Campbell, Ross. *How to Really Love Your Child.* Wheaton, IL: Victor Books, 1977.
Dobson, James. *Hide or Seek.* Old Tappan, NJ: Fleming H. Revell Company, 1974.
Roman, Mel, and Raley, Patricia E. *The Indelible Family.* New York: Rawson Wade Publishers, 1980.
Schaeffer, Edith. *What Is a Family?* Old Tappan, NJ: Fleming H. Revell Company, 1975.
Vigeveno, H. S. and Claire, Anne. *Divorce and the Children.* Glendale, CA: Regal Books, 1979.
White, John. *Parents in Pain.* Downers Grove, IL: InterVarsity Press, 1979.

MID-LIFE CRISIS
Conway, Jim. *Men in Mid-Life Crisis.* Elgin, IL: David C. Cook Publishing Company, 1978.
Conway, Sally. *You and Your Husband's Mid-Life Crisis.* Elgin, IL: David C. Cook Publishing Company, 1980.
Davitz, Joel and Lois. *Making It from Forty to Fifty.* New York: Random House, 1976.
Levinson, Daniel J. *The Seasons of a Man's Life.* New York: Alfred A. Knopf, Ballantine Books, 1978.
Petersen, J. Allan. *The Myth of the Greener Grass.* Wheaton, IL: Tyndale House Publishers, 1983.
Sheehy, Gail. *Passages.* New York: E. P. Dutton, Bantam Books, 1976.

EMOTIONAL/SPIRITUAL HELP
Augsburger, David. *Caring Enough to Forgive.* Ventura, CA: Regal Books, 1981.
Hart, Archibald D. *Feeling Free.* Old Tappan, NJ: Fleming H. Revell Company, 1979.
Mains, Karen Burton. *The Key to a Loving Heart.* Elgin, IL: David C. Cook Publishing Company, 1979.
Osborne, Cecil G. *The Art of Learning to Love Yourself.* Grand Rapids, MI: Zondervan, 1976.
Yancey, Philip. *Where Is God When It Hurts?* Grand Rapids, MI: Zondervan, 1977.

CAREER GUIDANCE
Bolles, Richard Nelson. *The Three Boxes of Life.* Berkeley, CA: Ten Speed Press, 1978.
Bolles, Richard Nelson. *What Color Is Your Parachute?* San Francisco, Ten Speed, 1970, rev. 1977.
Ward, Patricia, and Stout, Martha. *Christian Women at Work.* Grand Rapids, MI: Zondervan, 1981.

CHRISTIAN HERALD ASSOCIATION AND ITS MINISTRIES

CHRISTIAN HERALD ASSOCIATION, founded in 1878, publishes The Christian Herald Magazine, one of the leading interdenominational religious monthlies in America. Through its wide circulation, it brings inspiring articles and the latest news of religious developments to many families. From the magazine's pages came the initiative for CHRISTIAN HERALD CHILDREN'S HOME and THE BOWERY MISSION, two individually supported not-for-profit corporations.

CHRISTIAN HERALD CHILDREN'S HOME, established in 1894, is the name for a unique and dynamic ministry to disadvantaged children, offering hope and opportunities which would not otherwise be available for reasons of poverty and neglect. The goal is to develop each child's potential and to demonstrate Christian compassion and understanding to children in need.

Mont Lawn is a permanent camp located in Bushkill, Pennsylvania. It is the focal point of a ministry which provides a healthful "vacation with a purpose" to children who without it would be confined to the streets of the city. Up to 1000 children between the ages of 7 and 11 come to Mont Lawn each year.

Christian Herald Children's Home maintains year-round contact with children by means of an *In-City Youth Ministry*. Central to its philosophy is the belief that only through sustained relationships and demonstrated concern can individual lives be truly enriched. Special emphasis is on individual guidance, spiritual and family counseling and tutoring. This follow-up ministry to inner-city children culminates for many in financial assistance toward higher education and career counseling.

THE BOWERY MISSION, located at 227 Bowery, New York City, has since 1879 been reaching out to the lost men on the Bowery, offering them what could be their last chance to rebuild their lives. Every man is fed, clothed and ministered to. Countless numbers have entered the 90-day residential rehabilitation program at the Bowery Mission. A concentrated ministry of counseling, medical care, nutrition therapy, Bible study and Gospel services awakens a man to spiritual renewal within himself.

These ministries are supported solely by the voluntary contributions of individuals and by legacies and bequests. Contributions are tax deductible. Checks should be made out either to CHRISTIAN HERALD CHILDREN'S HOME or to THE BOWERY MISSION.

Administrative Office: 40 Overlook Drive, Chappaqua, New York 10514
Telephone: (914) 769-9000